UFOS:

REFRAMING THE DEBATE

UFOS:

REFRAMING THE DEBATE

EDITED BY

ROBBIE GRAHAM

www.whitecrowbooks.com

PRAISE FOR
UFOS: REFRAMING THE DEBATE

"Once in a while, when the study of UFOs sinks deep into stale complacency, a breath of fresh air blows in to wake up the participants and revitalize the discussion. This book is just such a refresher. Instead of the perennial standoff between believers, who treat extraterrestrial visitation as established fact, and skeptics, who dismiss the whole subject as obvious foolishness, the contributors to *UFOs: Reframing the Debate* find nuance and layers where too many others see only black and white or foregone conclusions. These essays honor the full scope of the phenomenon—the material, high-strangeness, experiential, psychological, social, cultural, expressive, mythic, and religious aspects alike—and recognize them as equally important, equally revealing dimensions of a complex whole. Each chapter will fascinate and infuriate readers with fixed ideas of what is true and important about UFOs, as well as set new ideas and connections buzzing in their brains. This brash, rejuvenating effort to lift ufology out of its intellectual morass is an achievement of Fortean thinking that Charles Fort himself might envy."

—THOMAS E. BULLARD, PH.D.
AUTHOR OF *THE MYTH AND MYSTERY OF UFOS*

"Robbie Graham's UFO anthology reframes the UFO from facile tabloid fare into its real challenge—how to interpret strange experiences offering hints of an Underlying Fundamental Ontology. To tackle such a difficult and at times bewildering task, a deep multidisciplinary dive is required. And that's exactly what you'll find in this thoughtful and stimulating book."

—DEAN RADIN, PH.D.
CHIEF SCIENTIST, INSTITUTE OF NOETIC SCIENCES
AUTHOR OF *SUPERNORMAL*

"Robbie Graham has assembled a set of essays with very subversive insights into the nature of UFO phenomena. If you intend to seriously study UFOs, you must read this book."

—GEORGE P. HANSEN
AUTHOR OF *THE TRICKSTER AND THE PARANORMAL*

"More than another recitation of the latest UFO events, *UFOs: Reframing the Debate* takes one giant step backward to get a good look at where the field as a whole stands in these early decades of the 21st century. Whether you are a hard-core materialist fan of the extraterrestrial hypothesis of UFO origins, gobsmacked and captivated by the frequency of 'high strangeness' UFO sighting reports, or a devotee of the 'space brothers' camp of UFO enthusiasts, there's something herein that is sure to delight and offend you, by turns. These thoughtful, critical essays deserve a thoughtful, critical reading by all who have ever wondered 'what about...' and 'what if...'"

—BRENDA DENZLER, PH.D.
AUTHOR OF *THE LURE OF THE EDGE*

"The UFO, to paraphrase a wise man who may never have lived, is a sphere whose center is everywhere and circumference nowhere. It might be a vehicle; it might be a passage between worlds; it might be a world in itself; it might be an intelligent other; it might be an intelligent us. It is a symbol representing everything we don't yet understand about the worlds we inhabit, and, most importantly, our relationships to them. Collectively, the contributors to this timely volume recognize this; they understand that there is no UFO phenomenon, there are only phenomena, just as there is no UFO story, there are only UFO stories. Despite the best efforts of some luminous minds, many of them included here, the UFO debate has, for far too long, been a circular one—this book should help that circle to become a sphere."

—MARK PILKINGTON
AUTHOR OF *MIRAGE MEN*

For information, contact White Crow Books
at 3 Hova Villas, Hove, BN3 3DH United Kingdom,
or e-mail to info@whitecrowbooks.com.

Cover Design by Red Pill Junkie
and Astrid@Astridpaints.com
Interior design by Velin@Perseus-Design.com

Paperback ISBN 978-1-78677-023-3
eBook   ISBN 978-1-78677-024-0

Non Fiction / Body, Mind & Spirit / UFOs & Extraterrestrials

www.whitecrowbooks.com

CONTENTS

ACKNOWLEDGEMENTS

My deepest gratitude to all those who contributed to this volume: MJ Banias, Greg Bishop, Robert Brandstetter, Jack Brewer, Mike Clelland, Curt Collins, Joshua Cutchin, Lorin Cutts, Susan Demeter-St. Clair, Micah Hanks, SMiles Lewis, Diana Walsh Pasulka, Red Pill Junkie, Chris Rutkowski, and Ryan Sprague.

Thank you also to Aaron Donaldson, Lesley Gunter, Michael Huntington, Lauren Kott, Regan Lee, Christian De Coninck Lucas, Jason McClellan, Kenn Thomas, and Frank Zero.

My special thanks to Greg Bishop, who consulted with me closely throughout the editing process and whose perspectives and advice have been invaluable; and to Red Pill Junkie, for his brilliant and original illustrations, and for creating our wonderful cover art. Finally, thank you to Jon Beecher of White Crow Books, for his encouragement, patience, and support.

ABOUT **THE EDITOR**

Robbie Graham has pursued the UFO mystery for more than half his life. He has lectured around the world on the subject and has been interviewed for the BBC, Coast to Coast AM, Canal+ TV, Channel 4, and *Vanity Fair*, among many others. His articles have appeared in numerous publications, including *The Guardian, New Statesman, Filmfax*, and *Fortean Times*. He holds first class degrees in Film, Television and Radio Studies (BA hons) and Cinema Studies (MA) from Staffordshire University and the University of Bristol respectively. He is the author of *Silver Screen Saucers: Sorting Fact from Fantasy in Hollywood's UFO Movies* (White Crow Books, 2015).

WITHIN

"Although adherents insist they are on a quest for 'truth,' their insistence they already 'know' such truth undermines attempts by UFO researchers and investigators to understand the true nature of the phenomenon."

"[UFO zealots] cannot be convinced to become more scientific in their approach, largely because they are faith-based and religious in nature. They operate on preconceived notions and a set of beliefs that preclude rigorous analysis. Their worldview is clearly metamodernist, accepting any and all claims and statements without critical examination."

—CHRIS RUTKOWSKI

"If these experiences are what they seem to be, then it should be no surprise that they [UFO experiencers] can come across like fanatical zealots."

"This weirder stuff gets ignored [because] some folks feel a need to be taken seriously. I would love to be taken seriously too, but I also feel a need to honestly share what's happened to me."

"This is an esoteric mystery and it requires esoteric methodologies to peel back its secrets."

—MIKE CLELLAND

"The UFO Mythological Zone... [is] the gap between fact and belief, what we see and what we want to see, what we experience and how we interpret it."

"People are forming highly personalized variations of the one core belief—the belief in a UFO reality. All else is up for individual interpretation via the UFO mythological zone. In the absence of facts, many people simply choose what they want to believe."

—LORIN CUTTS

"We might consider that understanding someone's point of view doesn't necessarily equate to agreement."

"A great deal of completely inaccurate—and often, at best, unverified—information is widely accepted, then spread as if it were reliable. We then tend to form beliefs and make up our minds about things which haven't actually been adequately explained. People subsequently not only reject revisions and corrections, but tend to embrace beliefs even more tightly when those beliefs are shown to be incorrect."

—JACK BREWER

"From materialism's ashes, a new model of reality will arise wherein the scientific establishment accepts the completely intangible, wholly interiorized phenomenon of human consciousness can manifest measurable effects in our physical world."

"Moving beyond materialism is about honestly confronting the fact that we know nothing for certain about UFOs, yet choosing to be inspired rather than frustrated by this realization, leading to a type of non-dogmatic gnosticism."

—JOSHUA CUTCHIN

"I can respect, communicate, and interact with people who do not share my own ideas."

"Modern skepticism can, I think, be summarized in many instances as an ideology, around which a social movement has been built—one that, today, also runs tangent with atheism—and as a paradoxically evangelical attitude about the supremacy of science above all other forms of knowledge."

—MICAH HANKS

"I advocate for a multi-theory interpretation of the UFO phenomenon. I don't think there is any one explanation that accounts for all the data. I think there are a number of things going on simultaneously."

"Human belief in alien Others creates cults, religions, and social movements of significance... it is clear that a wide variety of human agencies have manipulated the superstitions and myths surrounding stories of contact with non-human entities—folklore has been weaponized as a means to various ends."

—SMILES LEWIS

"What the Roswell Slides episode did was to expose the serious flaws common in standard ufology research practices... We were told that the evidence had been subjected to expert analysis, but the promoters themselves were the ones deciding which experts were qualified, only presenting findings supporting their existing beliefs that the body in the Slides was something non-human."

"By pooling our resources, we each had the best available data, access to the counsel of our peers, and the inspiration and encouragement to keep trying to find the truth. Groups can be great tools, but they have their limitations. Each of us must remain objective, seek the best evidence and ask challenging questions, whether as part of a team or as individuals."

—CURT COLLINS

"There is no future for ufology, and UFO discourse as a whole, in the mainstream. If a grandiose extraterrestrial contact event occurred tomorrow, and the UFO question was forced into mainstream ideology, ufology would die an instant death as the entire subject would become quickly negotiated into the general sciences, and therefore into capitalist ideological structures. If we assume that the status quo is maintained, and there is no public announcement regarding extraterrestrials, ufology will remain where it is."

"Many of my colleagues in ufological circles would argue that it is essential for UFO discourse to move away from the theological, and towards the scientific method. I would agree with them; however, the razor cuts both ways, and the ideological mechanisms of the sciences can be as dogmatic as the religious tenets of the UFO believers."

—MJ BANIAS

"Empires bloom and crumble to dust, and yet the mystery of the UFO lingers still—for it perhaps is not a puzzle meant to be unlocked by a consensus, but confronted and dealt with by each and every one of us when the proper time comes."

"I have successfully turned my lifelong obsession for UFOs into my personal alchemy, encouraging myself to pursue questions I know full well are without easy answers, and to grow both intellectually and spiritually for it. To assume one is certain of the phenomenon's true origins and intentions at this stage is beyond arrogant—it is childishly naive."

—RED PILL JUNKIE

"While I can appreciate and respect a 'nuts and bolts' approach to the phenomenon, the one clearly tangible vehicle central to any UFO story is the human witness. To ignore certain aspects of the experience that are described as 'paranormal' by the people who witness them is an act of folly."

"By cherry-picking reports and ignoring or being unsympathetic towards cases of high strangeness, researchers are losing valuable pieces of information and data that could work towards a greater understanding of the experience as a whole."

—SUSAN DEMETER-ST. CLAIR

"To even scratch the surface of the UFO enigma, we must move past the mentality that we are dealing purely with nuts and bolts, past the notion that the key to the UFO phenomenon lies in physical analysis."

"Instead of watching a phantom war between realists and dreamers, perhaps we might benefit from standing, if only for a little while, with one foot in each camp."

—RYAN SPRAGUE

"How much do we bring to the dance during a paranormal encounter? In other words, how much of the UFO experience is the result of our subconscious minds trying to make sense of unexpected, startling, and/or frightening input, and leaving us with an insane placeholder when it can't decide on anything else?"

"UFOs and anything walking out of them are never expected and always strange. In the act of first experiencing the event, and then, more importantly, in remembering it and telling the story about it to ourselves and others, we are adding many layers of cultural baggage and other input that help us to make sense of the experience. In so doing, we are taking ourselves step-by-step away from our original impressions."

—GREG BISHOP

"If we are to better know the UFO then we must learn first how to disentangle ourselves from the hallucinatory nature of seeing and accept that much of what is reported in closer encounter events is so very strange because it is beyond the borders of what can be witnessed."

In longing to make contact with the alien Other we can destabilize ourselves in ways that are not always healthy in how we endure our lonely existential hours... To dare to know the song the siren sings is to sink oneself into a void of self-design. The pursuit of the UFO mystery offers much of the same. There is a danger in surrendering the ego and identity, and so the call of the UFO may simply be one that is mirroring something much simpler to us. Do not try to penetrate the mystery, for that is not the way, but learn about yourself and what you are at the edges of the capacities of your biology."

—ROBERT BRANDSTETTER

FOREWORD

In early 2017 I sent a short essay, written in the thirteenth century, to my colleague who works for a contractor for NASA and the U.S. Space Program. My colleague is one of the world's leading experts in aeronautics, and I am a professor of Religious Studies, specializing in Catholic history. My colleague knew nothing about the source, and what it represented. I knew it was the first written account describing the stigmata of St. Francis of Assisi, the Catholic monk whom the current Pope chose as his namesake. It was written by a witness to the event, Brother Leo, the secretary of St. Francis. It describes an aerial anomaly that crashes through the earth's atmosphere to deliver what appear to be rays of light that rip open wounds on the hands and side of St. Francis. He later dies from these wounds, with Brother Leo at his side.

My colleague, who is not Catholic, was not aware that this event is famous and has been interpreted by Catholics as being the first case of the Catholic charism called the stigmata, or the wounds of Christ. He read the account and gave his interpretation. Brother Leo writes, "In the center of that bright whirlpool was a core of blinding light that flashed down from the depths of the sky with terrifying speed until suddenly it stopped." And there is more. My colleague wrote, "This appears to be a real object that has all the signs that it has broken through the atmosphere, created blue and white sparks, is spinning, and even appears to have given off some type of radiation, judging from the wounds that appear on the hands of the witnessing monk. There is a database of similar types of accounts of contemporary aerial phenomena."

Why did I send my colleague the description of this event? Am I suggesting that St. Francis' wounds and sighting of an aerial object, which occurred in the thirteenth century, were the result of a UFO encounter? I am not. Am I suggesting that modern accounts of anomalous aerial phenomena are sightings of angels, which is what Brother Leo called the spinning, living aerial object? No, I am not stating that, either. These conclusions would be too simple, and would probably be wrong.

What I am suggesting, however, is a research strategy that takes into account the real social and cultural effects of sightings like St. Francis' and Brother Leo's. I am not suggesting that, as researchers, we can know exactly what St. Francis saw, or experienced, or what modern experiencers see or experience. What we can know and study, however, are the cultural effects produced by these experiences. In my field, it is very obvious that this particular experience resulted in one of the longest and most enduring religious devotions and beliefs: the stigmata event of St. Francis, in which billions of Catholics believe. This is not insignificant. These events produce real effects. Their cultural impacts are substantial.

This brings me to the contents of this brilliant book. Each of the contributors in this volume is sharply aware of the futility of *concluding*. Instead, they offer strategies for *understanding*—understanding the phenomena, and understanding its social and cultural effects. In this way, their work is sophisticated and relevant. It is relevant because the latest research on belief in UFO phenomena places it on par with belief in God. More young people believe in UFOs and in the potential existence of extraterrestrial life than believe in God. *Let that sink in.* Roughly eighty percent of young people, and about sixty percent of older people, are believers.

Several essays in this volume consider the role of belief in the evolution of modern ufology, and how subcultural interpretations of anomalous events in fact tell us more about ourselves than about the phenomena. Of course, these contributors are not the first to have focused on the social effects of belief, instead of trying conclusively to solve the UFO riddle. Dr. Jacques Vallée, many years ago, proposed this very strategy to a closed group of global leaders at the United Nations. In that meeting, he stated that among its physical effects, and its potential objective nature, there is yet a third, more pressing aspect of the phenomenon to study. He wrote, "The third aspect is the social belief system which has been generated in all the nations represented on this committee by the expectation of space visitors." He also told the committee that the belief proliferates regardless of the objective nature of the phenomena. He continued, "The belief in space visitors is independent of the physical reality of the of the UFO phenomenon."[1] Although Vallée doesn't reject the objective nature of UFOs, he suggests that researchers seriously turn to the study of the phenomenon from the perspective of its effects on human society. *Regardless of its physical, objective nature, its social effects are very real.*

Ironically, what appears to be a "cop out" with respect to assessing the objective nature of the phenomenon is most likely the most effective means by which to understand it. Leaving behind the "nuts-and-bolts" approach and embracing the complexity of how the phenomenon affects and shapes belief frees researchers and allows them to gain a broader view of the mechanisms of the phenomenon. This view sheds light on its nature and reality. Although this might rankle hard core nuts-and-bolts theorists, it is the case that the phenomena commonly referred to as "UFOs" have been, and currently are, inextricably associated with religion and religious beliefs. The history of religion is, among other things, a record of perceived contact with supernatural beings, many of which descend from the skies as either beings of light, or on light, or amid light. This is one of the reasons why scholars of religion are comfortable examining modern reports of UFO events. Professor Jeffrey J. Kripal articulates this well. In his work, he has sought to reveal "how the modern experience of the alien coming down from the sky can be compared to the ancient experience of the god descending from the heavens."

These "contact events," which are the perceived interface between the human and the intelligent non-human being from the sky, spawn beliefs and interpretations. These beliefs and interpretations develop into communities of belief, or, faith communities. Kripal notes, "Some of the remembered effects of these fantastic states of mind have been taken up by extremely elaborate social, political, and artistic processes and have been fashioned by communities into mythical, ritual, and institutional complexes that have fundamentally changed human history. We call these 'religions.'"[2]

In analyzing the contact event and the subsequent interpretations that spawn beliefs about it, a researcher needs to keep a few things in mind. First, as in the history of religions, a contact event is not automatically a religious event, and the spotting of an unidentified aerial object is not automatically a "UFO event." These experiences become religious events, or UFO events, through *an interpretive process.* The interpretative process then goes through layers of shaping and sometimes active intervention before it reaches masses of people, and is finally solidified as a religious event, or a UFO event, or both. The processes are the same.

The strategy of "not concluding," or bracketing the question of what the phenomenon is, exposes the intricacies of how belief in the phenomenon works. Moving from a fixation on the objective nature of "what it is," allows one to focus on the social mechanisms that foster belief and how belief impacts human society. One can call it the work of angels, or demons, or UFOs, but those labels reveal more about the communities who use the labels than they do about the phenomena. Researchers can glean interesting data when they leave aside the potential cause and attend to the social effects that arise from belief in the phenomena.

The various formations of belief in UFOs can be traced as cultural processes that develop both spontaneously and intentionally within layers of popular culture and through intentional institutional involvement. It is important to remember that the actual objective nature of the events that inspire the interpretations and beliefs fade in comparison to the reality of the social effects. If one takes seriously Jacques Vallée's proposal that the phenomenon either is, or operates as, a control mechanism, then identifying its mechanisms—or *how* it controls—becomes a worthy matter to study. Here is a speculation: studying its social effects can help determine, as much as is possible, the nature of the phenomenon.

Whatever is the "UFO," whatever the triggering event, be it a misidentified aircraft, meteor, or a real extraterrestrial craft, one can agree that today it is the subject of mass belief. Leaving off the question of what it is, researchers can focus on the belief—how it forms, and how it impacts and influences history and human culture. The beauty of this volume is that it brings together both nuts-and-bolts materialists and those who favour more oblique approaches. Unusually, and refreshingly, it represents both objective observers of the UFO conundrum *and* subjective experiencers of it. The combination of these perspectives is necessary to better understand the phenomena. The non-dogmatic, self-reflective, and critical approach of each of these authors is urgently needed in the field of ufology, right now. They are its hope and its future.

—**Diana Walsh Pasulka, Ph.D.**
Professor and Chair of the
Department of Philosophy and Religion
University of North Carolina, Wilmington
Author of *American Cosmic: UFOs, Technology, Belief*
(Oxford University Press)

INTRODUCTION

Ufologists speak often of "The Truth." It's *out there*, they insist, and it must doggedly be pursued for the benefit of all mankind. But rarely are ufologists truthful with themselves. There is, of course, no such thing as "ufology," not in any meaningful sense of the term. If "ology" refers to a branch of knowledge or learning sprung from organized research, then ufology is a broken twig.

The UFO field has produced thousands of dedicated researchers over the years, and reams of literature; but to what end? What can we claim to know conclusively today about the underlying nature of UFO phenomena that we didn't know in the late-1940s? UFO study has always suffered from major organizational and methodological problems. It has also become dangerously self-referential. Few researchers are prepared to think critically.

Today, as ever, the Extraterrestrial Hypothesis (ETH) is the most popular ufological theory. It has become so popular that the already-flimsy architecture of the field has morphed into "exopolitics"—a movement born of the Internet and based on a blanket acceptance that UFOs are extraterrestrial vehicles, that the government knows this, and that, in time, "Truth" will break free and a new age of human enlightenment will begin. It is a myth, spun partly by external design, but largely by the UFO community's profound need to believe that universal truth is tangible, and within arm's reach. Today's UFO conferences bear an increasing resemblance to the spectacle of the Megachurch, where the cult of personality attracts thousands of believers, all hopeful their prophets can move them just an inch closer to UFO salvation.

If ufology is a New Age religion, then "Disclosure" is its Holy Grail—that ever-imminent announcement from officialdom that we are not alone in the universe, and, moreover, that "They" are among us. The problem with the Disclosure mindset is that it declares an end to the UFO enigma and discourages us from further study of the phenomenon, and of its cultural and societal effects. Why study when we can simply wait? All we need do is talk about UFOs in online forums and occasionally send a petition to the White House. Eventually, our leaders will see fit to share with us the aliens' world-changing information and technologies, ushering in a new era of cosmic consciousness. It's only a matter of time. Disclosure requires little more than our passive spectatorship.

The ultimate irony of the Disclosure movement is that, by imagining all answers to the UFO mystery to be out of public reach, deep in the bowels of the national security state, it places power into the hands of officialdom, while disempowering the individual. Modern "ufology," therefore, is no longer about asking challenging questions. Rather, it is about fitting predetermined answers into an established quasi-religious belief system.

If ever we are to further our understanding of the UFO enigma, we must fundamentally reframe our debate. We must wipe the board clean and fill it with new ideas, new theories, even new language. We must be willing to start from scratch when the field stagnates. We must be critical, sober, and free from dogma—ready to rinse away the residue of our own beliefs.

With the above in mind, in April 2016, I began approaching a select few individuals in the UFO research community—free-thinkers and iconoclasts—with a proposal for a volume of original essays presenting alternative perspectives on UFOs and the UFO subculture. Just under a year later, I find myself writing this introduction for the near-complete manuscript. It all came together relatively quickly and smoothly, if not without the usual amount of effort and sacrifice that goes into such an endeavor. All those who chose to write for this volume have committed to it wholeheartedly, and I have been inspired daily by their enthusiasm for the project.

I know I speak for all contributors here when I say this book was a challenge to write. I know it was a challenge to edit, and I also know it will be a challenge to read. Whether you're a "skeptic" or a "believer" (for lack of more nuanced terms), this book will irk you. And that, of course, is the intention. Indeed, it is structured such that it may provoke maximum discomfort in the reader and push cognitive dissonance into overdrive. For the first half of this volume, the essays spar back and forth between pro-and-anti-materialist approaches. Some of our contributors advocate extreme skepticism of any UFO claim, while championing traditional scientific methodologies—the dispassionate pursuit of objectively verifiable evidence—while other contributors see limitations in such an approach, preferring instead a more oblique path of engagement with what they see as a consciously oblique phenomenon. Other contributors explore why modern UFO accounts seem often to overlap with other mysterious phenomena, or how the UFO can be utilized as a looking-glass for profound introspection, one reflective of personal belief, stress, or trauma.

For all the unconventional theories presented herein, none of the contributors would be so bold or naïve as to discount the *possibility* that some UFOs are representative of extraterrestrial intelligences. We are suggesting, however, that today's UFO field is sorely lacking in meaningful debate and is close to the point of stagnation in its uncritical thinking and lazy acceptance of what may *seem* like the most logical theory for inexplicable aerial anomalies, but which, when tested against the full depth of data, falls desperately short as an exclusive hypothesis. To quote SMiles Lewis in this volume: "I advocate for a multi-theory interpretation of the UFO phenomenon. I don't think there is any one explanation that accounts for all the data. I think there are a number of things going on simultaneously."

Many of these "things" undoubtedly stem from what Susan Demeter-St. Clair refers to as "the one clearly tangible vehicle central to any UFO story"—the human witness. The role of the witness in UFO events typically is overlooked by UFO investigators, whose focus often is on *what* the witness has seen, rather than *why* they have seen it, or *how* they have interpreted it. The assumption, strangely, is that UFO witnesses are almost always independent of their anomalous experiences. Multiple essayists in this volume urge a fundamental redirection of UFO research, from the external to the internal—by seeking to understand the daunting complexities of human cognition and consciousness itself, we may better understand the UFO, and, perhaps more importantly, better understand ourselves.

If by some slim chance this is the first UFO book you've ever picked up, I'm afraid you've thrown yourself in at the very deep end of the pool, but that's all the more reason to push on with it; if you do so, I feel confident in stating that the wider ufological waters will seem clearer and more navigable.

∼

Chris Rutkowski's opening essay is a trial by fire for any reader who considers themself a UFO experiencer. He pulls no punches in his characterization of a substantial portion of the UFO community as "zealots." I know for sure that some readers will be inclined to set this book aside after just a few pages of Rutkowski's essay. Don't do that. If his perspective does not fall in line with your own, simply accept that from the outset, proceed with an open mind, and then ask yourself if any of his observations are objectively untrue. Rutkowski's essay is incisive and, to my mind, necessarily harsh. It is not, as some will undoubtedly see it, a piece of debunkery. Rather, it is a product of its author's frustration at those UFO enthusiasts whose wholesale rejection of all evidence at odds with their own beliefs justifies his view that ufology is more a religion than a science.

I've frontloaded this book with pieces on religion because the religious aspects of UFO belief are undeniable (again, this observation should not be interpreted as a dismissal of UFOs as an objectively real phenomenon. No one in this book attempts to make such a case). Make no mistake, ufology *is* a New Age religion; with this in mind, its followers should take caution, for many if not all strains of religious belief have been exploited throughout the ages by elite power structures for reasons of cultural and societal control—a case made by several authors here.

If UFO "believers" can pass the test of Rutkowski's essay—if they can override their cognitive dissonance—then they have the resilience and critical thinking to see them through all the essays that follow.

Next up, and in sharp contrast to Rutkowski's, Mike Clelland's essay is a deeply personal meditation on the author's direct experiences with UFOs and what he considers to be some form of non-human intelligence. Those of a traditionally skeptical bent may be inclined to skip Clelland's essay. Don't do that. Clelland's value in this volume is that he is unusually self-aware and self-analytical in the presentation of his experiences. He is certain he has interacted with anomalous phenomena in mysterious ways, but he steadfastly refuses to reach solid conclusions as to the ultimate nature and purpose of these phenomena. Clelland is an "experiencer" who shuns zealotry and who wears with discomfort any ufological labels that might be used to categorize him. He is compelled to share his story, and he wants us to hear it, but he also wants us to know he is incapable of objectivity in this arena. If more experiencers could adopt Clelland's considered approach, perhaps some bridges could be built between opposing ends of the UFO research camp.

Clelland's observations are largely subjective, and he places great value on the experience of the individual UFO witness. In contrast, the observations of our next contributor, Jack Brewer, are rooted in rationalism and the scientific method. Brewer seriously questions the value of UFO witness testimony, noting "...personal stories, interesting and entertaining as they may be, are often of very little value to the professional research process." He goes on to qualify this statement in considerable detail.

Brewer's essay is broad in scope and among the most constructive in this volume. It highlights numerous problems currently hampering serious UFO research, and then provides possible remedies and solutions. Again, it is the work of a man with a deep interest in the UFO mystery and a deep frustration at the lazy assumptions and shoddy practices of a great many—perhaps the majority—of UFO researchers.

Next in our line-up is Joshua Cutchin. Continuing with our back-and-forth approach, Cutchin's essay is a bold rejection of traditional materialist solutions to the UFO riddle and a challenge to "nut-and-bolts" researchers to engage with "high-strangeness" aspects of UFO phenomena from unconventional—even esoteric—perspectives. He encourages that we embrace uncertainty, noting: "Moving beyond materialism is about honestly confronting the fact that we know nothing for certain about UFOs, yet choosing to be inspired rather than frustrated by this realization, leading to a type of non-dogmatic gnosticism."

We're back to a materialist approach in Micah Hanks' contribution, which champions rigorous scientific methodology and ambitiously seeks to provide an entirely revised classification system for UFO reporting in the hope of more effectively sorting the proverbial wheat from the chaff. Still, Hanks seeks a union between those who operate within the structures of modern skepticism and those who roam beyond its walls, and he warns against scientific dogmatism, noting: "Modern skepticism can, I think, be summarized in many instances as an ideology, around which a social movement has been built—one that, today, also runs tangent with atheism—and as a paradoxically evangelical attitude about the supremacy of science above all other forms of knowledge."

We tread a middle ground in Lorin Cutts' essay, which acknowledges what its author considers to be a genuine mystery behind the UFO phenomenon, while advocating extreme skepticism towards almost all aspects of ufology. Cutts propounds similar ideas to those of Diana Walsh Pasulka and Jack Brewer in his discussion of what he refers to as the UFO mythological zone: "the gap between fact and belief, what we see and what we want to see, what we experience and how we interpret it." Cutts, himself a UFO witness, seeks to highlight what he sees as the major obstacles we must overcome—or at least *recognize*—if we are ever to come close to understanding the UFO enigma. The biggest obstacle, suggests Cutts, is *us*—our enthusiastic willingness to believe and to be led. He notes: "Many people are highly malleable and susceptible to new ideas and beliefs within the UFO mythological zone. Charlatans, fraudsters, and hucksters are free to roam and operate at will. Their contribution to the UFO subject should never be underestimated, for the conditions for successful deception are near perfect. Common sense, lateral thinking and balanced questioning are far superseded and outweighed by irrational belief. Contagion of ideas is rife."

Narrowing our focus in this volume is Curt Collins, whose essay is devoted entirely to documenting the skeptical investigation and successful debunking of the so-called "Roswell Slides," which were purported to show the image of a deceased alien entity. Collins was one of several members of the Roswell Slides Research Group (RSRG), and his contribution here is the definitive accounting of how the RSRG operated in tackling one of the greatest ufological blunders (or hoaxes, depending on your perspective) of the 21st Century. Collins' essay is intricate in its detail and reads like a true-life detective story of how a handful of researchers, separated in some cases by thousands of miles but united in cyberspace, took it upon themselves to expose as fraudulent the claims of dubious UFO personalities screaming from the hilltops that they had found the smoking-gun for Roswell, and that UFO Disclosure was now just a step away.

The reader can make up their own mind as to what motivated the Slides' promoters, but, for me, this was less a conscious hoax, and more a case of blind belief. The promoters wanted so desperately for the "evidence" to fit their firmly-established perspective on Roswell and UFOs more broadly, that they fooled themselves completely, seeing only what they wanted to see. And they fooled a great many UFO enthusiasts and researchers in the process. When the truth was exposed—that the Slides showed not an alien body, but something entirely down to Earth—it felt to many like the final nail in the coffin for popular ufology. Certainly, it can be said that the Slides debacle represents everything that's wrong with "ufology" today.

Collins presents the RSRG investigation here as a potential model for future UFO research and investigation—an example of how researchers can work together to solve definitively certain cases and prevent the spread of misinformation in the field. Collins reflects on the strengths and weaknesses of his group's methodology and observes: "Groups can be great tools, but they have their limitations. Each of us must remain objective, seek the best evidence and ask challenging questions, whether as part of a team or as individuals."

Next up is SMiles Lewis' adapted transcript of an epic public lecture he delivered, examining "The Fantastic Facts about UFOs, Altered States of Consciousness, and Mind-at-Large." It's a wide-ranging and deeply insightful piece covering everything from Gaian consciousness and planetary poltergeists, to the possible use of the UFO for "Covert Folklore Warfare" by government spooks. It also serves as an extensive bibliography of obscure but valuable literature relating to all themes explored throughout this book. For esoteric and conspiratorial bookworms, Lewis' essay is a treasure-trove.

We then move to MJ Banias. His ambitious contribution examines the limitations of subcultural UFO discourse within the constraints of modern capitalism. He argues that the ideologies of capitalism and UFO discourse are fundamentally at odds, and the result is that "ufology is forever trapped in a marginalized state."

Banias notes that, in stark contrast to the capitalist citadel under whose shadow it chaotically dances, UFO discourse has "no locus of control, no elites, and no ivory tower that establishes ideological truth. There is no established power in the discourse, therefore power moves openly between constant shifts in ideas." The UFO discourse, Banias argues, has no mechanism of governance: "it is democratized, with members of the subculture able freely to express their own ideologies, which vary from reasoned logic to utter speculative hokum... It is, in simple terms, a field of study which is completely democratized. It is an example of a living and functioning discourse that counters modern ideological capital—it creates a pseudo-reality that does not require mainstream official ideologies in order to exist; it is in this democratic state where modern ideological capital is impotent, unable to entrench itself and establish ideological order."

Unfortunately for ufology, it is this same dynamic that prevents even serious and legitimate UFO discourse from ever finding its way into official culture as anything other than a sideshow attraction. The future of ufology is bleak, says Banias, observing that, in the event of some form of official UFO "Disclosure" (if such a thing is even possible), "ufology would die an instant death as the entire subject would quickly become negotiated into the general sciences and, therefore, into capitalist ideological structures. If we assume that the status quo is maintained, and there is no public announcement... ufology will remain where it is. What can only occur then is a grassroots movement which always operates against the current ideological reality."

Continuing the sociological line of enquiry, our next contributor, Red Pill Junkie (RPJ), refers to the UFO phenomenon as a "disruption." Expanding on the theories of Jacques Vallée and John Keel, RPJ considers the possibility that UFO events may be the product of a trickster intelligence, gleefully and anarchically prodding us to provoke individual and societal reactions and developments. He notes, "The UFO disruption is not only a threat to the authority of scientific orthodoxy, it fundamentally defies every conceivable paradigm human society is built upon, in almost every sphere one can envision: religion, economics, communication, and state politics, to name but a few."

Equally, RPJ also considers it possible that certain UFO events are psychically-manifested by-products of collective stress and trauma during times of societal pressure or upheaval. Regardless of its possible stimuli or motivations, says RPJ, the UFO is the ultimate symbol of anarchist subversion in the modern world. Beyond its cultural and sociological musings, RPJ's essay is also a personal reflection on how its author has utilized the UFO as an instrument to better understand his own worldview in relation to others.

Susan Demeter-St. Clair's contribution is a focused discussion of how so many UFO experiences appear to overlap with parapsychological phenomena. Like Red Pill Junkie, she also makes a case for certain UFO events—particularly mass sightings—being triggered by the same psychic mechanisms as provoke poltergeist activity; such events, perhaps, being born of personal or social unrest and upheaval. As with others in this volume, Demeter-St. Clair urges UFO researchers to engage more openly and thoughtfully with the high-strangeness aspects of the phenomena. She argues, "UFO reports that include various types of psychic phenomena may be the key to a greater understanding of the UFO enigma, or, at the very least, trigger more meaningful questions in our ongoing efforts to understand it."

Ryan Sprague's essay draws from the work of theorists and researchers including Carl Jung, Jacques Vallée, Jenny Randles, David Clarke, and Greg Bishop. It considers the enduring appeal of the UFO in modern culture, ufology's long (and perhaps futile) struggle for legitimacy, and the questionable inclination of so many UFO researchers to label the phenomenon as "extraterrestrial."

Sprague does not discount the possibility of otherworldly visitation, but he ushers the reader gently down other avenues of enquiry and suggests we may sooner to come to grips with the nature of the UFO phenomenon by seeking to unravel the complexities of human cognition and our own perceptual apparatus.

Similar ideas are explored in great depth by Greg Bishop. His essay applies advanced theories of cognition to the experience of the UFO witness to highlight the foibles of human perception and how what we *see* is not necessarily an accurate representation of what is *there*, especially when we're confronted with phenomena at the extremities of human experience. The convolutions of human memory are also considered, as are the often-hindering approaches of the UFO investigator when eliciting witness testimony. Bishop notes: "In the act of first experiencing the event, and then, more importantly, in remembering it and telling the story about it to ourselves and others, we are adding many layers of cultural baggage and other input that help us to make sense of the experience. In so doing, we are taking ourselves step-by-step away from our original impressions."

Like others in this volume, Bishop encourages sharper focus on the role of the witness in the UFO equation. He posits that UFO phenomena may even be "co-created" events between the observer and the observed. This theory allows for the existence of anomalous stimuli or even non-human intelligences, but suggests that whatever the underlying cause of UFO events, it is likely far more complex and participatory than mere extraterrestrial visitation.

"How much do we bring to the dance during a paranormal encounter?" Bishop asks, "How much of the UFO experience is the result of our subconscious minds trying to make sense of unexpected, startling, and/or frightening input, and leaving us with an insane placeholder when it can't decide on anything else?"

Bishop's essay builds a compelling case for the power of the human mind to radically distort subjective extraordinary experiences—even in the moment of the experience. It raises serious questions about just how far off the mark popular ufology is in its simplistic conceptualization of this phenomenon.

Grasping for definitive answers to the UFO riddle is perhaps not the most productive approach, says Bishop: "The terms of the search may need to be changed. If we are looking for an 'answer' to the enigma, this assumes that there is an easy or understandable one waiting in the wings for just the right researcher who gets lucky or is amazingly smart. Perhaps the process should be referred to as a quest for understanding rather than any search for a specific truth. This may serve to keep the question open, and direct thought processes and models."

Our final essay, by Robert Brandstetter, again examines the perceptual limitations of the human observer, but it also serves as an impassioned plea for UFO witnesses—who often exhibit signs of real trauma—to be treated with empathy and compassion by those who might otherwise seek to exploit, ridicule, or ignore them. Whatever its root cause, the UFO experience is ultimately a human one, and all that that implies.

Brandstetter observes:

> Investigatory approaches towards the UFO witness have been haphazard and, in some cases, quite harmful, leaving the witness as something to both exploit and consume. Yet it is the witness experience that is the primary catalyst for ufology... What started as a story about seeing something strange in the sky has since been manufactured into a mythology... A return to the core component of the narrative is necessary and it must be done with more imagination, ethics and standardization that respect what it means to undergo a traumatic experience. A more compassionate approach to the witness, as well as an appreciation of how the act of seeing works during high-strange experiences, may allow us to gather much more valuable information about how the UFO phenomenon intersects with human perception.

Brandstetter ends his essay, and this volume, with profoundly personal contemplations on what it means to be a UFO witness, and the value of seeking to understand, to know, and to learn from those whose identity is bound-up in the alien Other.

This volume is critical but constructive. It combines ideas both abstract and theoretical, and concrete and practical. Some of these ideas gel and overlap; some of them clash and conflict. The goal is to shift and reframe the debate outside the prison of belief, yet also beyond the razor-wire of scientific dogmatism.

I encourage that you approach this book from the perspective of an anthropologist. Imagine your eyes are fresh to the UFO spectacle. What do you see in these essays? What do they communicate to you, individually and collectively? What do they tell you about their authors? What does your attraction and reaction to this book tell you about *you*? Pull this book apart. Dissect it. Dissect us. Dissect yourself. Consume every word. Muse on every theme and concept. If you feel riled or uncomfortable at any point, ask yourself why.

I provide no conclusion at the end of this volume because I am reluctant to further stamp myself on the material—I wish for the reader to be as free as possible in their own interpretations—and because I'm not sure there are any meaningful conclusions to be drawn of the phenomenon now beyond the theories and suggestions presented across the spectrum of these essays. Reach a conclusion if you can, but hold it lightly in the acceptance that letting go is no bad thing.

Understanding UFOs and related phenomena is a glacially slow process that is in its fetal stages. The UFO research field would do well to accept and appreciate this. Therein lies the freedom to explore—and to learn.

UFOs: Reframing the Debate is a cold, hard, slap in the face for "ufology," delivered with love. It is a call to break away from established ideas, approaches, and practices, and to boldly tread a new path in quest of understanding what may very well be the greatest mystery of all.

—**Robbie Graham**
March, 2017

OUR ALIEN, **WHO ART IN HEAVEN**

Chris Rutkowski

Of the many different cores around which a cult can form, possibly the most curious is the phenomenon of UFOs. Beyond the ostensibly pragmatic issue of whether or not aliens are indeed responsible for UFO sightings, there is a huge volume of discussion in formal and fan literature (and online in social media forums) regarding the interpretation of UFO reports as personal encounters with alien beings–physical and/or ethereal. In fact, such subjective discourse has almost completely supplanted any rigorous attempts to study the subject with anything resembling scientific methodology.

Given that much of ufology focuses on highly subjective interpretation of the UFO phenomenon as being due to an alien presence on Earth, how does ufology advance? And since there is a trend in modern ufology to embrace contactee-oriented discourse, having evolved from merely alien abduction accounts to more esoteric claims, what does this mean for the advancement of knowledge in the field today?

Modern ufology appears to have rejected science in favour of a more mystical and religious view. A simple look at a list on Amazon of best-selling books about UFOs on any given day will show that the top ten titles are conspiracy-based, religious, personal accounts of encounters, or are titles only peripheral to the subject of UFOs, such as ancient astronauts (which posits that aliens visited Earth during our early history or prehistory). Few can be classified as "scientific" in their approach.

This is likely an accurate reflection of the general public's view on UFOs. The populist consensus is that aliens are visiting Earth and are in direct contact with humans, whether conspiratorially, with one or another government organization, or invasively communicating and meeting with contactees. This in itself is an interesting phenomenon, because there is no incontrovertible evidence, from a scientific standpoint, that aliens exist at all, let alone are in contact with humans.

And yet, the belief persists. A recent Canadian poll released in August 2016 found the "vast majority of Canadians (79 per cent) say it is either definitely (29 per cent) or probably (50 per cent) true that intelligent life exists elsewhere in the universe." And when the random sample of the Canadian population was asked if they believe: "Extraterrestrial beings have already visited the Earth," 11 per cent replied "Definitely True," and 36 per cent replied "Probably True." Furthermore, 43 per cent of Canadians believe: "The U.S. government has covered up the existence and presence of extraterrestrial life on Earth."[1]

Polls done during the past 50 years throughout North America have found similar results; a significant percentage of the population believes that aliens exist and that they are visiting Earth. This is despite the fact that aliens have not been detected by terrestrial telescopes or other instruments, even though searches for extraterrestrial intelligence continue to be conducted by scientists and laypersons alike.

What, then, drives such a belief system? We can gain insight into the UFO belief mechanism by looking to other belief systems for comparison, such as mainstream religion. Religious adherents share a common set of beliefs that reinforce their behaviour and convictions. If they believe the universe was created by God, they will search for any indication that is so and adopt a set of tenets that lead directly from their belief system. In some fundamentalist sects, they will reject any negative evidence and dispute or indeed shun any sacrilegious attempt to undermine their strongly-held views.

More and more, ufology is the realm of UFO fans who describe their own experiences and encounters with denizens from other worlds or who promulgate extraordinary UFO stories. Few within UFO fandom dare to question claims of alien abductions or other kinds of contact with entities from "elsewhere."

We should also recognize the distinction between UFO abductees and contactees because they do seem to be different kinds of people in at least one aspect. Abductees tend not to proselytize the way contactees often do. In fact, most abductees insist on anonymity. For the most part, abductees are baffled by their experiences and that is why they appeal to researchers for help. In short, they don't appear to know what has happened to them and need some assistance in sorting out their lives, emotions and world view.

Modern contactees, on the other hand, need no one to tell them what happened to them. They know that they have encountered space aliens and have been selected for some important purpose. They can espouse great knowledge about how the universe "really is," and approach researchers not to get guidance, but for verification. What's more, many take it upon themselves to counsel other abductees and are sometimes regarded as experts themselves. Some feel they have been chosen by the aliens to help others of like mind.[2]

Fanatical UFO belief is essentially an anti-science movement. It rejects scientific evaluations and rational explanations for UFO sightings, often embracing an elaborate government cover-up of "the Truth" or ascribing near-omnipotent powers to aliens who manipulate reality. In this UFO subculture, patently absurd accounts and claims are considered not only possible, but likely.

This rejection of science by many in our culture has been noted by many scholars, most well outside of ufology. One recent study found: "Rejection of scientific findings is mostly driven by motivated cognition: People tend to reject findings that threaten their core beliefs or worldview... General education and scientific literacy do not mitigate rejection of science but, rather, increase the polarization of opinions along partisan lines."[3]

In this age where some people see a breakdown of society and where uncertainty dominates politics and economics, it may seem attractive to look for salvation somewhere other than from conventional paths to solutions. The reasoning seems sound enough: if aliens are truly advanced technologically—as they would need to be to have achieved interstellar travel—then they would certainly have solved problems such as environmental pollution, overpopulation, unequal distribution of wealth, world hunger, and war.

Psychologists have defined a theory of cognitive dissonance whereby people with strongly-held beliefs will protect their views by adjusting them to fit facts or, more usually, reject the facts that would negate their views. Such a process is clearly at work within hardcore UFO fandom, best defined in a classic study by Festinger et al., whose seminal work *When Prophecy Fails* documented the actions of a so-called "Doomsday Cult" who believed that aliens would save them from a disaster.[4] Even when the divinely inspired prediction of doom did not materialize, cult members still clung to their beliefs against all rational thought.[5]

It should be noted that not all individuals who are interested in the subject of UFOs are disaffected to this extent. Many are either simply curious about the subject because of pop culture representations of aliens, or are UFO witnesses who are merely trying to understand what they have seen. UFO belief becomes cult-like when adherents become closed to any interpretation of UFOs as conventional phenomena, and become something closer to religious zealots.

UFO zealots are certain that there is a real UFO cover-up preventing the truth of alien visitation from reaching the public. This can come from direct suppression of proof of alien visitation through the manipulation and control of mainstream media, or from silencing of selected UFO proponents who are "getting too close to the truth."

UFO zealots are certain that their own personal UFO experiences are proof of direct contact with aliens, even if they have only actually visually seen a distant light moving in the sky along the horizon. In many cases, they may have engaged in debates with ufologists, investigating their reports which have suggested some reasonable explanations, but have rejected these suggestions because, for example: a) explanations fail in their cases because of some minor differences; b) the investigators are not as enlightened as the UFO zealot witnesses; c) the investigators are part of the cover-up; or d) the witnesses received telepathic contact from the aliens, affirming their beliefs.

In rejecting explanations for or insisting on the reality of their subjective UFO experiences, zealous UFO believers often alienate themselves from other UFO fans. These latter individuals are interested in a search for "the truth" but do not "know" the truth as overly-fanatical followers claim. Rejection of a UFO zealot's sighting as having an explanation, or questioning their belief that they are in contact with aliens from, say, the Orion Nebula, will either cause a cessation in discourse or, more likely, an animated and vehement debate.

It is this kind of fervor that leads to the observation that much of what is called ufology today should be characterized as a religion, or, at the very least, religious in nature. Is there evidence in modern ufology that supports this approach?

There are two basic forms of fanatical UFO zealots: 1) adherents of overt spiritual/religious UFO cults; and 2) members of obsessive UFO belief groups. Both exhibit cultish behaviour.

Most UFO fan groups usually have no explicit spiritual relationship with the Space Brothers and simply believe with strong conviction that extraterrestrials are visiting Earth. They reject scientists' explanations of UFOs, and often insist that there is some sort of grand cover-up of the knowledge that aliens are among us. A good example of this is the Disclosure lobby, which is convinced there is an ongoing cover-up of proof that aliens are not only present on Earth, but that there is an international conspiracy to keep this information from the general public.[6]

The Disclosure lobby has a mandate to: 1) hold open, secrecy-free hearings on the UFO/Extraterrestrial presence on and around Earth; and 2) hold open hearings on advanced energy and propulsion systems that, when publicly released, will provide solutions to global environmental challenges. Ideally, what is envisioned is the U.S. President making an unannounced address to the nations on all TV networks, saying: "My fellow Americans, people of the world, we are not alone."[7]

Each year, some proponents of this movement predict that Disclosure is imminent, and each year, nothing substantive occurs to claim victory. Despite this, Disclosure proponents have adjusted their definition of Disclosure to include "soft disclosure," which is the release of official UFO-related documents by various world governments. Included in soft disclosure are the numerous times that politicians and officials have made public statements regarding aliens and UFOs, thus suggesting to Disclosure advocates that the public is being prepared for full Disclosure at a later time.

In some contrast to the Disclosure lobby (although not exclusively, since some adherents share views of both kinds of UFO zealots), spiritual UFO cults venerate omnipotent alien beings often called "Space Brothers," who are closely akin to deities. These entities are always much more advanced than humans, and their levels of advancement are such that these aliens exhibit apparently magical or mystical powers, including ESP and other psychical abilities. They use vehicles such as flying saucers to travel about the Earth (and inside the Earth) or across space and time to visit other planets. They are extraterrestrial in the same sense that God is "not of this world," and originate from distant planets that can be physical or ethereal.

Spiritual UFO cults each tend to cite a different planet of origin for their particular Space Brothers (and Sisters), including planets named Clarion, Korendar and Zanthar. In UFO cult mythology, for example, Clarion is said to exist "on the other side of the Sun," even though such a statement makes no sense whatsoever from an astronomical standpoint. Some groups select planets within our own Solar System as their aliens' homes, including Mars, Jupiter, Saturn and Venus.

An example of the latter is a woman who calls herself Omnec Omec, but was born Sheila Gipson.[8] Currently she lectures widely on how she was "born on the astral level of the planet Venus and came to Earth with her own physical body in 1955." She teaches adherents and followers about "raising consciousness" and achieving inner peace through meditation. Her lectures are a curious mixture of religion and quasi-scientific concepts, attracting UFO zealots who seek enlightenment and knowledge but lack the critical thinking skills that would allow them to realize Gipson's teachings are without any real meaning.

We know science can show Venus is uninhabitable by living creatures, but Gipson tells her followers that Venusian society and technology is so advanced they live in "a different dimension" and "vibrational state." Again, such phrases have no basis in science, but to adherents, they are considered possible.

Venus was also the origin of aliens according to several other contactees, including George Adamski and Howard Menger, the latter of whom even married a Venusian girlfriend in human form. At contactee gatherings, Menger passed along esoteric knowledge from the Venusians, such as: "Everything one creates must originate as thought, which consists of vibratory reflections under control of the mind or intellect. Whatever man thinks, he can do. People who have the ability to teleport themselves also have the ability to use this potential to the highest degree."[9]

At lectures, both Adamski and Menger displayed photographs of "Venusian Scout Ships" in which they claimed to have traveled in space. The photographs have been largely dismissed as fakes by experts, but that has not dissuaded their followers.

Some UFO contactee groups receive instructions directly from aliens through a leader's channelling, telepathic communication or automatic writing (in this way, parallels are drawn between ufology and parapsychology). Once members of a group are sufficiently immersed in the group's teachings, they can begin their own readings and receive messages from aliens. This sometimes leads to a distortion of original teachings. However, the motivation for individual members' own direct communication with aliens is that it allows them to experience their own spiritual "high." They, too, can become "chosen" emissaries of the aliens, much like the original group's leaders.

On the topic of the lack of proof of such alien visitation, Menger noted: "Science asks for proof, but how can we prove something which is beyond our sciences? Scientific proof is based on what we perceive with our five senses, not what we know with the use of even more valuable senses."[10]

This dismissal of science is encountered frequently among UFO zealots, who insist that their esoteric knowledge supersedes scientific methodology when it comes to considering the reality or non-reality of UFO stories or claims. The theme of UFO encounters as "beyond science" occurs repeatedly among contactees. They consider it completely unnecessary to prove the reality of their claims and, in fact, dismiss any attempt to quantify details of their experiences. At some contactee meet-ups, there are even strict rules about attendees not questioning experiencers' claims (reminiscent of 'Never mind the man behind the curtain!' mentality). In effect, in zealot contactee circles, anything claimed is considered as possible as any other claim, despite being apparently unlikely.

This approach is consistent with a view that our society has transitioned from "modernism" to "post-modernism" to "metamodernism." This new era is summed up succinctly as: "Anything goes." Anyone's view is as valid as any other. All opinions are valid and there are no real experts. Anything and everything is possible. From the *Metamodernism Manifesto*: "All information is grounds for knowledge, whether empirical or aphoristic, no matter its truth-value. We should embrace the scientific-poetic synthesis and informed naivety of a magical realism. Error breeds sense."[11]

The implications for ufology are devastating to those seeking "the truth." If even the simplest report of a UFO that is ostensibly just a distant light moving in the sky can be claimed to be a "scout ship," or if a contactee's claim of being impregnated by an alien abductor on board a flying saucer can be accepted without any attempt to question the storyteller, then any kind of real quest for truth must be abandoned. Not only is science effectively shut out of any such discussion, but it is supplanted by faith and belief, beyond the boundaries of orthodoxy.

In this realm of UFO zealotry is another claimed facet of the Space Brothers' characteristics: they are often said to be more "spiritually-attuned" than humans. Furthermore, humans who are in communication with such entities claim they can achieve "higher states of consciousness" and become more advanced as human beings though the influence of aliens.

What does this mean, exactly? This is clearly not the four levels of consciousness defined by psychologists such as Alain Morin: unconscious, conscious, self-aware, and meta self-aware.[12]

It seems to be something taken from Hindu or Buddhist philosophy, which holds that the world we see only becomes real through our observation of it.[13] This of course is parallel to some theories of quantum physics, and is best described by popular physics books such as that by Zukov (1979).[14]

Probably what is meant by UFO zealots describing consciousness is better defined as awareness. This is one's ability to perceive the environment through increasingly complex senses, and being aware of one's thoughts, emotions, ideas and the world.

One of the best-known examples of a group venerating the Space Brothers is The Society of Unarius, led by founder Ruth Norman (Archangel Uriel) for several decades until her death in the 1990s. The group owns dozens of acres in California and, for many years, awaited predicted mass landings of spaceships, which would save selected spiritually attuned individuals. They repeatedly retracted and refined their predictions, which failed to come to pass. Jesus, Mohammed and Einstein often were channelled by Norman, giving further teachings to the Society's followers.

Also a Venus-based group, Unarius, holds that Venusians have "energy bodies" and inhabit a "higher vibratory plane" that is invisible to ordinary, unenlightened humans. But again, what does that mean? In chemistry and physics, it is known that molecular vibration exists because atoms within a molecule can absorb energy and become excited.[15]

To say that a person can change the vibrational state of his or her complete body makes no sense whatsoever from a scientific standpoint. But to UFO zealots, this is a very profound dogma. Contactee Clifford Stone described a race of beings from the Arcturus star system thusly: "Arcturian society is governed by the elders, who are revered by the people of Arcturus for their advanced knowledge, wisdom, and extremely high vibrational frequencies. The higher the vibrational frequency, the closer one is to Light, or spirit, or God."[16]

Venusians, then, are apparently more spiritual than humans.

When challenged on these kinds of claims, UFO zealots will sometimes point to articles and papers in science journals in which terms such as "higher dimensions" and "quantum entanglement" are used, implying that modern science supports mystical concepts. This creates an interesting paradox, in which many UFO zealots reject mainstream science for its largely negative view of UFOs, but embrace quantum physics for its foray into esoteric realms that could be viewed as supporting ESP, interdimensional portals and parallel universes.

When questioned about frequent references to "consciousness" in discussions about UFOs, on December 4, 2014, one anonymous UFO zealot in a Facebook UFO discussion group noted: "Let me quote Sir James Jeans, 'The stream of knowledge is heading toward a non-mechanical reality; the universe begins to look more like a great thought than like a great machine. Mind no longer appears to be an accidental intruder into the realm of matter, we ought rather hail it as the creator and governor of the realm of matter. Get over it, and accept the inarguable conclusion. The universe is immaterial-mental and spiritual.'"

The implication was that reality is permeable and that mental processes create reality as we see fit. The quote is from Jeans' seminal book *The Mysterious Universe* (1930), in which he argues for the existence of an intelligent Creator of the universe. In that same book, he wrote: "… from the intrinsic evidence of the creation, the Great Architect of the Universe now begins to appear as a pure mathematician."[17]

Jeans, a Freemason (although an agnostic), was a mathematician as well as a cosmologist, and argued that the universe seems as if it was not designed by a mechanic but by a musician or a poet because of its beauty. He did not mean that the universe existed only as thought, but that it shows signs of elegant inspiration. Jeans was a pure mathematician, who saw the beauty of the cosmos reflected in elegant equations that described the motion of stars and the evolution of the universe. Taken out of context, Jeans' words seem to support the mystical nature of reality and suggest that science is incapable of explaining the universe.

Further, science writer Lisa Zyga in her review of a major work on quantum physics noted: "Does mysticism have a place in quantum mechanics today, or is the idea that the mind plays a role in creating reality best left to philosophical meditations? Harvard historian Juan Miguel Marin argues the former—not because physicists today should account for consciousness in their research, but because knowing the early history of the philosophical ideas in quantum mechanics is essential for understanding the theory on a fundamental level."[18]

To put it bluntly, by invoking mysticism and quantum physics, UFO zealots are misleading their audiences by implying that their views on the "higher consciousness" of alien contact is supported by modern science.

9

The determination of UFO zealots to hold onto their beliefs in the face of continued criticism for lack of evidence or proof has led to deep division within the UFO community itself. One outspoken ufologist, Trevor Wozny, noted on his blog: "UFOlogy MUST discourage this religiosity of the UFO subject. It helps no one, confuses most, and irritates to no end people that know better. Faith in anything is a bad thing. It robs a person of the burden of thinking too much and festers lies and deceit."[19]

He went on to note: "For some reason which I cannot fathom many, many people purposely and intentionally want and can believe anything. Facts do not sway them and anything that substantially threatens their topsy-turvy UFOlogical worldview is instantly labeled a conspiracy. Labeling anything with the conspiracy label without doing your due diligence is the height of intellectual laziness."

In review, we can identify several recurring themes in groups of UFO zealots:

1) Mankind's spiritual awareness is missing or weak. We are not "tuned in" to the true nature of the universe. This results in a lack of compassion, understanding, enlightenment and peace in our world.
2) Aliens (specifically Space Brothers) are trying to guide us back onto a path of spiritual understanding. It is only through continued interaction with such truly enlightened beings that we can hope to rise above our human failings.
3) There will be a Second Coming of aliens and/or a religious deity. Soon, if we are vigilant and can properly perceive the signs, there will be a revelation of the truth that will validate the claims of contactees and UFO zealots, revealing the presence of aliens among us.
4) Salvation is possible.

Even with these few common traits, we can see that UFO zealots and their groups are religious in nature. Such UFO religious cult-like groups are all concerned with the welfare of the human race. They are trying to spread the teachings of their "masters" in hope that mankind will be saved from itself.

Therefore, it can be argued that such UFO groups are essentially religious organizations that replace God with a being from another planet, higher dimension or parallel universe. They reject establishment science's dismissal of UFO reports, and, in doing so, adopt an anti-science attitude that is impressed on their followers. Distrust of government and rejection of establishment science reinforces their beliefs, and, because they consciously do not engage with those who would criticize or ask uncomfortable questions about their standpoints, their community of adherents bonds even more strongly.

Many variants of this have been noted. The Heaven's Gate UFO-based cult, for example, asserted that astronomers' observations of Comet Hale-Bopp supported their view that an alien spacecraft was heading for Earth to save selected cult members and physically transport them to a higher plane of existence (whatever that would mean; it was incongruous that non-corporeal beings would need a spacecraft at all). Tragically, in 1997, 39 members of the cult were found dead at one of the cult's centers, awaiting salvation after having ingested a poison so they could die and release their souls to heaven.[20]

This last point raises a concern that closed UFO-based religious cults could be dangerous. The Heaven's Gate incident shows that there are personal dangers from becoming too involved in one's faith in UFO salvation. In 1982, two people sat in their car for more than a month in North Dakota. They spent the entire time in their car, waiting for a spaceship to arrive. They were drawn by a "higher power" as they sat in below-freezing temperatures, snowbound in their vehicle. Eventually one of them died of a combination of hypothermia, dehydration and starvation, which spurred the other to seek help.[21]

A contactee named Vonnetta Chouinard claimed that at seven years of age, she died from pneumonia, but "rose again on the third day." At age ten, she "walked into another dimension" and began having visions. In 1968, Chouinard met the Space Brothers, who took her in their UFOs to other planets, and even inside the Earth. She says she was chosen by these entities "from the fourth dimension" to bring their message of peace to the world. She was directed to help convince mankind to stop pollution, cease atomic testing and repent to God.[22]

One thing that can be noted about present-day contactees, such as those who lecture at "Experiencers" conferences, is that their message has not changed from contactees from the early flying saucer era. Menger, Adamski and others from the 1950s claimed contact with Venusians who warned of environmental disaster, bemoaned humanity's lack of enlightenment and offered a prescription of peace, love and understanding. Nothing presented by post-Millennial contactees is any different, with almost identical content in their messages, channelled or otherwise. Even their descriptions of the physical appearances of aliens are virtually identical and without much more elaborate imagination: blonde-haired aliens (in some cases human hybrids), tall humanoids (sometimes blue in color) and the archetypal "little green man" (most often a shade of grey these days). In fact, one could say that the contactees from decades ago preached their messages with more flair and style, without resorting to vitriol often exhibited in Facebook forums, for example. That in itself is rather disappointing, and speaks to the dearth of actual information and lack of originality presented by modern contactees.

Some UFO-based religious groups' beliefs probably reflect anxieties about our present society and, more specifically, the possibility of nuclear war. In conversation with UFO folklorist Dr. David Clarke in 2002, *Guardian* journalist Paul Harris observed, "...the UFO craze began at the start of the Cold War, when the new threat of atomic war with the Soviet Union hung over the world." Clarke, in agreement, replied, "It was just simple to want to believe in something up there in the sky that could come and rescue us."[23]

Another possible motivation for strong belief in UFO visitation is the general angst felt by those oppressed, marginalized or otherwise "left out" of society. The classic work by Donald Warren (1970) found that people who were status inconsistent—who believe that they should be more valued by peers because of heritage, perceived privilege, or other social factors yet are marginalized—tended to report UFOs more often than those who were not status inconsistent. In this scenario, UFO contactees can raise their profile within a peer group of other UFO zealots by claiming to have personal contact with aliens, thus increasing their status within the group.

Warren noted: "UFO sightings are linked to status frustration and, especially, to perceived status deprivations relative to one's position on the social ladder... Thus, the marginal status persons report saucer sightings to break out of a social order in which they are not accorded the place that their situation, in their eyes, deserves. Alienation and distrust of official explanations and a general questioning of the merits of the "system" are common attitudes among status inconsistents."[24]

Other contact themes are the role of religion in a technological society, the need for peaceful international relations and the possibility of extraterrestrial visitation.[25]

According to most UFO zealots, the Space Brothers come from planets free from war, poverty and need. They have also achieved immortality through an emphasis on spiritual matters. In short, they exist in idyllic paradises much removed from terrestrial problems such as terrorism, economic uncertainty and government corruption. The Space Brothers' message also usually includes dire warnings to stop arms proliferation and prevent further war. Many early UFO religious cults were anti-communist but were paradoxically socialist in their structure. This was ironic, because both the FBI and CIA monitored the groups, which were viewed as dangerous, and often infiltrated the groups in order to keep watch on them.

Cult members' fear of death is lessened or eliminated by the belief that the aliens will prolong their lives or guide them towards reincarnation them on another planet. The groups often made Jesus a spaceman, but also defined him as a true messenger who died in His desire to teach us truth and love.

Menger noted: "Jesus said, 'Know the truth and the truth shall make you free.' Those who die on this planet without knowing the truth or having the gifts of awareness are prisoners of this planet and do not leave it; they are reborn in new bodies and continue in the school of life, bound to the wheel of karma."[26]

This corrupted mixture of Christianity and eastern religious theology is typical of those who reject religious dogma and instead selectively choose appealing ideas that fit with personal philosophy. Nevertheless, UFO cults almost always promulgate a "Christian" philosophy of love, peace and reconciliation. Most teach that humans should be kind to one another, respect all life and care for the Earth. Many have strong environmental convictions that in some cases move them to speak out against oil companies and large corporations.

However, by shifting their omnipotent deity from a spiritual God to a more technological entity, UFO cults place humans at par with their saviours. They believe that if only we were scientifically advanced enough, we could be like the aliens. This path to enlightenment is much easier than spiritual development, which requires somewhat more complicated things such as honest introspection, long-term commitment to a faith journey, altruism and true love for all.

The religious interpretation of abductions is not a trivial issue. Physiological psychologist Michael Persinger has suggested that religious experiences can be induced by the action of magnetic fields upon the brain. In particular, he points to conversion events as indications of alterations in brain function: "Beliefs that dominate a person's life are considered delusions only when they deviate extremely from culturally acceptable concepts. Psychologically, there is no difference in the belief that God protects a person from harm and the conviction that Omnipotent Space Creatures are spiritual custodians."[27]

He notes that dissociation, a common process, often occurs during intense personal events such as divorce, death and job changes. Periods of missing time and memories may change to the point where they are buried deep within our subconscious:

> When this occurs the concept of self is sometimes changed; in more religious traditions the period coincides with conversions... During periods of personal stress, these dissociated memories, modified by beliefs and expectancies, occur as experiences that are perceived as originating "outside" of the self. These experiences are perceived as real and are frequently ascribed to religious or mystical intervention. The consequent conversion in cognitive structure, alters the perception of the self and the sense of purpose.[28]

It is easy to envision a situation where someone is disillusioned or disappointed by a mainstream religion's dogma or church hierarchy and looks elsewhere for fulfilment and enlightenment. Perhaps he or she has been abused or slighted by a person of stature within the religion. Perhaps there is disagreement with one or more points within a particular statement of faith. Perhaps the commitment level required is too high or demanding. Regardless, this person is still seeking some form of spiritual guidance or enlightenment, and also something that will speak to his or her perceived higher intellectual level. In addition, the social/religious group will need to be non-threatening, help build self-esteem and have a minimum of dogma to which one should adhere.

What could be a better choice than a zealotrous UFO believers' community? A marginalized person would fit right in. A person who has been ostracized from other groups for radical beliefs could find a home in a group where orthodoxy is rejected. And by declaring him-or-herself as a fellow contactee, acceptance into the group would be guaranteed. There would be no questioning of motives, veracity or details. Such acceptance would drive up one's self-esteem and seemingly increase social status, at least within that community.

Such a UFO-based community also has expansive altruistic values, unlike groups such as dance clubs or book clubs. They are interested in far more than personal fulfilment (though that is one by-product of involvement) and are charged with raising the consciousness and/or spiritual level of the entire human race.

But such groups create a serious paradox within the broader ufological community. Although adherents insist they are on a quest for "truth," their insistence they already "know" such truth undermines attempts by UFO researchers and investigators to understand the true nature of the phenomenon. Their experiences cannot be investigated as "ordinary" UFO reports. Their experiences cannot reasonably be compared with most other observed UFO phenomena such as nocturnal lights, radar cases and photographic evidence. In effect, their experiences are not viable as data that can be considered in any scientific evaluation of the UFO phenomenon. As such groups and their outspoken proponents often proudly proclaim, they operate literally outside of science.

This is a concern for those looking to engage the scientific community in reasonable discourse regarding UFOs. The unwillingness of UFO zealots to conform in any way with scientific methodology with regard to testing claims within their community negates their value as sources of reliable information about the subject.

Having said that, what should the broader UFO community do about UFO zealotry? The most logical solution might be to consider the UFO zealot community as a separate, parallel track for ufological discussion. They cannot be convinced to become more scientific in their approach, largely because they are faith-based and religious in nature. They operate on preconceived notions and a set of beliefs that preclude rigorous analysis. Their worldview is clearly metamodernist, accepting any and all claims and statements without critical examination.

The delineation of such a "second track" within ufology might be the best option for identifying differences within the field of study. There could be recognition that one track would be for scientific discourse and analysis, such as case studies, in-depth investigations and data mining, and a second track would be the religious aspects of ufology such as contactees and spirituality.

Religious UFO zealotry is not congruent with a scientific attempt to understand the UFO phenomenon. And nor should it strive to be.

THE EXPERIENCE **IS IMPORTANT**

Mike Clelland

There's a joke about a guy standing out on the street at night looking down at the pavement under a lamp-post. His neighbor walks up and asks what he's doing, and he says, "I lost my keys." The neighbor asks if this is where he lost them, and the guy points to a tangle of thorny bushes off in the darkness, and says, "Oh no, I lost them over there, but this is a much easier place to look."

In many ways, this is the challenge of the UFO mystery. The pragmatic investigator might want to stay under that brightly lit lamp-post, yet the core of the mystery is somewhere off in the darkness. Yes, it's easier to frame the inquiry within the clarity of what we can comfortably wrap our minds around, and maybe that's a good starting point. But looking into what a UFO might actually be, or what it might mean, is peering through a doorway into madness.

I recognize that there's a need to cling to what can easily be understood. There is a belief that UFO abduction reports can be explained away as little scientists in metal spaceships visiting us to conduct experiments. We get in metal helicopters and abduct grizzly bears in Yellowstone National Park; we tranquilize them, subject them to medical exams, take samples and then release them—so this analogy is perfect, right? The pilots of those flying saucers are essentially us, just a bit further along their own timeline. This idea, that the UFO occupants are visiting from some other planet, star system or galaxy has been dubbed the Extraterrestrial Hypothesis (ETH), and it has permeated the UFO community to the point that most researchers treat it as certainty.

The problem is that this tidy metaphor falls apart when you really start to examine the accounts. It seems the only way to adhere to that simplistic view is purposely to ignore a lot of what gets reported. It would seem that we are dealing with something much more bizarre than can be explained by the ETH.

Of all UFO sightings reported each year, over half can't be described as anything like a metal craft. Instead, the majority of reports are of ethereal glowing orbs, most often orange in color. People are seeing something that might not be physical at all, at least in the way we understand it, yet seemingly under intelligent control. The orbs might glow brightly, but won't illuminate the things around them, as if incapable of projecting that light. This is just one point in a long list of things that just don't make sense.

Granted, visitors from far off planets may play some part in what is happening, but there are weird details that make this seem too simplistic.

One reader of my blog wrote this, and I agree: "I think the reality of what is going on is far stranger than the theories we've come up with. I think the idea of extraterrestrials is nowhere near as strange as what actually is." This from someone who awoke to a giant praying mantis standing at the foot of her bed.

There are aspects of this phenomenon that challenge everything. The web of little strings seems to go everywhere. Everything is on the table—life, death, sex, dreams, spirituality, psychic visions, genetics, expanded consciousness, mind-control, channelling, mysticism, miraculous healings, out-of-body experiences, hybrid children, personal transformation, powerful synchronicity, portals in the backyard, distorted time, telepathy, prophetic visions, trauma, ecstasy, and magic. It's as if our brains just aren't big enough to deal with the overload of so much weirdness.

If we talk about little lights in the sky, it shouldn't take long before we start talking about God. There is something about this mystery that forces us to confront the really big questions. Who are we? Why are we here? What does it all mean? These are the same questions that have followed us through the ages, and they well up again when wrestling with the UFO enigma. I'm always disappointed when a researcher avoids these deeper thoughts, never straying from the safety of that brightly lit lamp-post.

The focus of my obsessive research has been the issues surrounding abduction. There is a reason for this; it's because I'm an abductee. This is no easy thing to say, and I'm terribly conflicted by what that even means. It's something that evades easy answers. What I can say with complete sincerity is that something has intersected with my life, and these extremely difficult events point to some form of UFO contact. Coming to terms with this has been a profound challenge and it has altered the direction of my life.

My problem with "ufology" is my own personal experiences. I've been at the receiving end of enough weird shit that nobody needs to tell me this stuff is real. For this essay, I am going to mostly ignore all the sighting accounts and focus on what is pertinent to me—the so-called abduction phenomenon.

My other focus is owls, and how they seem to show up, either literally or symbolically, in relation to UFO contact. This traces back to my own first-hand experiences with owls, lots of them. When I first started seeing owls it coincided with a booming voice in my head that said, "This has something to do with UFOs!" Their arrival and that message consumed my life. I started collecting stories with both owls and UFOs and it culminated in a nearly-400-page book. This essay will steer clear of owls—there is plenty to be said without opening that can of worms.

Before going any further, I need to state something as clearly as possible—I am not an objective researcher. I am immersed in these dark waters and there is no way to separate myself from the tangled knot of emotions that come with what has happened in my life, things that go way beyond seeing little lights in the night-time sky. So, just know, whatever I say is coming from a place of obsessive self-examination, and how it ties into what I've heard from others. This would be true for any researcher who has had the direct experience. I don't know if it's possible to stay unbiased and detached in a field as highly charged as UFOs.

There has been a series of events peppered throughout my life that seem to imply some sort of otherworldly contact. As a boy I saw a weird orange flash in the sky while walking home from school and arrived home nearly two hours later than I should have. That same year I had a close-up sighting of a coffee-can-shaped UFO that vanished in the blink of an eye. As a young man, I awoke to see five skinny big-eyed "aliens" out my bedroom window. I could talk about any of these memories around the dinner table, but they were all framed as just a funny little anecdote. I have more stories like these, and they all implied the same thing, but I wasn't going there.

All that changed on Sunday, March 10, 2013. I call this my Confirmation Event.

That night, I was on a lonely road in southern Utah driving home from a UFO conference. Rather than getting a hotel room I simply pulled off and slept out under the stars. It was cold and beautiful, and at some point I awoke to see a giant round structure positioned on the top of a nearby hill. It had a ring of lights around its outer surface and my first thought was, "That looks just like a landed flying saucer."

I lay there probably for an hour, staring at it. I figured it was nothing more than a big house, and I eventually rolled over and went to sleep. This was the opening salvo in a long set of weird events.

As an aside, I went back to that same spot a year later to see if there really was a big round house on that hill spot. There was nothing.

The day after arriving home from the UFO conference, while standing next to my desk, I had what I can only call a psychic flash. I clearly saw a map of southern Utah with a straight yellow line running west to east with three points along its length. The image lasted no more than a second, and I immediately sat at my computer and began to create a map to match what I had seen.

I knew the easternmost point was the event from the previous day. I also knew the westernmost point—it was the sight of a terrifying experience in a tent from the spring of 2010. I was camping with a close friend, Natascha, just outside of Dolores, Colorado, and both of us woke up screaming. The next thing I remember was floating up, passing through the top of the tent and arriving in an endless white realm. The next morning I awoke with an eleven-inch scratch across my chest. It looked as if it could have been made by a single rose thorn dragged across my skin. But when examined closely, it wasn't a scratch at all. Instead, it was a row of tiny fluid-filled blisters all bunched together. I have no memory of how this could've happened.

The site along the center of the yellow line was an event from 2011, again with Natascha. We slept in a secluded spot in the glorious red rock desert of southern Utah; no tent, just lying out on the sand. It was a cold, clear moonless night with amazing stars, and Natascha decided to go for a walk along the dirt road. She hadn't gone very far when she saw something odd. Her first thought was there was someone with a very bright flashlight out in the sagebrush, but it was moving along too smoothly and too low. After a few moments, she realized she was looking at a glowing orb of light, maybe two-feet wide. She watched in amazement as it floated towards her, then suddenly exploded in a bright flash, and vanished.

Natascha was scared and ran back to our campsite. I'd been lying there awake the entire time she had been gone and I was listening to the loud hooting of a great horned owl, seemingly in the bushes right near my head.

While sitting at my computer creating this map, I was stunned when these three separate events all lined up exactly along a perfectly straight line, 231 miles long. You could zoom in to view the line at one-pixel thick, and it crossed right over the spot in the sand where I had been listening to the owl. Seeing the exactness of those three sites along that line changed everything. My old life had ended. From that moment on, I could no longer deny what had been happening to me.

There is so much more to this story, and to tell it properly requires about an hour, or over 20 pages (with illustrations) in my book. A flood of other events reverberated outward from this moment of confirmation. Synchronicities, more psychic flashes, number sequences, ethereal floating mandalas, a shamanic ceremony, birthdays, and coyotes, all play a part in this frenetic narrative. It's impossible truly to describe what it's like to be swallowed up like this. It's not just one isolated event; it's a lot of them, and this barrage can take its toll.

That was a long story that seems to imply something, but what that might be is unknown. Each weird experience is like a spoke on a wheel, but I want to know what is at the hub holding them all together. It's an abduction story without an abduction.

Though imperfect, I'll be using the term 'abduction' throughout this essay. I'm also using a few other imperfect terms: abductee, experiencer, and contactee. These words might seem interchangeable, but they all imply something different, each having its own conflicting baggage.

"Abductee" would imply something negative—individuals being taken against their will by UFO occupants. "Contactee" would imply something positive. Such people might see themselves as being asked to take part in a grand cosmic fellowship. "Experiencer," in the middle, is a little more neutral.

There seems to be an induced amnesia created by the UFO intelligences, making the issues of contact terribly difficult to study. Someone might have had a lifetime of repeated experiences, yet remember nothing. These profound events might be buried in the unconscious, yet with impressions that can still influence the person. If so, we should expect some repercussions from these hidden experiences, enough to create personality quirks, like phobias or compulsions.

The word "alien" is used throughout this chapter, and some object to this because it implies a being from another planet (an assumption). Others prefer visitors, ETs, UFO Occupants, or Star Beings. I know one woman who refers to them only as "creatures." The dictionary has several definitions for "alien." One of them is: "differing in nature or character typically to the point of incompatibility." For me, this seems entirely acceptable. Sadly, all these words fall short because none of this is straightforward.

Abduction accounts can be exceedingly complex. A person might remember just little bits of the beginning and the end of an event, with their memories erased between these bookends. They might recall only a fleeting image, or have clear memories of events in their entirety. I struggle because there's no simple way to sum up the conflicting experiences that get reported by people.

Some will tell hellish nightmare stories at the hands of their alien kidnappers. Others will tell blissful stories, as if they are communing with angels. I try my best not to weight one side more than the other. Something real is happening. There is both deep trauma and mystical transcendence woven into this phenomenon, and these opposite extremes need to be acknowledged. Ignoring one aspect means wilfully denying part of the mystery. There can be an overlap and blurring between these poles; a disparate gray zone where easy answers seem impossible.

Dr. Leo Sprinkle is one of my heroes in this field. This big-hearted man has been actively researching UFO contact for over 50 years, and his biography reads like a checklist of every major event in the modern era of UFOs. He has a Ph.D. in Counselling and was a Professor of Psychology at the University of Wyoming.

I sent Leo a copy of my owl book right after it was published, and, a few weeks later, he sent me a handwritten letter scolding me for using the word abductee. I love this man dearly, and my heart sank on reading his review. He had been a college professor for decades, and I sensed this role in his stern feedback. He argued that the better word should be 'inductee.' Induction means being brought to something, while abduction means being taken away. Fair enough, but "abduction" and "abductee" are the words we are stuck with.

Leo told me a wonderful story about a reporter asking him this question: What do you say to skeptics?

First, he clarified the difference between skeptic and a debunker: "Well, if they are truly skeptics that's one thing, but if they are debunkers I don't really like to talk to them because they're no fun (laughs). But if a person is truly skeptical and wants to know how to be involved with the UFO research, I say read a thousand reports, talk to a hundred witnesses, have your own experience and then we can really talk."

The reporter replied, "Oh, I guess the experience is important."[1]

Yes, the experience is important, but it's also messy and confusing. With these experiences come mixed-up emotions and ideas, everything getting filtered through our own fragile psyches, and all the assumptions that come with it. It's also important to know that Leo has seen strange flying objects at several points in his life and has come forward with his own memories of direct alien contact.

A UFO researcher with abduction experiences is very common. When talking to researchers I will ask if they are an abductee, and, more often than not, they'll cautiously share their memories of contact. I'm at this point now where I just sort assume that most of the researchers in this field are also abductees. But what does it mean if so many of the people investigating UFOs are abductees? One way to look at it would be that such a defining life event would create an interest in the subject. Or, could they have been zapped with a psychic ray gun that derails their normal life and puts them on the thankless path of obsessive UFO research? On some subconscious level have they been ordered to study UFOs? How many UFO books are the result of this kind of manipulation? I'm wrestling with exactly these questions—I mean, why did I write my book?

If we are trying to reframe the UFO debate, just know that many of the debaters on the stage have probably been abducted. If these experiences are what they seem to be, then it should be no surprise that they can come across like fanatical zealots.

In the summer of 2014, I interviewed the editor and staff of *Open Minds*, an online UFO news source. The audio interview took place shortly after they ended their paper magazine and switched over to digital content. Alejandro Rojas, Maureen Elsberry and Jason McClellan were all full-time UFO journalists, and that seems remarkable given the hostility, which this topic generates.

The site does an excellent job of covering the mainstream accounts of UFO sightings, and would occasionally cover abduction accounts.

The articles on abduction were most often a review of classic cases from decades ago (Betty and Barney Hill, Pascagoula, The Allagash Abductions) or they would cover pioneering researchers such as Budd Hopkins.

I had immersed myself in abduction research and felt the three UFO journalists were barely dipping below the waterline, and avoiding the strangest reports and their implications.

During the interview, I pressed them, telling them they should dig deeper and cover more of the bizarre aspects of this phenomenon, especially in connection with abduction accounts. Their response was a polite but firm, "No." Listening back now, my pleading came across as sort of desperate. It's awkward to hear me acting so pushy, telling a magazine to change their editorial stance. I was almost, but not quite, acting rude.

They were unyielding, not wanting to stray from journalism and into conjecture. Maureen said, "It's almost like mixing religion and news... there's a fine line with this and it would be difficult to do."

Alejandro was aware of the magazine's focus and said, "We try to balance this as best we can... If there's a mission of ours, it's to penetrate the mainstream."[2]

Listening again to that audio interview for this essay, the anxiety and tension in my voice was clear. There was a neediness in how I was acting, and it was hard for me to hear. I was tempted to edit this exchange from the podcast because I sounded like such an impatient zealot. These were my true emotions, so, although it was awkward, I left it in.

Author, blogger and researcher Christopher Knowles wrote to me afterwards: "I listened to your interview with Open Minds. I think you should realize that at this point the only people who are interested in abduction material are mostly abductees. So I think they did have a point there."

Yes, but here's the problem—I feel strongly precisely *because* I'm one of those abductees.

Within the literature are repeated statements that most abductees feel burdened with a strong sense of mission. I hear this all the time, but rarely have I heard anyone say just what that mission might be. There is something about this that just feels so terribly important—it's like living your life with a flashing red sign that reads "urgency" front and center in your mind's eye. Adding to this is a burning need to make sense of my experiences, and this angst can get overwhelming.

After my pleas during that interview, Jason suggested I write something for their site. He was right. What I had asked was for them to publish more of the articles that I would want to read. So I sat down at my computer, began typing and, two months later, they posted my article with the headline "The Possible Unsettling Implications of UFO Sightings."[3]

The ideas in the article came from a series of conversations I'd had with the late Elaine Douglass. She had been with MUFON for 25 years as the state director for Utah and Washington DC, and most of her research had focused on abductions.

While conducting a sightings investigation she would ask the witnesses the standard set of questions—what time, how big, and so on. But she would follow up with deeper, more personal questions, asking them to describe any unusual personal events. She would ask, "So, what else, in your whole life, has ever happened to you that you cannot explain?" More often than not, a big story would emerge. Many of the witnesses told Elaine about unusual events that might imply some sort of direct contact experiences. Her conclusion, after a quarter century of research, was that over half the people who see UFOs are abductees.

This may seem like a bold statement, but it's very similar to what other investigators have concluded. Abduction researcher Budd Hopkins spoke openly that if someone sees a UFO, they are most probably either seeing it arrive or leave, and some length of missing time is hiding an abduction event. The implication being that memories have been erased by the "occupants" of these elusive "craft." Hopkins also publicly speculated that there are probably more abductions than UFO sightings, a comment that surely rankled some of the more conservative researchers.

Assuming the role of journalist, I called a bunch of abduction researchers and asked each of them the same question, "What percentage of people who are reporting an unambiguous UFO sighting are actually abductees?" The word unambiguous was included in the question to separate the more close-up structured reports from just little dots of light way off in the distance.

The article quoted five researchers, and, although they all felt it was impossible to come up with an actual percentage, most agreed with Elaine's conclusion. The others were more cautious, yet still acknowledged her point.

When asked the same question, abduction researcher and hypnotherapist Yvonne Smith was quick to agree with Elaine's conclusion, saying the majority would be abductees. She said, "Many of the close-up sightings will have clues that this was a probable contact experience, things like distorted or missing time, or a car engine sputtering and mysteriously stopping."

Joe Montaldo is both an abduction researcher and an abductee, and he said, "ET never has to show himself to anybody. There is no need to ever let anyone see a craft, ever." This implies that their technology is so advanced that making their craft invisible is effortless, meaning if anyone actually sees a UFO it's because they want to be seen for a reason. When asked to give a percentage of how many people who see a UFO are actually abductees, Joe said, "I'd put it at 100 percent."

Any of these statements would be terribly difficult to quantify, yet one thing all the researchers agreed on was that the closer the UFO to the witness, the more likely an abduction event has occurred. There is an implication that many, if not most UFO sightings have a buried abduction component.

The thought that most sighting reports might be abductions is more than a little bit disturbing. It's at odds with how most of us are even capable of thinking about the issue, and this includes seasoned UFO investigators.

My article generated a lot of traffic for the Open Minds site. There was a stat counter that displayed the online hits, and the numbers were quite high. This gave me the sense that there are plenty of people out there who are eager to read about some of the stranger aspects to the UFO phenomenon. The only other post I could find with higher hits was an article where the actor Dan Aykroyd recounted his personal UFO sighting.

Early on in my research I had a long talk with Miriam Delicado, someone who would fit the definition of a contactee, a term implying an ongoing communication with benevolent aliens. She has been an outspoken presence, sharing her experiences since the publication of her 2007 book, Blue Star: Fulfilling Prophecy. During that conversation, I asked her what she tells people when they ask about the reality of these experiences and, without skipping a beat, she said, "Just look at my email inbox."

In the years since that conversation, I've been speaking out about what has happened to me. And now, like Miriam's, my email inbox is overflowing with people reaching out to me. They are telling me their experiences, and most of these letters have a desperate tone. I understand this deep need for someone simply to listen.

This journey has been terribly confusing, especially when I first started looking into my experiences. During those initial years, I sent out letters just like the ones I'm now receiving. I mailed them off to the researchers and experiencers who, I thought, might be able to offer help. What I am receiving, for the most part, is coming from abductees. Even if they don't say it, their stories certainly include clues and events that imply a hidden abduction experience. I read their accounts, try to offer some kind words, answer their questions, and then new ones arrive.

Each one of these stories should be investigated, yet that isn't happening. Just from the number of emails I receive, this phenomenon is much more pervasive than anyone would dare consider. Yet, there isn't the money, manpower or time, truly to deal with the magnitude of what is being reported.

At the heart of each account is a real person, and, in many cases, a family who are struggling with something beyond comprehension. It's one thing to catalog the reports and compare the details, but it's something altogether different to try to come to grips with what it all might mean. Any attempt to reframe the UFO debate requires a deeper awareness that these experiences are terribly complex and deeply personal.

There's a lot of subtle (and not so subtle) clues that imply abductions are something widespread and common. If this is true—and from my point of view it certainly seems to be—shouldn't it be considered important?

UFOs are not ambiguous, they are a part of us, they are interwoven into our human consciousness. But what does this even mean?

The word consciousness has become a sort of catchphrase for anything that might deal with the mind, or perhaps the higher mind. Telepathy, psychic weirdness, collective memories, spiritual awakenings and divine transformations all get lumped into the big consciousness basket. I've heard established UFO researchers being warned by their peers not to go down the path of consciousness. Better to stick with the pragmatic details, like government documents and reports from credible witnesses. The fear is you'll lose all credibility by even considering something so intangible.

Anything seen as new-agey gets ignored by many who want to cling to something tangible, things like metal spaceships. The more ethereal aspects are swept aside for fear of "turning off" the greater public. Better to frame it as something easier to wrap your mind around.

Another reason this weirder stuff gets ignored is some folks feel a need to be taken seriously. I would love to be taken seriously, too, but I also feel a need to honestly share what's happened to me.

I have spoken to a few abductees who are out there telling their stories in a very public way. They keep to their script, and what they share is both remarkable and strange. But, when I take them aside and ask if anything else is going on, they will whisper something extremely bizarre—I mean like really freaky shit. When I ask why they don't share that part too, they'll say they need to be taken seriously. I get this, yet the dilemma remains. Much of this phenomenon is just too outlandish even to bring to the table.

While at a UFO conference, I spoke briefly with journalist Lee Speigel, who covers (among other things) UFOs for the Huffington Post. I asked him why I never see any articles about abduction in his reporting. He told me that he doesn't want to write anything that would "turn off" the readers. The way he said it was very matter-of-fact and practical.

Moments later I talked with filmmaker James Fox. I asked him if his upcoming feature-length UFO documentary would include anything about abductions. He pretty much gave the same answer, "No, we've decided we want be taken seriously, we don't want to lose our audience."

I've heard this a lot. Journalists, authors or filmmakers who specialize in UFO reporting will shy away from the topic of abductions. Or, if they do cover it, they'll only reference events that are decades old, like Betty and Barney Hill.

The problem with the abduction subject is that it seems to have two layers. The surface layer is what we've all seen on late-night cable TV documentaries—creepy gray aliens taking people from their cars on lonely roads. The deeper layer is much more challenging. Things become absurd; alternative realities get jumbled up with mythic imagery. This is obviously a simplistic way to look at it, and the whole thing probably goes ten layers further down. Hardly anyone wants to address that surface layer, and pretty much nobody wants to go any deeper.

Anne Strieber, the late wife of author Whitley Strieber, had a simple way of evaluating the validity a report of UFO contact. She said, "If it's not weird, I don't trust it." She referred to this little phrase as her BS detector. Author Nick Redfern has said something similar. When trying to describe the complexities of UFO research, he's said, "It's not just that it's weird, it's too weird."

This is what I'm drawn to: the accounts that are so weird they defy any logical explanation. I am pulling on this thread because it's been my own direct experience.

I've been finding that, within some stories, is a confusing collision of overlapping experiences, a mess of twists and turns, and all the details are so weird. Things feel mixed up with threads running off everywhere and synchronicity spills over the edges like an unattended sink. For me, this chaos is a sign to trust the event as legitimate. The more complicated the interwoven details, the more valid it seems. For me, this is a shaky form of proof, but proof of what?

I've been using the term paradox syndrome to describe this frenetic pattern. A paradox is an attempt at sound reasoning, but the conclusion appears unacceptable. A syndrome is a group of related or coinciding things, events, and actions. I don't understand why it works this way, but all the messy threads must tie into some core event, and the challenge is not to get lost in the mayhem. I've been collecting and cataloguing precisely these kinds of stories. My own Confirmation Event, told earlier, is one of those stories.

If we are trying to reframe the debate, we need to be aware that these more complex accounts are not easy to categorize or share. It takes a great deal of patience to sit and listen to what people have been through. The bar is set pretty high for what I consider too weird, yet I've met plenty of people who tell me stories that stretch what I can fathom. It would be easy to dismiss these folks as unreliable, but I feel strongly that the clues to unravel this mystery are tucked away within their experiences. Here's my advice to any UFO researcher, you need to listen to the abductees, even if what they tell you is challenging.

I spoke to a researcher with a focus on sighting reports and he told me, "I used to do abduction research, but it just took up so much time." My heart sank, yet what he said seems fair—it's easier and less time-consuming to study UFO sightings than to get dragged down into the bottomless pit of abduction research.

I had a friend call me out on how I do my research; he was frustrated and said I wasn't being scientific. My response was 'what do I care, I'm not a scientist.' He was right by pointing out that I'm not objective. I'm not trying to approach this muddle of divergent experiences with science as a tool. Instead, I see my role as more of a folklorist. I'm simply collecting stories and letting these narratives speak for themselves.

There are cries that the UFO phenomenon should be studied scientifically. Perhaps it should, but that isn't my concern. The scientific community has either ignored or denounced the UFO phenomenon for close to 70 years. With very few exceptions, UFO researchers, who try to wrestle with this mystery using any kind of scientific rigor, end up framing it merely as metal spaceships from another planet. They want to measure burn marks in a farmer's field. They don't want to cloud their tidy documentation with the strange invasion of consciousness that gets reported when you listen carefully to what experiencers are saying. These challenging stories are being lived by real people, and I sense an even deeper story hidden below the water line.

To examine this subject rationally seems tenuous, so I've been putting more of my efforts into trying to read the symbolic clues. I've come to see these experiences playing out with a sort of dream logic. Instead of looking to a pragmatic UFO investigator for answers, it might be better to ask the gypsy fortune teller.

At this point, I see the skills of a dream interpreter being an appropriate tool when analyzing someone's experience. Scrutinizing reality as if it were a dream has become normal for me. This kind of thinking probably puts me on the "outs" with most of the mainstream researchers, but I can't help it. This is an esoteric mystery and it requires esoteric methodologies to peel back its secrets.

If you see a UFO, is it better to call a MUFON investigator, or the local shaman from the nearby Indian Reservation? The no-nonsense investigator will ask what time you saw the object, and to describe what it looked like. The shaman might ask very different questions. What has been going on in your spiritual life leading up to your sighting, and what has changed in the aftermath? He might inquire about dreams, premonitions, gut feelings and intuitions.

This is not a call to dismiss the role of the nuts and bolts investigator. There is a responsibility to walk out into the witness's yard and measure the burn mark in the grass, then write that down in your notebook so it can be compared with other cases. This is an important part of the role of the overall process. But it's equally important to look beyond the physical clues. They'll need to ask the witness how their soul has been influenced by what they've experienced—and then pay close attention to the answers. We are dealing with a phenomenon that can seep its way into our reality in ways that are both outlandish and profound. My advice to any new researcher would be to expect absurdities and to trust their gut.

Leo Sprinkle spoke with me about his own journey, from UFO researcher to an instantaneous realization that he was himself an UFO experiencer. It happened in a group meeting where he listened to a witness describe the uniform worn by an alien being—the pants had feet connected, like a child's pyjamas. He was hit with a flood of memories and was suddenly sobbing. One of his patients said, "Good, now Leo is suffering like the rest of us!"

Suffering with these experiences is entirely accurate. Leo described the challenges of coming to terms with this realization: "It was a long journey, but finally I accepted that I was on the path, and the way to follow that path is to not only be conscious of what is happening at the head level, but also to be accepting at the heart level or the intuitive level."

This is good advice for self-examination, as well as for looking at the overall contact phenomenon. Many of the people involved have endured something traumatic, and they need help as well as compassion.

Jeffrey Kripal is a historian of religions, and a professor of Philosophy and Religious Thought at Rice University in Houston, Texas. He is the author of multiple books on the mystical experience, including The Super Natural, which he co-authored with Whitley Strieber.

Jeff has studied ancient manuscripts and also worked with people who tell of their own anomalous experiences. These might be religious epiphanies, or a UFO contact event. In the quote below, Jeff describes what I've encountered many times. He articulates clearly the challenges of listening to people as they share what has happened to them and the task of making sense of these stories.

> This is the thing about this material, you think you've heard the last strange thing, and then it gets stranger. What the debunker [rationalist] thinks is that, no—if we just had enough information it would all make sense and all the strangeness would go away.
>
> But my experience with these folks is exactly the opposite. The more they tell you the weirder it gets. Part of the reason is that they don't quite trust you in the beginning, so they tell you just sort of the surface of the story. And then they tell you a little more, and a little more. And the more they tell you the stranger it gets. It does not make more sense; it makes less sense. And I think that this is important. I think that is part of the phenomenon, that it's absurd, and that it's meant to confuse us. And I think that, when we look for it to make sense, I think we are going down the wrong path. Because it doesn't.[4]

I understand this in my bones, because I have lived it. Seeing a UFO on a clear starry night is just the smallest part of my story. There is so much more. Coming to terms with what I have been through has required abandonment. I was desperate for a pragmatic answer, but any hope of that stayed beyond my reach; it just floated away and then disappeared. I had to give up and, in doing so, I've reached a place of calmer waters. I've had to leave the comfort of that brightly lit lamppost, step off the pavement, climb into the thorny bushes, and be content in the darkness. In many ways, this describes the owl, a creature at home in the dark.

After the publication of Communion in 1987, Whitley Strieber received a flood of letters, this in an era where people wrote on paper and mailed them in envelopes. His wife, Anne, spent the next few years reading upwards of a quarter of a million of these letters. What she read were heartfelt accounts sent by people describing their own contact experiences at the hands of alien visitors:

> Mr. Strieber, I'm scared. After this happened, I felt like I had been standing on bedrock, and that it had dropped out from under my feet, leaving me floating in an ocean whose bottom I could not see. I felt as if everything I thought I'd been clear about for seventeen years— the things that people learn—were lies, and that this was what was important. But it scared me, and I wasn't sure that I wasn't crazy. I in fact tried to commit suicide because I didn't want to be a lunatic.[5]

This kind of personal testimony is common; I've heard it often. These experiences can be horribly traumatic. Even the good experiences will leave people adrift without any easy way to deal with the sudden disappearance of their sense of reality. Your old way of thinking crumbles, and then something new needs to be rebuilt to take its place.

For me, this has already happened. I have suffered through the realization that I am, for lack of a better word, an 'abductee.' These trying events would make normal life for anyone nearly impossible. This new awareness is sometimes referred to as the trauma of enlightenment.

A collective myth has blossomed within the UFO community: "Disclosure with a capital D." Many of the true believers foresee a press conference where the President of the United States will declare that UFOs are real, but I'm not holding my breath.[6]

I don't need someone in authority to tell me what I already know, and I certainly won't wait for some kind of approval. Fuck all that.

Trying to frame it all as something simple isn't working. We want a nice British actor with a deep voice stepping from his shiny flying saucer like that scene in *The Day The Earth Stood Still*. I've spoken to hundreds of abductees, and never once have I heard anyone describe seeing an alien walk out of a landed craft (that said, I've read some accounts like that, but very few). Instead, a lot of people have told me of little beings just stepping into their bedroom through a swirling vortex in the wall. But this is rarely mentioned out under that lamp-post.

I am no longer in a position to wait for others to make ripples in this pond. It's my job to say what I feel in my heart in a way that will be heard. This is an arena that most people will ignore, or dismiss with contempt. Simply talking about these ideas is considered crazy in the eyes of many.

But there is a need to be brave. Mythologist Joseph Campbell wrote about the challenge of the inner quest, "You enter the forest at the darkest point, where there is no path." He was referencing the Knights of the Round Table, as they embarked upon their quest for the Grail. The UFO subject is just a long list of unknowns with no path to follow, yet you can still press on in that darkness.

Everyone is fragile and we all bring our own baggage to the table. Trying to grapple with these ideas seems to reflect some deeper part of ourselves back at us. The reporter who spoke with Leo Sprinkle was right when he said the experience is important—it has the power to change you.

I really have no idea what is happening and what it all might mean; my thoughts change with the wind. What I feel strongly on Monday fades away on Tuesday, replaced by some new perspective on Wednesday. Ideas form, shape up into something viable, and then collapse. We are confronted by a mystery, and nothing would be more gratifying than to actually solve it. But I don't expect that to ever happen.

This is a deeply personal journey, and it feels like a mistake to depend on others for approval. There are times when I feel like I'm chasing my tail, stalling out, or just plain overwhelmed. Yet I wallow forward, trying to make sense of the madness. There is something about this stuff that just feels important, I don't know how else to say it.

It's not my job to remedy problems in the UFO community, but it's my responsibility to proceed onward doing the best I can. This is hard work, and the hardest of all is looking inward.

THE FUTURE LEADS **TO THE PAST**

Jack Brewer

It seems to have been with us a long, long time, whatever "it" may be. Researchers such as Jacques Vallée suggest humankind's dance with the strange, including odd sights in the sky, is virtually inherent to our existence. The unknown and misunderstood apparently manifested in tales of fairies, trolls and, of course, aliens and their flying machines.

Are such stories due to overactive imaginations and hoaxes, or do some of them actually represent brushes with truly interesting phenomena? Perhaps each of those is true, as well as combinations thereof, at different times.

The popular John Keel contemplated similar notions as Vallée, reporting that early European settlers in America interpreted lights moving across night skies as witches on broomsticks carrying lanterns. Intriguing as it all may be, a reasonable argument could be made that the extraterrestrial hypothesis (ETH) is just as indicative of deeply held yet questionable beliefs.

One of the few items most members of the UFO community agree upon is that the modern-day era of UFOs took significant shape during the mid-20th Century. Reports of what came to be known as foo fighters, ghost rockets and flying saucers ushered in an age of assumptions that the earth was being visited by extraterrestrials. Despite wide acceptance and adamant proclamations, validation of an alien presence remains as elusive as ever.

Among the most damning aspects of the ETH is its overwhelming lack of direct evidence. It also doesn't account for details of interesting cases such as the Mothman saga or reports of high strangeness where it is nonetheless boldly evident.

A lack of verification of visiting aliens does not necessarily translate into a lack of phenomena worthy of investigation. It may just mean the ETH is wrong, at least for the vast majority of cases to which it is typically applied, if not all of them. It is entirely possible we've jumped the gun in suggesting and drawing conclusions, as did our superstitious forefathers who were convinced the covert spread of witchcraft and its suspected satanic nature were responsible for misfortune and misunderstood phenomena throughout their communities. Parallels could certainly be drawn.

In order to view more recent circumstances in sharper focus, let's consider how assumptions evolved. Let's also take a look at some challenges that consistently hinder a search for truth. We'll consider what we, as community members, can do to encourage best practices, and we'll explore how integrating such information into our perspectives and research leads to a healthier, more functional community and reframes the debate.

Rocky Beginnings

Hoaxers have been a significant and constant wrench in the gears ever since the early days of ufology. In some instances, it was Uncle Sam failing to be entirely forthright about activities in the UFO arena.

The late-1940s were a time of tremendous flux and reorganization within the U.S. intelligence community. Whatever spy games and deception operations were afoot, the morphing of the Office of Strategic Services into the Central Intelligence Agency coincided with notable UFO cases of the era.

The former International Director of MUFON, James Carrion, demonstrated via official declassified documents that the 1946—1947 ghost rockets saga conclusively involved elements of deception.[1] His research additionally showed that a classified operation, Project Seal, was actually shelved prior to being misrepresented as a continuing effort to develop an airborne weapon more powerful than the atomic bomb. The apparent propaganda campaign happened literally right alongside the UFO-related events of the summer of 1947 to the extent that one paper carried the "news" of the supposed airborne super weapon on the same page as a story about the Kenneth Arnold sighting. Such events should be considered worthy of deeper study.

As of this writing, Carrion's growing list of intriguing circumstances include the work of Col. Carl Goldbranson, a high-level career intelligence officer whose specific area of expertise was planning and implementing deception operations. Interestingly, the colonel was corresponding with the FBI about flying saucers during what became that famous summer of '47, representing what we now know to be a link between deception planners and official UFO investigations.[2]

Whatever the reasons for such incidents, they deserve consideration. They may also be the tip of the proverbial iceberg.

Researchers noted the potential significance of such documents as a 1950 RAND (Research and Development) Corporation report compiled for the Air Force and titled, *The Exploitation of Superstitions for Purposes of Psychological Warfare*.[3] Similarly, the activities have been widely noted of such skilled deception artists as British Maj. Jasper Maskelyne and an American officer by the name of Edward G. Lansdale. Maskelyne was a professional magician who proved to be remarkably successful at creating advantageous battlefield grand illusions during World War II. Lansdale was an advertising executive turned CIA man who applied his marketing skills to the exploitation of beliefs surrounding such topics as vampires and soothsayers. He is well known for his deception activities in Southeast Asia. According to the *Journal of the American Folklore Society*:

> The Filipino army had not been able to evict a squadron of Huks from the area of a garrison town. A combat psychological warfare squad was brought in and, under Lansdale's direction, planted stories among town residents of an asuang or vampire living on the hill where the Huks were based. A famous local soothsayer, they said, had predicted that men with evil in their hearts would become its victim. After giving the stories time to circulate, the squad set up an ambush on a trail used by the Huks and, when a patrol came by, snatched the last man. They punctured his neck with two holes, held the body upside down until it was drained of blood, and put it back on the trail. The next day the entire Huk squadron moved out of the area.[4]

Such darkly fascinating stories are numerous and span several divisions of the U.S. intelligence community and its allies. It could therefore be considered potentially significant that USAF Project Grudge concluded, "Planned release of unusual aerial objects coupled with the release of related psychological propaganda could cause mass hysteria."[5]

The August, 1949, Grudge report went on to recommend, "That psychological Warfare Division and other governmental agencies interested in psychological warfare be informed of the results of this study."

The editor of this book, Robbie Graham, has shown how the long arm of the CIA and its UFO-related interests reached well into Hollywood. Graham's work includes exploring how two confirmed propaganda specialists were employed as a production chief and a script writer on the set of the 1951 extraterrestrial contact film, *The Day the Earth Stood Still*.[6] It is reasonable to suspect the intelligence community had interests in influencing the movie and subsequent public opinion of its extraterrestrial-themed subject matter. While the specific purposes of such influence may be debated, its actuality is clear.

Interestingly, production of *The Day the Earth Stood Still* happened during the same era in history, 1950—1953, that Col. Edward Lansdale was running around the Philippines spreading stories about vampires among the Huks. He soon took his craft to Vietnam where he covertly engaged in "political-psychological warfare," which included putting words in the mouths of astrologers and enrolling the assistance of soothsayers to exploit their followings.[7] Lansdale, who eventually retired a major general, operated with the support and backing of Director of Central Intelligence, Allen Dulles.

By 1953 the CIA covertly sponsored a scientific committee, the Robertson Panel, briefed on military intelligence related to UFOs. Air Force Capt. Edward J. Ruppelt, charged with studying UFOs via Project Blue Book, later wrote about the existence of the committee in his published work, causing the UFO community to push for the release of its resulting report. According to today's CIA, the document offered was less than transparent, failing to disclose Agency interest in or sponsorship of the Robertson Panel. "As an alternative," the CIA website currently explains, "the Agency prepared a sanitized version of the report which deleted any reference to CIA and avoided mention of any psychological warfare potential in the UFO controversy."[8]

A now declassified CIA cable shows that the very next year, 1954, after forming the Robertson Panel, Agency assets in Guatemala were instructed to consider creating a UFO hoax. The intention of the deception was to serve as a public distraction from bad press cast upon the CIA due to its sponsorship of a coup in the Central American nation.

"If possible," the CIA cable read, "fabricate big human interest story, like flying saucers, birth sextuplets in remote area to take play away."[9]

Further jamming up the gears for UFO researchers is the fact witnesses have been retracting stories—and spooks have been inserting themselves in those stories—since the outset of the modern-day phenomenon. The chain of events that formed what many consider the cornerstone of ufology, the cases of the summer of 1947, is riddled with discrepancies and unanswered questions.

The Maury Island so-called UFO incident of June 21, 1947, in Tacoma, Washington, began with a fantastic story of falling saucer debris. An investigator of the case was none other than Kenneth Arnold, who soon reported his own celebrated UFO sighting, but not before he became enmeshed with the intelligence community. A primary witness in the Maury Island case later retracted their story, drawing the entire incident into heavy question.[10] The unusual events of that summer included the Roswell Army Air Field issuing a press release stating the 509th Operations Group recovered a "flying disc"—and then issued another statement advising a "weather balloon" was what had been retrieved.

Where the rubber meets the road, we can't say for sure if those specific 1947 events, which significantly shaped ufology as we know it today, even included a flying object of unusual origin. Possibly not.

We could go on at length, but, suffice it to say, the involvement of the intelligence community in the UFO controversy is well established and, in my opinion, suspect. To further complicate the search for truth, a vast number of hoaxes were perpetrated on the community by garden variety charlatans. While some episodes were more consequential and well known than others, scrutinizing false claims and unsupported assertions came to be standard operating procedure within ufology, at least among its more discriminating community members.

Investigative techniques and data presented as evidence in the UFO genre continue to stretch the limits of tolerance, even among many who consider themselves quite open-minded and to have experienced strange phenomena. Memory-enhancing techniques, conclusively discredited long ago by qualified professionals, are still promoted by organizations and investigators questionably claiming to prioritize scientific study, and a recent prematurely celebrated case turned out to be built upon nothing more than an old photo of a mummy in a museum (see Curt Collins' essay in this volume). Such circumstances are all too common, drain valuable time and attention, and arguably characterize the genre more so than events of legitimate interest.

The UFO community appears to have been led astray since its very beginnings. It is entirely possible the ETH was built on false premises in the first place, leaving future generations of sincere researchers and interested parties struggling to gain traction on a poorly laid foundation. Beliefs seem to have been manipulated by a combination of deceptive opportunists, intelligence officials, and various demographics consisting of individuals harboring suspicious motives. Hoaxers, charlatans, and well-meaning yet misguided people influenced by such charlatans, swamped the genre in waves of alien-themed movies, books, conferences and dead-end claims.

A Fundamental Problem

Let us again consider that if the foundation of present day ufology was built on shifting sand and is unstable, that doesn't necessarily mean there's nothing worth investigating. It doesn't mean people don't experience things they don't understand, and it doesn't have to mean none of it is interesting. It might just mean popular explanations are falling short in some instances. We might be looking in the wrong places for what answers are to be found.

If we're going to reframe the debate, we might be wise to promote inclusion rather than exclusion, as well as promote tolerance rather than an atmosphere of closed minds—and that goes for offering those with critical questions a seat at the table along with everyone else. We want to attract competent community members with renewed ambition and fresh eyes, rather than repel them.

We might consider that understanding someone's point of view doesn't necessarily equate to agreement. Lines of reasoning can be understood without fully supporting or endorsing them in all circumstances. Whether or not we agree, there are some dynamics important to understand, and demonstrate we understand, while at least empathizing with why others might introduce them into a debate or discussion.

One such dynamic is that personal stories, interesting and entertaining as they may be, are often of very little value to the professional research process. That's just how it is. Anecdotal evidence is problematic for reasons including that scientists form studies, which in turn form insights and paradigms, from repeated observations, not from single events. Clinical trials, for example, typically involve sets of research subjects whose conditions and activities are closely monitored so that important patterns can accurately be identified. Failing to follow such protocol increases the chances of forming faulty conclusions.

An example of faulty conclusions drawn from limited observations can be found in the early days of blood transfusions. Crude experiments produced hit and miss results, sometimes fatal, before researchers learned of blood types and the critical importance of their compatibility. The full ramifications of the procedure were better understood after more factors and their importance were revealed.

The value of personal stories is further questioned by the strides made in memory research. Qualified experts have demonstrated that memories are filled with errors. It is conclusively established. What's more, the ways questions are asked can significantly alter responses.[11] Such circumstances should be considered of great significance to a UFO community consisting of often minimally trained, overeager investigators who regularly employ hypnosis to solicit witness testimony. At the least, it is important to understand why such practices draw criticism, and to realize the burden of proof is upon those investigators to corroborate the questionable statements and arguably induced memories. Concerns are entirely reasonable and should be expected, particularly from individuals who stay current on material published by qualified experts.

Even without using hypnosis, it could be well argued that investigators typically put more weight on witness statements and interpretations than is warranted. This doesn't necessarily mean witnesses are confused or fabricating their testimonies; certainly not in all cases, and it doesn't even have to mean investigators are necessarily biased, at least not always.

I am suggesting it is problematic that, in the UFO community, patterns are often presumed to be identified from repetitive witness narrations. Then, it follows that characteristics of suspected paranormal phenomena are more widely accepted, based on those narrations and assumed patterns. This is risky and we should tread cautiously because the presumptions are derived from subjective witness reports. Specifically, there is no way to know, absent corroborating evidence, whether witnesses are experiencing things as they interpret, or whether they are actually misinterpreting experiences in similar manners. It is certain that in at least some instances we are seeing testimonies stemming from cultural influence, ill-advised investigation techniques and resulting false memories, not from unusual phenomena and alien-related activity. Therefore it stands to reason we should thoroughly explore the much more likely possibilities before accepting the thinly supported fantastic.

Each progressing episode and story passed around ufology increases the chances that future incidents will be interpreted in ways that support past perspectives. Think of water seeking its way through well-worn drainage ditches with each successive rainfall. In addition to such subjective perception and personal conditioning, witnesses are also likely to continue to interpret future events in preconceived ways due to peer pressure: The ongoing emotional support of investigators and community members who offer encouragement is understandably valued.

The future leads to the past, not just in identifying how assumptions will collectively be formed and premature conclusions will be drawn, but in understanding the roles that media, pop culture, and even the UFO community itself play in influencing how witnesses will interpret experiences that haven't even happened yet. The accepted paradigm doesn't have to be accurate, just well-known, for it to serve as a bandwagon.

There is simply no substitute for verifiable evidence. Its absence in most UFO cases doesn't necessarily mean nothing of potential interest is happening. Researchers might just be lacking in ways to get misunderstood phenomena under a glass. However, we, as a community, stand to be taken much more legitimately if at least acknowledging the problematic aspects of relying heavily upon witness testimony, unreliable investigative techniques, and similar activities that diminish credibility.

To be fair, anecdotal witness reports in any number of non-UFO subjects can, at times, involve circumstances that prove to be worthy of study, leading researchers to form better understandings of relevant phenomena. However, it could be emphasized that potential opportunities to gain insight into uncharted waters makes it all the more important to proceed carefully, refraining from swaying witnesses and being careful not to draw premature conclusions.

It could further be argued that the UFO genre includes many cases of reasonable interest, and all of the reported phenomena may not be attributable to hoaxes, misunderstandings and variations thereof. Perhaps so. Be that as it may, the combined influence of charlatans, spooks, and researcher bias is among the greatest challenges to the community, making it prudent to exercise healthy skepticism when engaging in UFO-related discussion and contemplation. To ignore that this is the case is, in itself, to enable the problem, failing to cultivate intellectual honesty while decreasing the likelihood of legitimate research being produced or more widely acknowledged.

Studies indicate that once the damage of accepting inaccurate information is done, it is extremely difficult to reverse. Research conducted at the University of Michigan showed that when misinformed people were exposed to corrected facts, they rarely changed their minds.[12] Actually, they tended to dig their heels in deeper. Researchers found that facts did not cure misinformation, but, quite the opposite, often led to inaccurate beliefs being held even stronger.

See a fundamental problem here? A great deal of completely inaccurate—and often, at best, unverified—information is widely accepted, then spread as if it were reliable. We then tend to form beliefs and make up our minds about things which haven't actually been adequately explained. People subsequently not only reject revisions and corrections, but tend to embrace beliefs even more tightly when those beliefs are shown to be incorrect. To reframe the debate, effectively and competently, we must not only acknowledge that such dynamics are happening, but make consistent decisions to swim against the undertow and be more of the solution than the problem.

It would be helpful to exercise some understanding when people choose not enthusiastically to embrace fantastic stories supported by witness testimony and various questionable types of less than convincing evidence. We might choose to remember that if we desire others to share our beliefs, it is our responsibility to demonstrate those beliefs to be accurate. Otherwise, people are completely entitled to believe or suppose differently. It is simply unreasonable to demand agreement without conclusive evidence. What's more, it is after applying reasonable skepticism that the proverbial cream will rise to the top. If there are events of legitimate interest to be found, accurately identifying them will involve careful, systematic research, which rejects sensationalism and accepts critical review as an important and fundamental part of the process.

Researchers, Investigators and Consumers

As researchers, it would be very helpful to emphasize differentiating between suppositions and facts. I advocate presenting a proposed possibility—a potential explanation for a certain case, for example—then citing fact-based resources as supporting evidence. Cite facts, then present opinions of what the facts may indicate.

Work could further be legitimized by relying more heavily upon sources recognized as credible within the professional research community. These include such resources as authenticated documents, newspaper clippings, journals and similar media that offer valuable use as reference materials. I accept researchers speculating as much as they want, but my respect is particularly earned when they differentiate between speculation and what can be demonstrated as factual.

I also advocate aiming attention at specific circumstances, as compared to discussing wide scale topics in general terms. I am suggesting it is much more practical and potentially productive to consider a specific case in-depth, or even a single aspect of a particular case, than the validity of circumstances too broad to cover effectively. Get down to details. Certain time periods might be researched, or the work of a particular individual, rather than discussing and debating generalities while failing to drill down through more interesting details that might actually resolve select circumstances.

As investigators, community members must cease employing conclusively unreliable techniques if there is to be any hope at all of gaining credibility and reframing the debate to a more sensible perspective. This cannot be overemphasized. The time for experimenting with hypnotic regression as a memory enhancing tool of alien abduction is long gone, much less relying on it as a primary investigative technique. There is no credibility to be found in either practicing or supporting such dated and potentially harmful activities.

It would also be helpful if investigators encouraged one another to further educate themselves on such topics as memory, witness testimony and emotional trauma. The beliefs and hopes of investigators should not permeate their cases, and more effort could be invested in promoting objectivity if the UFO community is to earn the wider acceptance and respect it has long claimed to seek. Embracing and addressing points contained in the skeptical argument is part of the path to credibility, particularly as compared to averting from the issues.

Among such points demanding reasonable attention is emotional trauma. To neglect to accept its substantial relevance to the UFO community, and to enable investigators to continue to gloss over it through intentional omission or lack of understanding, is detrimental to the wellbeing of witnesses, to the quality of information reported, and to a sincere search for truth.

Emotional and psychological trauma is the result of extraordinarily stressful events that shatter a sense of security.[13] It is not the objective facts that determine whether an event is traumatic, but the subjective emotional experience. Individuals suffering from untreated trauma are likely to undergo future traumatic events, and that is particularly the case among those who experience childhood trauma. Symptoms include confusion, anxiety and fear. Limited abilities to think critically are common, as are difficulties in keeping chains of events in accurate chronological order. Untreated trauma may cause individuals to misinterpret the original traumatic event and to find variations thereof to be happening over and over again.

Emotional trauma may very well be among the most significant and least discussed aspects of the UFO community, particularly concerning reports of alleged alien abduction. It would be reasonable to question why community leaders and investigators are not more commonly encouraging people, who describe themselves as repeatedly experiencing traumatic events, to seek qualified treatment.

To encourage proper treatment for trauma and, in effect, promote good mental health, qualifies the advocates as more competent and better informed to discuss the cases. Demonstrating a willingness to acknowledge the relevance of trauma shows commitment to accuracy, concern for witnesses, and helps create an atmosphere more conducive to authenticity and good quality discussion. That would be the case regardless of the origins of the reported experiences. It might indeed be questioned why trauma specialists and related mental health professionals are not more actively consulted. Their areas of expertise and understandings of behavior are extremely relevant.

Another point deserving of more attention is physical evidence. Investigators could improve credibility and the quality of summaries of cases if they clarified the presence or absence of supporting physical evidence. Explaining what was done with any such evidence would also be very helpful, particularly as compared to emphasizing and dwelling on witness testimony. Advancing technology now allows cost-effective procedures conducted by qualified personnel for everything from photo analysis to forensic testing. It should be used. Reframing the debate includes taking advantage of such opportunities, following the trail of evidence to what logical conclusions it provides, and acknowledging when physical evidence is either entirely absent or if investigators questionably fail to pursue it.

As consumers, personal responsibility can be taken in choosing to support writers and researchers whom, we feel, frame the relevant dynamics in reasonable and accurate context. We also have the choice not to support those we feel do more harm than good.

There is unprecedented access to information and those who report it. Blogs, podcasts and websites addressing the UFO controversy are plentiful, as are books on the subject. A multitude of sites host book reviews and related discussion, and most researchers are readily available via personal web pages and various forms of social media. The witnesses, researchers and trendsetters of ufology are, in many cases, more accessible than ever before, and public discussion is certainly easy to find.

I encourage taking advantage of such accessibility in order, morally and financially, to support those we value and those we feel conduct themselves responsibly. Not only will they appreciate it, but we are doing a service for community members who will read our discussions and reviews, both currently and in the future.

In the same ways, support may be offered to those we feel worthy; we have the choice to refrain from attending events and buying products from organizations and individuals whom we identify as failing to make constructive contributions. No organization or individual researcher should be considered the only game in town. An abundance of sources is now available to choose from for information and discussion, ranging from Fortean to skeptical, so we can offer our valued support wisely. Be heard.

Similarly, intentional decisions could be made about the types of community we wish to cultivate. Consumers and witnesses would be well served to choose specifically what type of support they are seeking when they venture into the UFO community. Services offered by therapists and investigators, for example, are entirely different and should not be confused with one another. A therapeutic relationship with a psychoanalyst should be considered much differently from what one should expect from an investigator conducting what should be an objective inquiry into facts and evidence. It would be beneficial to identify whether one is seeking emotional support, as in the form of sharing experiences and receiving empathy and acceptance, or investigative support, in which critical thinking should be prioritized and a list of likely explanations compiled.

Caution should be exercised in selecting sources for emotional support, be it through group meetings or private therapists, and consulting qualified professionals would be a wise choice. Working with an investigator should be given ample consideration as well.

Consumers are completely entitled to ask a potential investigator, therapist or other service provider to state their objectives and clarify terms in writing, as well as means of recourse. Identify what is wanted and seek it from appropriate sources.

Researchers, investigators, and writers, in turn, have responsibilities to clarify what they are seeking when interacting with others, as well as what they are willing and able to provide, and act accordingly. It would be helpful if they refrained from participating at events and conferences sponsored by organizations promoting sensationalism and engaging in less than best practices. Such efforts would contribute to improving the community and increasing its opportunities to gain respect.

I contend that a great deal of information circulated around the UFO community—the vast majority—is simply incorrect or, at the least, unsubstantiated, while detrimentally accepted and promoted as common knowledge. I am suggesting the present community and its sizable list of urban myths evolved out of decades of cultivating and marketing stories to those of us admirably open-minded enough to be willing to consider them further, yet ultimately led astray. Some of the perpetrators were well-meaning, some were not, and some may have just been doing their jobs.

If we are to find events of interest at the heart of what became a truly phenomenal social occurrence, we would be wise to drop preconceived notions to the best of our abilities. If we're going to reframe the debate, we'll be well served to know the history of how we got here, where we've been, what worked and what didn't, and how to proceed both intelligently and competently. It's not always easy, but things worth doing often aren't.

IN FOR A PENNY, IN FOR A POUND: MOVING UFOLOGY
BEYOND MATERIALISM

Joshua Cutchin

SIR BAR: Look you Sir, Truth may be blam'd, but never sham'd. I cou'd give you farther proof if occasion serv'd. But Truth is not to spoken at all times.

ALD: Yet it concerns you to speak, and to prove what you speak, this is no jesting matter.

SIR BAR: Well than, O'er shooes, o'er boots. And In for a Penny, in for a Pound.

—EDWARD RAVENSCROFT, *THE CANTERBURY GUESTS, OR, A BARGAIN BROKEN A COMEDY*

In the late sixteenth century, Tycho Brahe proposed a model of the solar system wherein all the known planets—five at the time—revolved around the Sun, while the Sun itself orbited the Earth.[1] Referred to as the Tychonic System, the concept was not altogether new, having precursors in the fourth century B.C.[2]—nonetheless, this hybrid geoheliocentric model was closer to the truth than contemporary theories, which held the Earth as the fixed point around which the entire cosmos rotated.

The Tychonic System maintained popularity among progressive scientists until the early-1600s when Galileo proposed his heliocentric model, wherein the Sun is the fixed point around which all other celestial bodies in the solar system orbit. Though persecuted by the establishment, Galileo's proposition was eventually accepted.[3]

Centuries later, Albert Einstein would christen him "the father of modern physics—indeed, of modern science altogether,"[4] a sentiment Stephen Hawking would echo in his *A Brief History of Time*: "Galileo, perhaps more than any other single person, was responsible for the birth of modern science."[5]

While Brahe is not exactly a minor footnote to history, at the same time he enjoys neither the accolades nor the man-on-the-street familiarity, which Galileo does in the twenty-first century. Brahe could commit to everything that made Galileo immortal except for the Earth's rotation around the Sun. To do so would have been revolutionary. His significance to science would be enormous had he not engaged in half-measures and committed to a fully heliocentric model of the solar system.

In for a penny, in for a pound, as it were. Ufologists take note.

If there is such a thing as "mainstream ufology," it focuses upon a "nuts-and-bolts" (N&B) interpretation of sightings in support of an Extraterrestrial Hypothesis (ETH). Advocates of this grounded approach assume—perhaps naïvely, though not entirely illogically—that an extraterrestrial civilization would mirror our own dreams, desires, and abilities as a species. Humans wish to explore the galaxy, therefore aliens wish to explore the galaxy; humans would accomplish this goal by building metallic flying machines, aliens would as well; humans would study and catalogue alien life, aliens vice versa. To make a gross reduction, it is a quaint mid-twentieth century proposition wherein little green scientists in physical spacecraft regularly visit Earth.

In this model, the materialist paradigm—the dominant philosophical doctrine of science, wherein matter is the fundamental constant of reality and all other phenomena, including human consciousness itself, are illusory byproducts of matter—reigns supreme. N&B/ETH researchers hold that the UFO problem can and will be solved by physical evidence: burn marks at landing sites, a stunning video, a compelling photograph, a crashed flying saucer, an extraterrestrial body.

While plenty of cases superficially support the N&B/ETH view, its materialist foundations are shaken when confronted with the High Strangeness characteristic of a majority of UFO close encounters. Alleged "alien" abductees report profound synchronicities manifesting in their lives, battle poltergeist phenomena in their homes, and occasionally encounter loved ones during their brief sojourn to the Otherworld.

These pernicious data points serve as constant reminders that we are swimming in a very strange pool indeed. Of all the fantastic motifs reported by eyewitnesses, telepathy—the ability of aliens (or even just lights in the sky) to exchange ideas with witnesses via thought—is most common.

"Of 124 cases with the means of communication specified, 98 (79%) involve telepathy, thought transference, or the witnesses being able to understand or 'hear' the beings without their mouths moving or any apparent auditory input," wrote Eddie Bullard in his comprehensive 1987 work, *UFO Abductions: The Measure of a Mystery*.[6] While no study of similar magnitude has been compiled in the intervening three decades, even a cursory survey of the literature suggests that this trend has not abated.

"Regarding UFO contact, we would do well to recall that most contactees and abductees have claimed some form of telepathic connection with these other beings," wrote Richard Dolan in *UFOs for the 21st Century Mind*. "In fact, such connections are often felt by people who have UFO sightings, without even experiencing the extra level of abduction or contact. In other words, these beings appear, somehow, to connect to us telepathically." He later adds this aspect is "not fully appreciated by current science."[7]

At first blush, accepting the presence of telepathy in alien abduction cases seems as though it would be anathema to N&B ufologists of the ETH persuasion. After all, their position firmly seeks scientific answers to the UFO question, while telepathy is regarded as New Age bunk by the materialist establishment. In practice, however, most ETH advocates seem quite keen to declare this peculiarity a reality of the UFO experience.

Prior to his death in 2011, Budd Hopkins suspected not only that extraterrestrials were responsible for the abduction phenomenon, but also that they possessed telepathic abilities. In 1981's *Missing Time*, he sidestepped any possible contradiction by suggesting the telepathic component could represent extremely advanced technology.[8]

Alien abduction researcher Dr. David Jacobs, though initially skeptical of telepathic communication in his early work,[9] later warmed to eyewitness testimony of "Mindscans" and telepathy as a reality: "In virtually all abduction accounts, the communication between the aliens and the abductees is done through 'telepathy,' and not aurally through their ears," he wrote in 1992.[10]

Stanton T. Friedman—someone who has arguably done more than anyone else to legitimize UFO research while holding a firmly N&B paradigm—most overtly articulated his acceptance of telepathic communication in UFO encounters on a January 21, 2012 episode of Alex Tsakiris's popular *Skeptiko* podcast:

> I'm convinced that any advanced civilization will know about telepathy and mind control and communication at a distance. It really came home to me when I was standing at the exact location where Barney Hill was standing when the saucer was over their car and he's looking through binoculars at the crew on board.
>
> For no good reason, they jumped back in the car, very frightened, and they get off the main road, Route 3, and they go onto a secondary road. Then they go onto a dirt road—which Barney would never have done. And he winds up alongside the only place in the area where you could land a, let's say 80-foot in diameter, flying saucer... It was clear proof to me that these guys were directing his actions.
>
> It seems to me eminently clear that these guys have capabilities—as the only simple term I know—to do things that we don't look upon as being respectable. Such as mind-reading, mind control, and getting people to forget.[11]

In short, telepathy is regarded as *consensus gentium* among N&B/ETH ufologists, as well it should be. If we tossed out every account involving telepathic communication, we would be left with only a tiny fraction of the cases reported. The question stands, however, whether or not those in favor of the N&B/ETH solution have wrestled fully with the implications raised by telepathy in UFO and abduction reports.

The Slippery Slope

The most obvious repercussion of a belief in telepathy is how it normalizes a host of other psi phenomena in a domino effect, which in turn busts the perceived N&B/ETH ufological monopoly. After all, it seems arbitrary to draw a line in the sand at telepathy, which is but one point on a robust spectrum of psychic abilities. The UFO literature is rife with witnesses who experience such activity, from the comparatively mundane (precognition, clairvoyance) to the dramatic (psychokinesis, astral projection). Telepathy, a phenomenon whose existence is roundly accepted by N&B/ETH advocates, accompanies nearly all such examples.

Wrote Jacques Vallée in the mid-1970s:

> I have long had an interest in both UFO manifestations and such psychic manifestations as telepathy, poltergeists, and psychokinetics, but I have refrained (until a few years ago) from attempting to build a bridge between these two fields. To be sure, I have been aware that many UFO cases contained elements indicative of psychic phenomena. At the same time, I have found in the literature of psychic history many observations that were suggestive of either the presence or the interference of UFOs. It would have been impossible not to recognize these connections and yet, to give just one example, when I was recently invited to speak about UFO research at a University of California extension course on psychic phenomena, my decision to accept the invitation was greeted with disbelief among astronomers privately interested in the subject. One of my physicist friends who was studying the material aspect of the sightings even called me to ask, 'Why are you getting such a solid field as UFO research mixed up with the disreputable area of psychic phenomena?' implying that by speaking of the analysis of UFO sightings before specialists in brain research, meditation, biofeedback, and brainwave analysis, I might jeopardize my chances of ever capturing a real, material flying saucer!
>
> At the same time, it was amusing to observe the initial reluctance of those who had spent all their lives studying poltergeists, telepathy, and the human aura to consider the subject of UFOs.
>
> But once the connection was established, there could not be any more doubt that we had to deal with one, not with two, subjects; not with two sets of phenomena but with a single universe of events in which a single set of laws was in force.[12]

It is easy to illustrate how this inevitable connection declaws the traditional N&B stance. Starting in the 1970s, the United States government began pouring funds into research on remote viewing, an alleged psychic ability wherein a sitter is given a series of coordinates and asked to articulate what impressions and sensations come to mind. The Stargate Project, as it was called, cost Americans at least $20 million before it was shut down in 1995 for "failing to produce any actionable intelligence information" (one suspects that if this official narrative were true, the project would have been terminated after one, five, or even ten years rather than twenty, but that is a topic for another day).[13]

A list of those attached to this endeavor reads like a rogue's gallery of 1970s parapsychologists and psychics: Russell Targ and Hal Puthoff spearheaded the research, enlisting the help of individuals such as Joseph McMoneagle, Pat Price, Uri Gellar,[14] and Ingo Swann in various capacities.[15] Swann is of particular note for an anecdote he related in his 1998 book, *Penetration: The Question of Extraterrestrial Telepathy*.

Just prior to Stargate's formation, a mysterious government agent calling himself "Mr. Axelrod" contacted Swann and asked him to remote view a set of coordinates on the far side of Earth's Moon. Swann was initially frustrated with his results, which seemed to produce visions of very un-Moonlike things, including artificial structures and evidence of some sort of mining operation. After Axelrod assured him these results were consistent with their intelligence of activity on the Moon Swann, gobsmacked, continued with his session.

> There were "nets" over craters, "houses" in which someone obviously lived, except that I couldn't see who—save in one case.

> In THAT case, I saw some kind of people busy at work on something I could not figure out. The place was dark. The "air" was filled with a fine dust, and there was some kind of illumination—like a dark lime-green fog or mist.

> The thing about them was that they either were human or looked exactly like us—but they were all males, as I could well see since they were all butt-ass naked. I had absolutely no idea why. They seemed to be digging into a hillside or a cliff...

> But there in my psychic state, as I felt I was, some of those guys started talking excitedly and gesticulating. Two of them pointed in my "direction."

"I think they have spotted me, Axel. They were pointing at me, I think. How could they do that... unless... they have some kind of high psychic perceptions, too?" [16]

While the story is likely fanciful, it raises a host of compelling possibilities if true. We have no idea how these moon inhabitants would have described Swann to their peers.

Was there a visual component? Did he appear like a ghost to them? Or perhaps Swann appeared to the Moonites as an anomalous light in their sky, or as a flying saucer? Perhaps when *we* observe such things in *our* skies, we do not see physical extraterrestrial spacecraft, but manifestations of advanced intelligences remote viewing Earth. Perhaps only the psychically sensitive among us can see them—those of us receptive to telepathy.

Why build a clunky metal disc and travel 40 light years to observe Earthlings when you can do it from the comfort of your living room? N&B spacecraft are not *fait accompli*. This is one of a myriad of possibilities rendered plausibilities when ufologists endorse psi phenomena.

Rejecting Materialism

Less obvious but far more profound is how this endorsement of telepathy in UFO encounters draws irreconcilable battle lines between ufology and materialism. In the eyes of modern scientists, belief in telepathy and psychic abilities further degrades the already-sullied topic of ufology; they despise these concepts and reject them outright, because they directly threaten the scientific method.

Scientific literature is littered with sentiments such as those espoused by philosopher-physicist Mario Bunge:

> Precognition violates the principle of antecedence ("causality"), according to which the effect does not happen before the cause. Psychokinesis violates the principle of conservation of energy as well as the postulate that mind cannot act directly on matter. (If it did no experimenter could trust his own readings of his instruments.) Telepathy and precognition are incompatible with the epistemological principle according to which the gaining of factual knowledge requires sense perception at some point.

Parapsychology makes no use of any knowledge gained in other fields, such as physics and physiological psychology. Moreover, its hypotheses are inconsistent with some basic assumptions of factual science. In particular, the very idea of a disembodied mental entity is incompatible with physiological psychology; and the claim that signals can be transmitted across space without fading with distance is inconsistent with physics.[17]

Lest we assume this is an isolated opinion, consider the conclusion of a 1988 panel commissioned by the United States National Research Council to study the paranormal: "Despite a 130-year record of scientific research on such matters, our committee could find no scientific justification for the existence of phenomena such as extrasensory perception, mental telepathy or 'mind over matter' exercises... Evaluation of a large body of the best available evidence simply does not support the contention that these phenomena exist."[18]

It doesn't matter that this statement is demonstrably false (more on that in a moment). What matters is that ufologists make no friends in these circles—*the circles they so desperately wish to be included in*—by endorsing telepathy.

How do N&B/ETH ufologists seeking mainstream acceptance hope to reconcile extraterrestrial visitation with something science declares a fundamental impossibility? Who cares about evidence like burn marks on the ground, radar data, radiation effects, or government documents when the eyewitness adds, "The aliens spoke to me without their mouths moving"? Inadmissible by association.

Any ufologist worth his Fortean salt will point to recent advances in the field of consciousness studies as legitimizing such data. It is true: while plenty of dreck exists as "evidence" of psychic phenomena, a handful of well-qualified researchers are tearing down the materialist paradigm brick-by-brick, producing top-notch research and even publishing in highly regarded peer-reviewed journals.

Rupert Sheldrake has conducted a great many consciousness research projects, but perhaps none more famously than his "pet telepathy" work. His rigorous experimentation, conducted with utmost dedication to the scientific method, suggested that dogs rush to wait by a door or window the moment their owners begin the return journey home. One dog in the study, Jaytee, boasted an 85% success rate, despite Sheldrake randomizing departure times, drivers, and vehicles.[19]

Dutch cardiologist Pim van Lommel conducted one of history's largest longitudinal surveys of cardiac arrest patients with the express purpose of examining their Near Death Experiences. His subsequent article, which appeared in the prestigious British medical journal *The Lancet* in 2001, concluded that no current medical explanation satisfactorily explained the patients' experiences.[20]

Before his 2007 death, University of Virginia School of Medicine psychiatrist Ian Stevenson practically ended the reincarnation debate. Just one of his works, 1997's *Reincarnation and Biology: A Contribution to the Etiology of Birthmarks and Birth Defects*, chronicled the past-life memories and anomalous birthmarks of over 200 children, each corresponding to the lives and wounds of the deceased they claimed to have once been.[21]

Cornell University professor Daryl Bem published a paper in 2010 suggesting that intense emotions may directly enhance psi phenomena. In his research, over 1,000 subjects exhibited greater aptitude in guessing the location of erotic images over neutral images (53.1% versus 49.8%—statistically significant).[22]

This is but a taste of the reputable work currently underway in consciousness studies. It is required that if you are unfamiliar with any of the individuals above—who are but a handful of the researchers pushing back on materialism—you avail yourself of their work *posthaste*.

In light of this admittedly stellar research, some will counter that the N&B/ETH approach will be exonerated if psi abilities are one day accepted within the scientific establishment. In that event, these human capacities will not be regarded as *supernatural* phenomena, only poorly understood *natural* phenomena.

These individuals could not be more wrong, at least in the way materialism has forced us to define "natural" over the last few centuries. Materialism holds that only the tangible is real. Extended consciousness effects have no place in a materialist paradigm, period.

At the same time, remember that non-materialist does not equal non-scientific. Science is nothing more than a set of guidelines and tools to evaluate reality honestly and objectively, whereas materialism is an assumption based upon the notion that only things replicable in a laboratory setting are worthy of labeling "real" (though, as illustrated above, not even controlled repeatability satisfies this arbitrary standard). Confirming the objective reality of telepathy, remote viewing, clairvoyance, or any other psi effect would devastate our understanding of natural laws, which would in turn cripple the surety with which the scientific method operates. It would shatter materialism.

Alex Tsakiris deftly explains this in his book *Why Science is Wrong... About Almost Everything.*

> If my consciousness is something—anything—other than a product of my brain, then science is out of business until it figures out exactly how my consciousness interacts with this world. If my consciousness is more than my physical brain, then consciousness is the X-factor in every science experiment. It's the asterisk in the footnotes that says, "We came as close as we could, but we had to leave out consciousness in order to make our numbers work."[23]

The good news is the tide of consensus is beginning to favor researchers like Sheldrake, van Lommel, Stevenson, Bem, and company. Scientists are speaking and behaving less like materialist drones and more like open-yet-critically-minded truth seekers (in other words, more like actual scientists). There are well-placed individuals in the materialist establishment entertaining ideas like the multiverse, or the notion that we may be living in a simulation. Granted, they're still banging the antiquated drum of eighteenth century materialism, but at least a dialog is starting.

For a more specific example of how mainstream thought is sounding weirder by the day, consider the sentiment expressed in a 2015 press release from The Australian National University. Upon confirming that particles exist in a state of abstraction until they are observed, quantified, and measured (basically saying that events at the quantum level are defined by the future, *not* the past), Dr. Andrew Truscott said, "At the quantum level, reality does not exist if you are not looking at it."[24]

Talk like that from a ufologist in the 1990s would have been greeted with men in white coats.

Once the last tile falls in the "psi acceptance domino chain"—and it will, through fits and starts—it will be patently obvious that materialism is, if not outright falsified, at least undermined to an irreparable degree. From materialism's ashes, a new model of reality will arise wherein the scientific establishment accepts that the completely intangible, wholly interiorized phenomenon of human consciousness can manifest measurable effects in our physical world.

Does this sound like any unexplained aerial phenomena you may have run across?

Either materialism is correct or materialism is incorrect. If it is correct, how can N&B/ETH researchers believe in telepathy? If it is incorrect, then why do so many still feel obligated to explain UFOs using the exact materialist paradigm that telepathy's existence refutes?

Telepathy in UFO accounts or scientific materialism—one must be rejected. No middle ground. No half measures. In for the penny that is telepathy, in for the pound that abandons materialism. Why continue playing by scientific rules when you've already broken them by ascribing to telepathy and, more to the point, *the rulebook is being rewritten in your favor as we speak?*

Granted, none of this precludes the possibility of telepathic extraterrestrials visiting Earth in sophisticated spacecraft; nor is it suggesting that plenty of N&B/ETH researchers have not already adopted a post-materialist, consciousness-based paradigm. But it is fatiguing to read convoluted descriptions of crash site "memory metal" nanotechnology or hear lecturers suggest elaborate proposals on how faster-than-light travel could be achieved. Such materialist apologies become completely unnecessary when operating in a consciousness-based paradigm.

A magical paradigm.

A Consciousness Paradigm or: How I Learned to Stop Worrying and Love Magic

Orthodox ufologists will likely recoil from the term "magic." Admittedly, it sounds like the least scientific thing possible. But to take an Arthur C. Clarke-ism and turn it on its head, if any sufficiently advanced technology is indistinguishable from magic then it follows that magic is indistinguishable from any sufficiently advanced technology.

Those straddling the magical-ufological line are in good company. The United States government, as evidenced by The Stargate Project, has a long history of keen interest in both UFOs and magic for decades (perhaps the big secret of UFO Disclosure, should that day ever come, is that they've been studying the two as a single phenomenon). The dynastic families of America have long been rumored to empty their pocketbooks into a variety of occult projects. A quote apocryphally attributed to J.P. Morgan says, "Millionaires don't use astrology—billionaires do."

To make the term "magic" further palatable, let us turn to the perennially articulate chaos magician Gordon White, who said in a 2015 interview:

> Magic is a culture-specific response to naturally occurring consciousness effects like telepathy, and precognition, and all these normal things that as humans, with a normal-functioning mind, we experience ... If you look from Australian Aboriginal tribes to chaos magicians in 2015 London, the quote unquote "powers" or the quote unquote "effects" that you can achieve with magic pretty much boil down to the same four or five things: telepathy, precognition (so seeing the future, clairvoyance, whatever you want to call it), visiting the Otherworld, and in some way, trafficking with the spirits.[25]

Much less frightening, no? It is easy to entertain the objective reality of magic once we cast aside the restraints of materialism, to which magical practice stands diametrically opposed. It is but another domino. If you believe in telepathy, you have a *de facto* magical worldview—in a manner of speaking, hardline N&B/ETH researchers have endorsed magic for decades.

It is difficult to imagine the well-read ufologist arguing against White's description of magic. The greatest amount of pushback would likely focus on his last two points—visiting the Otherworld and trafficking with the spirits—but doesn't that perfectly describe alien abductions? If the magically operant have been correct about the reality of psi effects for millennia, while science tumbled down materialism's rabbit hole, perhaps we should give that community the benefit of the doubt when it claims that disincarnate spirits exist?

Viewing ufology with a magical eye is not novel (early pioneers like Allen Greenfield advocated this approach for years). It *is* novel to declare that we shouldn't feel ashamed at this interpretation. It *is* novel to predict that, one day, *their* science will look a lot more like *our* science. All we have to do is keep our heads down and wait out materialism's death throes. In the meantime, it is imperative that ufologists familiarize themselves with magical resources and thought.

One of the biggest things holding back ufology is that two thirds of researchers have never cracked open a grimoire. Had they done so, they would realize that the hodgepodge array of spirits, catalogued therein, mirror the varied appearance of extraterrestrial species in UFO literature. They would see how communing with deceased loved ones in alien abductions isn't so odd when your paradigm encourages the construction of ancestor altars. They would see that there is very little difference between a tenth century mage summoning Ashtaroth and Steven Greer calling down UFOs from the night sky in 2017.

And they would begin to understand how non-human logic works.

"Magicians have personal experience of non-human logic; what it feels like, how it manifests in life and culture, and so on," White wrote in his 2016 book *Star.Ships*. "It is characterized by atemporality, high levels of coincidence, repetition of motif and symbol in entirely unrelated contexts and a quasi-fractal capacity to look weirdly resonant at whatever level you observe the phenomenon, from the micro to the macro."[26]

White describes the forces behind this non-human logic as "Magonian," a term borrowed from Jacques Vallée's invaluable 1969 book, *Passport to Magonia*. Vallée's intercontextual examination of the UFO phenomenon drew parallels not only to faerie folklore of Northern Europe but also to medieval French stories of airship-piloting wizards from the cloud realm of Magonia.[27] Calling these phenomena "Magonian" is connotation-free and handily strips away the artificial barriers, which mainstream ufology has erected between accounts of extraterrestrials, spirits, the fae folk, and Blessed Virgin Mary apparitions.[28]

In 1918, magician Aleister Crowley famously claimed to have repeatedly summoned an entity named "Lam," which he sketched with a bulbous-head, highly evocative of modern descriptions of Gray aliens.[29] Ufologists view Crowley's interaction with Lam as extraterrestrial visitation; the magically operant view it as conjuration, but calling the experience "Magonian" gives us a much-needed *lingua franca* facilitating interdisciplinary discussion between these communities.

This heady ufological-magical blend is a promising avenue of exploration. Moving beyond materialism is about honestly confronting the fact that we know nothing for certain about UFOs, yet choosing to be inspired rather than frustrated by this realization, leading to a type of non-dogmatic gnosticism. Magonian phenomena encompass any number of answers to the UFO problem: aliens, yes, but also time travellers, demons, spirits, cultural poltergeists, interdimensional entities, the Jungian collective unconscious, daimonic higher selves, faeries, ghosts—or infinitely hybridized theories therein.

"If there are physical [extraterrestrial] lifeforms ... I posit they are subject to the same nonphysical interaction and subsequent wobbles in technological complexity [as us]," wrote White. "Granted, it gets a little blurry when you allow for the fact that a universe-spanning spirit world must contain the Dead of numerous alien races and hence interaction with it implies a roundabout transfer of technology from one species to another... only separated in time."[30]

The truth of the matter is that, as a ufological community, we have left the door open to a consciousness-based—and, by logical extension, magical—view of reality since the field's inception. The cognitive dissonance of accepting telepathy in UFO encounters while simultaneously striving for mainstream scientific acceptance is a recurring stumbling block to contemporary ufology ... we are collectively treading water by clinging to notions of flesh and blood extraterrestrials in nuts-and-bolts spacecraft.

There is yet hope, however. A field which is constantly marginalized need not be on the wrong side of history—the materialist paradigm will fall apart given time, and consciousness studies is the proverbial star to which ufology should hitch its wagon. The study of UFOs and alien abduction has zero obligations to a N&B/ETH model. What it *does* owe an obligation to is, to quote Alex Tsakiris, "follow the data wherever it leads."

Perhaps Gordon White articulated this sentiment most evocatively:

> To abandon interpretation to scientism is to shirk natural philosophy's most sacred duty. Your tribe deserves better. And if you feel some residual squeamishness over who has legitimacy of interpretation in our culture, consider this. We are wholly justified in turning the question on its head and asking the scientists what it is they think they are doing swimming in our pool in the first place.[31]

You now have permission to wade into the deep end.

TOWARD A BETTER **UFOLOGY:** APPLYING SCIENCE TO **THE STUDY OF UAP**

Micah Hanks

"Of all the questions the Gallup pollsters have asked the American public, why have UFOs struck such a resonant chord with the average adult American?" This was a question asked by Allan Hendry, UFO investigator for the Center for UFO Studies (CUFOS) throughout the late-1970s, whose work alongside J. Allen Hynek resulted in his book, *The UFO Handbook: A Guide to Investigating, Evaluating and Reporting UFO Sightings.*[1] Hendry observed: "It is true that the average individual is woefully ignorant of the way stars, aircraft, and balloons can manifest themselves. Yet so many of them have "flying saucers" registered in their subconscious and it is imprinted so strongly that there must be something about UFOs that has become important to our psychic makeup since the end of World War II."[2]

Many who become entangled in the slowly evolving quagmire that has become "ufology"—that is, the effort toward scientific study of Unidentified Flying Objects (UFOs), or, as I occasionally prefer, Unexplained Aerial Phenomena (UAP)—begin to get jaded with time. This is because, despite thousands of books written on the subject, and numerous studies conducted by scientific and investigative groups on both civilian and government levels, no serious headway has been made toward a consensus opinion about what the UFO phenomenon truly represents.

The majority of those interested in the subject, who advocate the existence of anomalous aircraft, gravitate toward an extraterrestrial theory of origin. However, this position remains controversial due to a lack of physical evidence that would conclusively help make this determination. Indeed, many leading UFO advocates would argue that there is no need for further "study" of UFOs at all; the data before us, scant though it may seem to any scientist, is already enough to have ushered in the era of "Disclosure," which replaces ufology altogether.

This *Disclosure*, roughly defined, is the notion of pushing for release of government data about UFOs that may be withheld from the public, and it has become fundamental to the majority of the work carried out by UFO researchers, advocates, and personalities in the broader field of modern "ufology." However, despite the passion and enthusiasm it has aroused in the UFO community for a number of years, there are a few reasons why it may not be the best focal point for obtaining knowledge about UFOs.

The Pitfalls of UFO Disclosure

The "Disclosure" idea, and the social movement that has formed around it in recent decades, is not without merit. It seems highly likely that at least *some* information on the UFO subject is being withheld from the public. History shows that groups like the CIA had secretly involved themselves in studies of unexplained aerial craft and other phenomena, while publicly downplaying the subject, for fear that knowledge of their role in ongoing studies might actually *encourage* belief in UFOs. As former CIA Chief Historian Gerald Haines has noted, this was considered undesirable at the time, since the CIA worried that rising interest in UFOs among the general public might foster social movements capable of destabilizing government authority (as had been a concern with many other, non-UFO social groups and movements, particularly throughout the 1960s and 1970s).

Thus, there is some historical precedent for why governments have withheld UFO data. However, as a ufological avenue of enquiry, the Disclosure movement may very well be a dead-end; certainly it is seen as such by an increasing number of researchers who hope to *apply scientific study to the UFO mystery.* By this, I mean gathering reliable information (as well as finding better ways to gather it, with the help of new, innovative technologies), and attempting properly to assess what that data yields.

This is not to detract from the idea of pressing for greater government transparency on subjects like UFOs. Nonetheless, a persistent danger exists in the *presumption* that such information exists, or that by lobbying for its release, something akin to an "Ark of the Covenant" for ufology will be revealed, laying out plainly, and for all to see, the "reality" behind the UFO phenomenon... whatever that might be.

Put more simply, overconfidence in the assumption that government agencies *already have* the answers, and that ufology is purely an aim toward gaining access to that information, may in fact be entirely counterproductive should it transpire that either of the following is true in relation to the UFO question:

1. No such information exists in the possession of government agencies, or
2. It *does* exist, but it continues to be withheld, despite political activism

I speak the above with full knowledge, of course, that many serious UFO researchers in years past *have* managed to garner new information through the FOIA process; three individuals that come to mind here are Stanton Friedman, John Burroughs, and Nick Redfern, each of whom I have spoken with personally about this subject at some length.

Thus, the argument remains that *scientific UFO research*, which really is the simple definition of the term "ufology," is of utmost importance to the study of UFOs if it is to be determined that there is anything more to the subject than the simple misidentification of prosaic natural and manmade phenomena, paired with a variety of factors that contribute to the ways humans interpret it on a case-for-case basis.

Returning to Allan Hendry's book, he offers the following analysis of the term "UFO," as well as what it means, and how this applies to the scientific study of unexplained aerial phenomena:

> The definition of a UFO given here is quite unusual, really; unlike other definitions that say what an object is or what it is like, this one describes a UFO by what it is not, or not like. If UFOs are, in effect, "everything in the sky that we don't understand," then this suggests

65

that the number of kinds of UFOs is hopelessly large. Is this the case in practice? If ufology is composed of a chaotic jumble of dissimilar, unrelated events, then it can't be amenable to study and therefore can't really be a science.[3]

This assessment, without additional context, may sound hopelessly bleak. Hendry, however, *though scientifically skeptical* in his assessment of the subject, had not been a debunker of UFOs (in fact, he argued against the ideology that, "if 90 percent of all UFO reports can be explained simply, then why not 100 percent?").[4] Anyone who takes time to read Hendry's comprehensive analysis of the subject, as presented in *The UFO Handbook*, must see that it is among the most thorough, non-biased scientific studies ever to have been presented on the subject; in fact, it may be the *very finest* instance of scientific UFO research collated in a single publication.

On the varieties of the UFO experience—and the oft-asserted notion that the term "UFO" refers to *all varieties* of unexplainable aerial phenomena, Hendry wrote: "In the past, UFO theories have shared one thing in common: the reductionist opinion that all UFOs belong to one generic class, i.e. that all unexplainable accounts of flying objects, ranging from distant Nocturnal Lights to exotic encounters with UFO-nauts, share a common blanket explanation scheme."[5] Thus, the majority of Hendry's book examines what UFOs *are not*, with detailed surveys that examine how easily (and consistently) common aircraft and other aerial objects or phenomena have been misinterpreted by observers.

Of particular importance is Hendry's emphasis on the way that "flying saucers," as a social meme, have broadly influenced people's interpretation of unidentified objects seen in the skies, particularly at night. This has led to a consistent trend toward assessment of natural or manmade things as being "UFOs," "alien craft," or other similar things. This is carried over into close encounter reports, where many claims of interactions with UFO occupants (though not all of them, perhaps) seem to indicate fantasies conjured by the observer, in response to this ever-present "flying saucer" meme. Hence, the differences between reported experiences from one UFO case to the next are almost infinite in their variety, further complicating the serious scientific treatment and categorization of such data.

With all the aforementioned in mind, Hendry offers a number of breakdowns and designations, which include extrapolations on possible sources that may account for many UFO reports, while allowing for the possibility that a minority of these cases do involve exotic or, at least, as-yet unexplained phenomena.

Still, a lot has changed in the world since 1979. The proliferation of drone technologies has added to the number of things we see darting through the sky on a daily basis. Also, the prevalence of smart phones and other handheld devices have allowed for the effective containment of small UFO investigative facilities carried within one's pocket, thanks to apps that range in focus from astronomy and star gazing, to oscilloscopes, police radars, and even satellite and aircraft tracking programs.

With the changing of times, the ways that UFOs are studied, and the designations applied to the collective UFO data, must change as well. Yes, modern researchers must take into account the prevalence of drones operated both by civilians, as well as government agencies. This, in addition to a number of similar innovations since the beginning of the 21st century, all further complicate the way UFOs are studied, and what their underlying sources may be.

The prevalence of "IFOs"—that is, objects that account for the majority of UFO reports, but which can be ruled out as prosaic sources through careful scientific research—greatly informed Hendry's work, and helped lead him to the novel concept of proposing what he called:

> ...a non-extraordinary plan to account for UFO reports at least as well as others mentioned (these "others", it should be noted, are the common sensational or extraordinary theories proposed by UFO advocates, in view of the seemingly exotic elements many UFO cases appear to represent).[6]

Thus, a "non-revolutionary, alternative UFO theory" is useful, because it helps whittle down the sensational claims that surround the majority of UFO research and to bring things down to a level that may allow scientific study to be useful in solving the broader UFO mystery (and none of this is to say that there cannot be an exotic or otherwise unusual explanation for some UFOs, but merely that we would better serve the subject by not assuming such a position from the outset, since the data may indeed reveal otherwise further on down the road).

Out with the Old: A New Classification System for UFOs

Over the last several years, my attitudes toward the UFO subject have changed greatly. At the outset, my own neophyte views fell very much in line with generally accepted attitudes: UFOs were probably evidence of alien visitations. With time (and with virtually no evidence of anything that could rightly be considered "extraterrestrial"), my skepticism grew, and I began to consider alternatives to the extraterrestrial hypothesis that might still account for some UFO reports, in addition to whether much of the phenomenon could have terrestrial origins.

My present hope, as a UFO researcher, is to propose a new set of designations for UFOs, which involve possible origins of various UAP that are subject to scientific inquiry, given our current level and understanding of applicable science and technology. These will incorporate new sources of possible UFO sightings (such as drones), as well as the reformulation of older elements, with consideration given to new technologies and innovations. My reason for wanting to do this is twofold:

1. New technologies, as well as new scientific discoveries, have helped broaden the range of possible sources for UAP since the day of Allen Hendry and J. Allen Hynek; the kinds of "IFO" sources they were comfortable working with have also broadened to include things like drones.
2. The previous classification systems first employed by J. Allen Hynek were too general, even for the period in which they were created; by today's standards, they no longer appear to provide a workable criterion for many modern UFO reports (we'll expand on this in a moment).

Hence, I argue that a "modernized" UFO classification system, which draws from the sort of crude classification system first employed by J. Allen Hynek, should be instituted. Of his original classification framework, Hynek wrote in *The Hynek UFO Report* that, "A number of years ago, I devised a simple classification system based solely on what was reported as observed and not on any preconceived idea of what the actual nature of UFOs might be. It was purely an observational classification system, much like an astronomer might use to classify the different types of stars or a zoologist different types of beetles that he came across in his explorations."

Hynek's observational classification system was composed of the following: What Hynek called NOCTURNAL LIGHTS, followed by DAYLIGHT DISCS. For instances where radar data corroborated a sighting, Hynek employed the term RADAR VISUALS, and for observations that occurred close at hand, Hynek used a three-tier grouping called CLOSE ENCOUNTERS (CEs), which accounted for a UFO observed close enough to discern relative detail (CE I), a UFO observed interacting physically with its environment in some way, and possibly leaving residual evidence (CE II), and a UFO observed along with its apparent occupants, or entities otherwise associated with the object (CE III).[7]

In later literature, two additional observational classes were instituted after Hynek's passing; these include cases that involve some apparent mental or physical transport of an individual between locations in conjunction with a UFO observation (CE IV), and a disputed fifth category (CE V) that may involve UFO physical injury cases (as proposed by Jacques Vallée), or human-initiated interactive encounters with UFOs (as proposed by Steven Greer).[8]

As we already see with the differing opinions about what constitutes the "CE V" cases, a number of other issues arise from these early classifications. Namely, the fact that Hynek's term for "Daylight Discs" borrowed from the heavily inferred "flying saucer" meme that became popular after the famous Kenneth Arnold sighting of 1947. Even Hynek, as did Hendry after him, noted that the term "Daylight Discs" actually referred to any number of different types of objects —not just "discs"— as they appeared when observed in the daylight. These ranged from *actual* discs, to egg-shaped objects, cylindrical craft, and a host of other shapes.[9]

There are many UFO reports that have described little more than amorphous illuminations, whether seen by day or by night; the primary difference here being that a *nighttime observation* would presumably leave far more to the imagination than a daylight observation. Imagine some vague, luminous form observed in the night sky; it is easy to see that this may in fact represent any number of things, perceived only by the apparent presence of lights. Do these lights envelope the object, or merely represent fixed points on a much larger craft? If two parties were to see the exact same amorphous, luminous object, with one group observing at night, while the other observed it during partly overcast conditions in afternoon daylight, one could easily guess that the interpretations of this hypothetical object might vary greatly.

Introduce *a small group* of these lights, rather than a single luminous orb, and the nighttime watchers might consider them lights along the perimeter of a larger craft, while our afternoon observers would liken it instead to a small "fleet" of orbs flying in formation.

Right off the bat, it begins to make logical sense to do away with the entire concept of "Daylight Discs." We also see that it may be important to draw distinctions between objects seen in daylight hours that are structured-looking "craft," versus those which are merely luminous phenomena that may otherwise resemble the "Nocturnal Lights" Hynek originally designated. Based on our earlier examples, we might do well to introduce separate designations for the nocturnal and daylight luminous phenomena as well, based on the likely differences in the ways each may be interpreted dependent on on visible conditions.

At the time Hynek began to devise his initial classification system, military bodies in the U.S. government and those elsewhere around the world, gave far more credence to the UFO situation (as made obvious by Hynek's work as a scientific advisor to the USAF's UFO study program, Project Blue Book). Hence, UFO incidents that occurred in close enough proximity to military installations, airports, or aircraft in flight might be able to produce radar information to corroborate visual sightings. While still relevant today, the lessened interest by military bodies in the UFO subject, paired with a range of new technologies that may serve as useful ways to corroborate visual sightings, presents a case for modifying and expanding Hynek's "Radar Visual" category as well.

While a close-hand UFO observation (CE I cases, generally recognized as being within 500 feet) may provide useful data, such observations in the past have failed to provide significantly useful new data about UFOs in the broader sense. Additionally, the Vallée definition for a CE V case would appear to be very similar to Hynek's CE II classification, in that each presents evidence of physical interactions between the UFO and its surrounding area (by area, here I also mean any individuals operating in that space). Given these criteria, CE IV may also qualify, in that a person being transported between locations also infers that the UFO has interacted with its physical environment and those within it.

Lastly, while UFO literature from the last several decades reveals a plethora of case studies that purport to involve interactions with UFO occupants, many researchers today will recognize that such claims have seen a sharp decline since the 1990s. Whether this is due to cultural factors, changes in belief systems, or some other stimuli (or the lack thereof) remains undetermined. Regardless, the marked decline in exotic UFO craft and occupant cases that once littered the UFO journals and publications is a noteworthy observation.

Now that we have observed the problems with the older classification systems, in addition to having noted certain changes in the way the UFO subject is being studied in the present day, I have assembled a new classification system, which I feel is more efficient, in addition to being less reliant on the prevalent memes and staples from the ufology of yesteryear (things like "flying discs" and "abductions").

This new proposed classification system is as follows:

1. Nocturnal Luminous Phenomena
2. Daylight Luminous Phenomena
3. Aerial Craft or Structured Objects
4. Objects Corroborated with Radar, Satellites, Photos, Video or Smartphone Apps
5. Objects that Interact Physically with Individuals or the Environment
6. Objects Accompanied by Beings or Apparent Operators

I expect, with time, that many of these designations and guidelines may change, or will otherwise be met with challenges, such is always the case, as we have seen, when new data forthcoming presents a case for re-thinking old ideas.

In order for the proposed classification system to be effective, I feel it is also pertinent to have a filtering system through which possible IFOs (Identified Flying Objects) may be easily grouped and discerned, at least in the majority of cases. Using a filtering system in this way will help prevent the absent-minded collection of endless reports of lights seen at night, or of vague descriptions of structured objects seen by day. As Hendry and the CUFOS had done in the late 1970s, proactive research that involved phone calls to local airports, Air Force Bases, National Weather Service centers, advertising plane companies, and other sources of useful information will nearly *always* reveal a common source behind some otherwise strange-sounding UFO reports.

Bearing this in mind, the following designations of UAP constitute circumstances that range from little-understood natural phenomena, to manmade aircraft, and even some speculative technologies for which a good amount of data exists to support a basis for their existence. Psychological interpretations of possible UAP are also considered. These are all areas where science, if applied in a proper, discerning manner, may yield new results or confirmations, in addition to helping understand their relationship to the study of unexplained aerial phenomena:

Natural Phenomena
    Celestial
    Atmospheric / Meteorological
    Geological
    Refractions / Mirages / Illusions
    Biological (birds, insects, etc)

Psychological Phenomena
    Misinterpretation of prosaic occurrences
    Delusions / Fantasies
    Mental Disorders

Manmade Non-Vehicular Aerial Objects
    Balloons
    Kites
    Satellites / International Space Station
    Spotlights
    Rockets / Fireworks

Drones / Unmanned Aerial Vehicles (UAVs)
    Civilian UAVs
    Military UAVs

Conventional Manmade Piloted Aircraft
    Hobbyists / Inventors
    Misidentification of Known Commercial or Military Aircraft

Experimental / Secret Government Aircraft or Technologies
    Secret / Undisclosed Military Aircraft
    Privately Funded Research & Development Operations

Note the inclusion of a "biological" subcategory within the designations for "Natural Phenomena" listed above. Implausible though it may seem that a bird or an insect might be mistaken for being a

UFO, this often *does* occur in photos and video. It happens when a much smaller creature in flight passes near the camera lens, giving the appearance of a larger, faster-moving object further off in the distance. Adding further confusion is the fact that, under some circumstances, physical characteristics of a fast-moving object or animal may be distorted in photos and videos, as with the so-called "rods" that result from traces of the wingbeats of insects as recorded by interlaced video systems.

Also note that the designations presented in the category system above *do not* include such things as "alien craft," "strange humanoids," "inter-dimensional phenomena," or other presently unproven or speculative sources for UAP reports. The reason for this, rather than to eliminate any possibility of the existence of such things, is because *in the event that all of the above can be ruled out, then all we are left to consider, with any certainty, is the presence of some "unknown."* In order to extrapolate further upon the possible source of the resulting "unknown," we would require more data... but we must reach that point first.

At the present time, despite the kinds of "evidence" the UFO community has offered over the last several decades, little has been forthcoming that would satisfy the biologist, chemist, or physicist. Granted, this is not to say that *some* evidence does not warrant further review; merely that no such evidence appears to offer irrefutable "proof" of an anomalous source behind UAP reports, at least at present. Perhaps this will change in the future, either with the acquisition of new data, or with the utilization of new technologies that may help us learn new things about existing evidence on hand.

The Merits, and Problems, With "Modern Skepticism"

My views presented here are, I feel, *necessarily* skeptical, and hence it may seem questionable why one of such disposition would seek further to commune with the broader "UFO Community" today—a community whose greatest names and personalities largely still champion the extraterrestrial hypothesis, or at least some variation of it.

The reason, to me, is very simple: I can respect, communicate, and interact with people who do not share my own ideas. Despite my skepticism, I have been shown great respect by many within the UFO community, and have made lasting friendships with many people whose own ideas about the phenomenon differ greatly from my own.

Conversely, in my personal experiences, I have found that my inter-actions with those who identify with the ideology of modern skepticism are not as warm or friendly; while this is not *always* the case, often, the modern skeptic will shun anyone who is willing to give consideration to the notion that there may be more to the world than any of us are presently aware (Hendry might have identified these individuals as the "why can't we just debunk 100% of all UFOs?" crowd).

Modern skepticism can, I think, be summarized in many instances as an *ideology*, around which a social movement has been built—one that, today, also runs tangent with atheism—and as a paradoxically *evangelical* attitude about the supremacy of science above all other forms of knowledge.

Obviously, science and, more importantly, the scientific method, rest at the cusp of what I seek to address in the present missive. Hence, in pointing out the adoption of a dogmatic "scientism" amidst the modern skeptic movement is not to detract from the *proper* applications of sci-ence by any means. Neither is it meant to disregard skepticism, when applied scientifically, rather than as part of an ideology one adopts, or in order to garner favor from others within any proposed social move-ment, which modern skeptics might seek to join. These are elements that I feel, unfortunately, *do* inform the minds of many modern "skep-tics," which has led them to the dismissal of a wide range of beliefs and disciplines; no less unfortunate among these than the current conflict surrounding physicists and their disregard for philosophy.

To the contrary, I hope to instill in the mind of the reader that prop-er adherence to scientific methodology, and a reasonable, open-mind-ed skepticism, will be of great benefit to the study of UFOs. To quote the notable skeptic Gary P. Posner, M.D. (someone whose views toward the UFO subject, though often different from my own, I certainly do appreciate), "The great irony is that we "skeptics" are the open-minded ones. As certain as we may be that UFOs are not ET... we are capable of—indeed committed to—changing our minds, should compelling evidence be brought to the fore."

Perhaps, with careful thought, analysis, and an equal willingness to be open-minded in our skepticism, science can help us move toward a better ufology than we have seen in years past... and with it, perhaps, more answers than we have managed to attain previously.

ALMOST **EVERYTHING** YOU THINK YOU KNOW **ABOUT FLYING** SAUCERS IS WRONG

Lorin Cutts

T he modern UFO era has presented us with a set of problems that we have been unable to deal with in any rational or responsible way for over seventy years. Popular UFO mythology would have us believe that it all started when businessman and pilot, Kenneth Arnold, set off in his small plane from Chehalis Airport for Yakima, Washington State, at around 3pm on June 24, 1947 and reported seeing nine blinding, crescent-shaped objects flying at incredible speed towards Mount Adams. But even this is wrong.

The Yakima region, with Mount Adams just to its western perimeter, is still, without doubt, one of the busiest hotspots for UFO activity in the United States.[1] Another one hundred miles as the crow flies east-northeast of Mount Adams lies the vast Hanford Nuclear Site. If we were to name anywhere as the birthplace of the modern UFO era, it would arguably be more accurate to give this accolade to Hanford. This was home to the Manhattan Project that spawned the world's first devastating H-bombs that destroyed the Japanese cities of Hiroshima and Nagasaki in August 1945. Is it any coincidence, around the time and location of the first crude plutonium enrichment, that the first modern flying disc reports began to come in with any regularity?

It is now clear there were dozens of UFOs reported both visually and on radar for many months prior to June 24, 1947 around the nuclear facility. These included a sighting of three discs at 2.30pm that afternoon, some 30 minutes prior to Arnold's take-off.[2] By late June of 1947, UFO reports were exploding across the USA in numbers never seen before: a report by Ted Bloecher, later used by The Rand Corporation, suggests 853 sightings of unexplained aerial phenomena in June and July of 1947.[3] Of course, it is open to discussion that all kinds of aerial phenomena had been reported for centuries or millennia. But the fact that one of the most highly classified projects in the United States at that time was having its airspace penetrated by objects of unknown nature and origin was not only a cause for alarm, it was also highly embarrassing.

With these very early flying disc reports lie the origins of what would become an important factor in the way the US government and military would publicly deal with the modern UFO enigma. There was evidently a need to classify, deceive and obfuscate in order to cover up these inexplicable incursions into restricted airspace. And by the time UFOs had really grabbed the public's imagination, those responsible for keeping Hanford's secrets (both of a nuclear and a potentially more esoteric nature) would certainly have had no issue with Arnold's sighting (which made no mention of Hanford) being placed front and center. Kenneth Arnold's famous sighting was by no means the first UFO sighting, but it was the first to capture mass media attention. Just over two weeks later, Roswell would hit the newswires. Mythology was in the making.

So, over the next seventy years, how did we go about attempting to assimilate into our culture those things that continued to defy rational explanation or didn't fit within our scientific understanding? On the one hand, we ridiculed or ignored them and said that they didn't exist. On the other, and in the absence of much real information at all, we mythologized—we made much of it up. The modern UFO era heralded the arrival of the flying saucers. Whatever their true nature, it seems fair to say they were and are "vehicles" for the hopes, dreams, and fears of a New Age.

I'm going to attempt to explain why I think almost everything you think you know about flying saucers is wrong.

UFO Social Engineering 101

i.   The Subject That Covers Itself Up

Back in April 2012, I interviewed the stalwart UFO investigator Stan Gordon. For over fifty years, Stan has been a frontline investigator in Pennsylvania, his primary focus gathering thousands of field reports of all things paranormal. He told me that some of the things reported in his cases were so weird, so bizarre and unsettling, that the subject covers itself up. Nobody wants to go near them.[4]

The following year, *The Citizens Hearings on Disclosure* was held in Washington D.C. This was an attempt to present the UFO subject in a respectable light to former members of Congress in a mock congressional hearing. Ufologists wore ties and sensible footwear, spoke with authority on ET contact, and finally got a chance to feel how real UFO Disclosure might one day feel. It was certainly a great dress rehearsal. But that's only part of the picture, if that's even part of any picture at all. Where, oh where, were the tales of aliens offering pancakes, the beings that wanted our fairy cakes and our Oreos, the encounter with the giant blob beings, or the brown, dung-like flying objects? They weren't talked about, and the people who witnessed these things were not invited, and with good reason: they'd make the entire UFO subject seem even more ridiculous.

"High Strangeness" was the term coined by Allen Hynek to label the inexplicable effects and synchronicities of events related to and occurring before, during, and after UFO encounters. I prefer to think of it simply as all the stuff that doesn't fit into our comfort zone—the experiences people report that challenge our preconceived ideas of what UFOs and the paranormal should be. High Strangeness feels at times like the Death Metal of ufology—and no Death Metal band has ever been invited to the Grammys. But how can we seriously claim to be studying the UFO subject properly without taking all the data into consideration? Should UFO Disclosure day ever come, will High Strangeness even be invited to the big coming-out party? I very much doubt it, for it would make any official announcement, consisting of a singular explanation for UFOs as being of extraterrestrial origin, seem somewhat simplistic and premature. Indeed, it would appear to be screaming, "Not so fast, blithering earth fools!"

One of the people I've come into contact with in Portland, Oregon, claims a series of encounters with UFOs and non-human beings. I've talked with him at length about these, and some of them also involve his wife. She had a history of UFO experiences prior to their meeting and it was whilst in bed together one night in 1997 or 1998 that things took a decidedly bizarre turn.

On several occasions during the preceding days, James and his wife had been disturbed in the night by odd sounds, and both had the sense that someone or something had been in their bedroom. Growing more and more fearful and frustrated, James had secretly wished that whoever or whatever this was would just show themselves. Earlier that day James had bought a packet of Oreos. He opened the packet, ate a couple, and placed them on the sideboard on the other side of the bedroom in case the late-night munchies should arise. He went to bed but, an hour or so later, was awoken by the sound of the rustling Oreo packet. Out of the very corner of his eye, and lit by the streetlamps outside, James could make out the silhouette of an approximately five-foot-tall, greyish, non-human entity. It was stealing his Oreos! "Why, that bastard!" he thought. With the exception of the tips of his fingers, which he wiggled frantically, he was alarmed to find that he could not move. He tried to scream out to his wife but all he could manage was a whisper. The intruder made off with a sizeable stack of Oreos at incredible speed past the foot of the bed and disappeared through the wall and James suddenly found himself able to move again. In the most abstract of ways imaginable, James had finally gotten some personal proof that these nocturnal visitations were, in some way, real. The missing Oreos were never to be seen again.[5]

Tony Watkins was a mechanical engineer who recalled coming into contact with several small grey beings in some woods near his home in Nanty Glo, Pennsylvania, in 1958. He was convinced he'd been implanted with something, and began to have different dreams. His black-and-white dreams were normal, but the colored dreams were sometimes prophetic and seemed to contain real information. If he thought about his contact experience he would get severe headaches. In 1990 his stepdaughter asked him where he thought these beings had come from. Something replied to Tony at that exact moment, by telepathy and in a mechanical voice, "the seventeenth state of matter" where "all knowledge is constructed in a pyramid form." He immediately got another headache.[6]

Ann Druffel, together with the late D. Scott Rogo, researcher and writer on parapsychology, co-authored an incredible book on early UFO contact, *The Tujunga Canyon Contacts.* Within a number of these cases, the non-humans encountered gave information relating to an alleged cure for cancer. This became almost like a calling card to the researchers during their investigations, and they began to take it as a sign that the experience, which was being recounted to them, was in some way genuine. After all, how could so many people, unbeknown to each other, report the same piece of information within their contact experiences? The message was kept secret and eventually given to medical professionals as potentially groundbreaking information. The cure for cancer given to the contactees was acetic acid—household vinegar. While there are some New-Agey schools of thought that link apple cider vinegar with killing cancer cells, I think it's safe to say that acetic acid is not a reliable cure for most cancers—at least within our current scientific understanding.

So, what does all this say of a phenomenon, and perhaps the intelligence(s) behind it, when we have, at least on the surface, seemingly nonsensical experiences or false information being imparted? At best, we can say that the phenomenon appears to have a sense of humor. At worst, it seems to be continually attempting to confuse us or cover itself up. Or is there something else happening entirely? Do some aliens simply like Oreos? Is the intelligence attempting to communicate with us the best it possibly can? Are some of these contact experiences steeped in symbolism or interacting with our subconscious minds? Or is this all a by-product of something else entirely?

Within many UFO and paranormal experiences, there does appear to be some kind of an external intelligence interacting with us in a variety of ways. Yet, for obvious reasons, the nonsense and trickster elements are all too often overlooked. Certainly, building any kind of literal belief system around the UFO contact experience would—to say the very least—appear hugely problematic.

But, for the best part of seventy-five years, this is exactly what we've been doing.

ii. **UFO Sociology and** The UFO Mythological Zone

"They said that I was the center of the universe. My spirit and ethereal body covered the whole of creation and all dimensions in between. I was cosmic mind spread throughout the infinite universe. Creation emanated from my senses and emotional body. I would shapeshift through the elements and disperse light and colors. They said they had never seen anything like it and could barely put into words what they saw."[7]

LAURA MAGDALENE EISENHOWER

ON MAY 10, 2016, LAURA BEGAN A GOFUNDME CROWD-FUNDING CAMPAIGN TO RAISE MONEY FOR A NEW CAR.[8]

"Hello everyone and welcome to this month's Sirian star language, so just sit back and relax and enjoy the transmission: Myassalanto-kahanosayantokah Elyayahantokayayantaskoyanasah."[9]

SOLRETA ANTARIA

Laura and Solreta are just two of the speakers who attended events in 2016 at the Gilliland Estate (formerly known as ECETI—Enlightened Contact with Extra Terrestrial Intelligence). Here, ranch owner and "visionary"[10] James Gilliland holds regular sky watches and "ascension" events at the base of Mount Adams.

The view of the mountain from the Field of Dreams is stunning. Not only have I personally witnessed dozens of unidentified lights in the sky at the ECETI ranch, I've also witnessed many more in the Yakima/Mount Adams region outside the ranch.[11] These experiences have also included anomalous lights on the mountain, lights appearing to come out of the mountain, green fireballs, orbs, apparent psychic interactions and even a couple of episodes of high strangeness. Most of these were with various other witnesses, too.

To my mind, there can be little doubt that there is a range of genuine phenomena occurring on a regular basis in this area. Other UFO researchers, such as Allen Hynek and Jacques Vallée, have also examined Yakima, and the area has been the subject of several studies over the years.[12] The ranch would appear to be the least of it—in fact, there appears to be far more activity on the eastern side of the mountain and in the Yakima Valley itself.

Gilliland calls these UFOs in the sky at ECETI "Ships," "Pleaideans," or "Motherships." But all I have seen, and all anyone has recorded on video at ECETI, are various lights in the sky. There appears to be a huge gap at ECETI between what is actually being *seen* and what is being *reported* and *interpreted*.

Let's call this the *UFO mythological zone*. This is just one example of it, but throughout the UFO subculture it's everywhere.

It's the gap between:

- Fact and belief
- What we see and what we *want* to see
- What we experience and how we interpret it

Many people are highly malleable and susceptible to new ideas and beliefs within the UFO mythological zone. Charlatans, fraudsters and hucksters are free to roam and operate at will. Their contribution to the UFO subject should never be underestimated, for the conditions for successful deception are near perfect. Common sense, lateral thinking and balanced questioning are far superseded and outweighed by irrational belief. Contagion of ideas is rife.

Look at many of the UFO stories on the internet or in the media; look at the UFO Disclosure movement and the characters within; look at the FREE study for abduction research; look at MUFON; look at many of your favorite researchers; look at ufology as a whole—the vast majority lies within this mythological zone. And while there is nothing wrong with open discussion, speculation and hypothesizing in a field so vast and mysterious, there is a world of difference between these things and passing off totally unfounded statements as absolutes. Indeed, one of the worst things about the UFO mythological zone is that it often shuts down any meaningful conversation about what we are possibly dealing with or how it might operate.

It turns this into a cult.

Most of these organizations don't even question the idea that the UFO issue could be anything other than extraterrestrial visitation. They've already made their minds up. Based on what exactly? There's the UFO mythological zone again. The UFO subculture is no different from any other cult except in two major aspects:

- There is no *single* belief system
- There is no *single* cult leader

People are forming highly personalized variations of the one *core* belief—the belief in a *UFO reality*. All else is up for individual interpretation via the UFO mythological zone. In the absence of facts, many people simply choose what they want to believe. Some think they are the center of the divine universe, some channel in an alien tongue, and others take their cues from various individuals—be they UFO researchers, contactees or new-age gurus.

Feeding off this belief-driven, unscientific and highly mythologized subculture is the mainstream media. This is the way the subcultural dysfunction and the UFO mythological zone really start to affect our culture. In the click bait age, the mainstream media uses UFOs and their followers as entertainment like never before. It makes little difference if the stories are obvious hoaxes or real accounts—they all serve the same purpose: to grab attention, entertain, generate revenue and sometimes steer narrative.

Primed for this assault by a steady diet of sci-fi and clichéd National Enquirer-type headlines from our earliest memories, the last few decades have given birth to *The X-Files* and, more recently, a barrage of poorly produced reality/fake TV shows, including *Ancient Aliens*, MUFON's *Hangar 1* (complete with paid actors posing as real ufologists),[13] *Chasing UFOs, Fact or Faked, UFO Files, UFOs: The Untold Stories*—the list goes on and on. This barrage of half-truths and fiction has helped turn huge amounts of interest toward the UFO subject; of that there can be little doubt. Indeed, most surveys since the advent of *The X-Files* have thrown out staggering numbers of the U.S. population who "believe" in UFOs, aliens, or extraterrestrial life.[14] But, given that virtually nothing is really as it seems, what do many of these people actually believe?

Firstly, many now associate the UFO term exclusively with the subject of *extraterrestrial* contact. Thanks to a frivolous media and a potent cultural pairing of expectation and imagination, the UFO acronym has largely changed from meaning *Unidentified Flying Object* into what we simply wanted and expected UFOs to be.

Secondly, in the mainstream culture—just as with the UFO subculture—there is no *one* belief system. I state again: people are creating highly personalized variations around the one *core* belief—that of a UFO (read: *extraterrestrial*) reality.

Extraterrestrial contact may turn out to explain some UFO reports. But even if this is the case, I would suggest that's only part of it. Furthermore, by simplifying the UFO issue into one neat explanation, and sidelining the parapsychological aspects of UFOs, are we not likely to miss something of even greater importance? What we are calling genuine UFOs could actually be several different things that emanate from multiple sources, including some here on Earth. They may even be different types of phenomena altogether. So, given this highly confusing backdrop, what would an official announcement about extraterrestrial life mean today? Our failure to deal with UFOs in any responsible way and the creation of this vast mythological zone would indicate even larger cultural problems ahead. Far from real UFO Disclosure being closer than ever, are we not now perfectly positioned for the biggest deception of all?

iii. The Mirage Men

Mirage Men is the title of a book and documentary by Mark Pilkington (author) and John Lundberg (director) that details the organized attempts by various branches of the U.S. intelligence community to mislead researchers within the UFO field. Book and film focus on the tragic case of Paul Bennewitz, a gifted military contractor, who had observed UFOs on various occasions over Kirtland AFB from his home in Albuquerque, New Mexico. He was eventually driven to the verge of insanity by apparent joint intelligence campaigns between the U.S. Air Force Office of Special Investigations, the CIA and the NSA. I would argue these Mirage Men have not only been extremely successful in polluting the UFO field with false information, but that such operations continue to this day and that many UFO researchers are now wildly off course as a result.

Attending today's UFO conferences can be a confusing affair. On the one hand, luminaries of the UFO research community will stand there and rightly tell you not to trust the big, bad government that has covered all of this up for decades. On the other hand, they will hold up government documents (yes, from that same big, bad government you shouldn't trust) claiming that they *prove* a myriad of facts about UFOs. Some of these researchers laughably expect the government suddenly to stop lying and come clean about all of this any day now. Some are even associated with the intelligence community themselves.

These are just some of the many dichotomies one will confront when faced with the collective narrative of modern ufology. It can be schizophrenic, irrational and full of contradictions. The misdirecting of UFO research has been going on long before the days of the highly controversial (and utterly bogus) Majestic Twelve documents. UFO iconoclast James Carrion recently suggested that Mirage-Men-style activities may even go as far back as 1946.[15]

Newsflash: If the government releases any official documents, through the Freedom of Information Act or any other official channel, then chances are that some of these documents may partially contain exactly what they want you to think and know—disinformation. I am constantly surprised by how many in the UFO research community continue as if disinformation isn't even a consideration. We need to show far more discernment when considering anything coming from alleged, official sources. In fact, we need to show far more discernment, period.

I would also suggest the same caution when it comes to many UFO research organizations and groups.[16] The largest of these, the Mutual UFO Network (MUFON), has a decidedly questionable past with many of the best cases going into that great big vault in the sky, never to be seen again (and no, it's not called Hangar 1).[17] In my opinion, MUFON is still, amongst other things, a UFO data collection and funneling scheme. One has only to look at their official mission statement—*The scientific study of UFOs for the benefit of mankind*—and then look at some of the research they actively promote (e.g. data gleaned from hypnosis,[18] psychic channeling dressed as "remote viewing," etc.[19]) and some of the highly dubious people they invite to speak at their conferences, to know that, at the very least, they appear to be deeply confused about what the word "scientific" actually means.[20]

Jack Brewer detailed the pitfalls of using hypnosis in his book, *The Grays Have Been Framed,* and I would also urge everybody to read *Operation Mind Control* by Walter Bowart. Hypnosis is virtually useless in retrieving accurate memories without the contamination of imagination and expression from the subconscious mind. Cultural expectations are also an issue, and, perhaps most alarming of all, real memories of events can be altered with relative ease. It isn't hard to imagine why the Mirage Men would want hypnosis—the ultimate mythology machine—to be placed front and center as an important tool in so-called UFO "research" today.

Did UFO abduction lore really come from just a handful of individuals? Was one of the primary trailblazers a hobbyist hypnotist with no training?[21] Was another such trailblazer an MK-Ultra-related, mind control participant and a best-selling fiction writer with a million-dollar book advance?[22] Did a huge chunk of our cultural narrative about alien abduction come from the hobbyist's hypnosis data or the million-dollar book? The answer to all of these questions is a resounding YES. Of course, I'm talking about Budd Hopkins and Whitley Strieber.

Strieber's book, *Communion*, went on to sell over two million copies and became a Hollywood movie, while Budd Hopkins's *Intruders* was made into a primetime TV series.

There is little doubt that Mirage-Men-type psychological operations have been employed in the mainstream. Could these operations be rolled out further for mass cultural consumption on a scale hitherto unseen? Given the technological advances that have been made over the past few decades, I would suggest that certain factions within the military-industrial complex could instigate seemingly magical, pseudo-paranormal or pseudo-extraterrestrial experiences with ease. Furthermore, I would say that the gap between what is *truly* paranormal and what is covert human technology has been closed to the point that it has been indistinguishable for some time now. Has the window for getting to the bottom of all of this therefore closed forever? Or will we discover and harness new technologies that might allow us to finally rip off the masks and reveal the intelligences behind the UFOs, the paranormal and the Mirage Men like never before?

UFO Social Engineering 101 — Revision

So how do we attempt to disentangle this giant ball of mythological wool? I would suggest the first step, as in dealing with most problems, is to acknowledge that we actually *have* a problem. We then need to consider this mess at every turn as we move forward. While undoubtedly there is much to suggest that there is a genuinely anomalous component to the UFO enigma, we must now acknowledge the fact that the UFO subject is as much about social engineering as anything else.

The three components of social engineering in ufology can be summarized as:

- **DECEPTION:** THEM. The subject that covers itself up—the external intelligence(s) or entities behind the UFOs (whoever they may be and wherever they are from) and the mythology created, either by accident or design, by them.
- **DELUSION:** US. UFO sociology and the UFO mythological zone—the widespread effects of UFOs on we, the people, and our culture, and, in the absence of facts or scientific proof, the mythology we've created around them.

- **DISINFORMATION:** GOVERNMENTAL. The Mirage
  Men—The stage management and cover-up of UFOs (either of
  the genuine phenomenon or as cover for secret projects, psy-ops,
  etc.), and the many aspects of governmental/military-industrial/
  intelligence operations and the mythology the Mirage Men have
  created around them.

Whichever way we choose to look at it, it's a damning statement on
how we deal with things when faced with the prospect of the unknown,
both collectively/culturally and often individually.

We tend to:

- Ignore data that doesn't fit with our preconceived ideas and
  expectations
- Mythologize and fantasize about the things we don't know
  about—to the point of cultism
- Look to authority for answers and leave ourselves wide open to
  manipulation

I propose, therefore, that 99% of everything written and said about
UFOs is total bullshit, and that almost everything you think you know
about flying saucers is wrong.

A Pause for Reason

Let's take a deep breath for a moment and pause.

Imagine a meadow with beautiful flowers. It's a late summer's
evening; butterflies float around on the breeze and the tranquil calm
of the wind caresses your sun-kissed face. Ahead of you is a beautiful mountain. The remainder of last winter's snow has almost melted
to reveal a striking volcanic mound. If you shut your eyes, all you can
hear is the soft wind and the vague excitement of the children picking
their huckleberries in the distance.

I'm about two miles as the crow flies from the ECETI Ranch. The
sun will be going down soon. I am not only in prime position to see
all events on the mountain, I am in a place where I am free to think
clearly and to see for myself. Without someone telling me that these
are Pleiadean spaceships, what exactly do I see? Can I interact with the
intelligence behind this spectacle? Is it different from being around the

thoughts and beliefs of others and the potential contagion that these thoughts and beliefs may bring?

Much like during many previous visits, what I observe appear to be intelligently controlled, anomalous bright lights coming out of the mountain or appearing in the sky above. But, if absolutely anyone can study this, why don't they? Why are we still re-hashing and trawling over decades-old cases when we could be investigating this and the people that experience it in real time? Do we really want answers? Or do we want to keep the questions alive? Maybe the answer lies in the fact that the phenomenon here in Yakima appears to work on a subtle level. In a culture that screams for a landing on the White House lawn or that leads people to feel the need to embellish and make this even more cosmic and mysterious than it already is—we are probably at odds with whatever this is.

In Yakima, as in many other hotspots around the world, there is much work to do. A modern, scientific study utilizing cutting-edge technology, super-high resolution cameras and full access to the Yakima tribal reservation would be of potentially huge benefit. The problem with trying to study this purely with science is that it's been pretty elusive to track down. In my seven years of experience at Yakima, I don't think that's necessarily the issue here. I think more of an issue might be: how do we measure the human experience in all of this? If the UFO subject is to move forward in any meaningful way, the human experience (with particular emphasis on the interaction with the subconscious mind), as well as the parapsychological and other more esoteric aspects of the UFO experience, can no longer continue to be ignored. Yakima is a veritable trove of all kinds of high strangeness, not just UFOs. We should start to study all aspects of non-standard human experience together. We can no longer continue to treat the UFO phenomenon as separate from other paranormal, spiritual, religious, esoteric, highly synchronistic or other currently uncategorized phenomena. Whether we utilize science or also include other methodologies and philosophies, one thing is certain: we need to stop trying to fit the UFO subject into what we want or expect it to be. This has gotten us virtually nowhere in over seventy years and would be the least "scientific" thing of all to do.

UFO Truth in The Post-Truth Age

"When enough of us peddle fantasy as fact, society loses its grounding in reality. Society would crumble altogether if we assumed others were as likely to dissemble as tell the truth. We are perilously close to that point."[23]

—RALPH KEYES

Although I've considered only the cultural and sociological implications of UFOs thus far, I would now suggest the possibility that we are facing a far greater issue: a widespread cultural informational crisis. The mythological zone is not only confined to UFOs or paranormal beliefs. The Internet revolution, for all the benefits it has brought, has also bombarded us with false information, hoaxes, nonsense, junk science, spin, and outright lies. This has affected mainstream media as it attempts to keep viewers from drifting towards alternative media. All of this is now challenging our beliefs and changing us like never before. Far from social engineering, could this situation lead to social chaos or a time when truth is simply lost in the noise—a total informational breakdown? We now appear to be living in a *post-truth* age where flat-earthers 2.0 can become a cultural movement in a matter of months; where lies can be celebrated as truths, dumb can be celebrated as genius, and even Donald Trump can be President. Ralph Keyes wrote his book, *The Post-Truth Era,* about our eroding cultural values in relation to the telling of truth and lies. But, just like the mythological zone, the post-truth concept relates to the wider informational crisis with frightening relevance too.

It is, perhaps, more than a little ironic that now, of all times, given the arrival of the post-truth age, some would be campaigning for UFO Disclosure. There are many reasons why I think UFO Disclosure can't and won't happen, but they can best be distilled into one simple sentence: Disclosure is like attempting a prison break by asking the prison guards for the keys. Far more likely is a solution that delivers everybody what they want and need, and one that provides a convenient get-out-of-jail card for those in the corridors of power—an announcement that we have found extraterrestrial life and that we are finally not alone. This would not, however, amount to anything close to full UFO Disclosure,[24] nor would it come close to solving the UFO problem. On the contrary, our problems regarding UFO truth in the post-truth age would only just be beginning. And if you think things are a mess now—unless we can come to grips with the informational crisis and our cultural issues in dealing with the unknown—just wait.

What would such an announcement mean for the Mirage Men? Would the Men-in-Black quietly cash-in their pensions early, park up their Buicks and hang up their black hats and suits for good? Or would their superiors be rubbing their hands together at the prospect of putting into mass circulation those methods they'd so stealthily perfected over the years? Those responsible for the illegal, criminal and unconstitutional activities surrounding UFOs and the national security state over the decades would certainly never be called to justice. They would gradually move with relative ease from the subterranea of the black world into the blinding sun of the white. Those bulk-purchased, iconic, Men-in-Black shades might never be more useful.

Escaping the Mythological Zone

So, do we, as a civilization, choose science or do we choose belief? Can science and belief ever coexist healthily alongside one another and make compatible bedfellows? Do we stand on the cusp of unison between science and spirituality or—in a desperate attempt at unifying these two opposing constructs—does the mythological zone bind us forever?

Have we not always been wrestling with these two opposing forces? Have we not always had an uncomfortable and contradictory relationship—part curiosity, part fear—with the unknown? Have we not always felt a sense of wonder, loneliness and insignificance when looking up at the seemingly incalculable number of stars above? How could we not? These human traits have driven some of our greatest scientific discoveries and achievements.

But these traits have also been used against us and allowed us to be deceived.

Current scientific understanding will never be the truth of the entire universe. Science, while the foundation of societal development, will always be something of a paper god. Belief is the fixer with which we attempt to fill the void behind that ever-fluid line of current scientific knowledge and beyond into the great unknown. Meanwhile, from within this void come magical, high strangeness, and human experiences that continue to mystify and confuse. But rather than becoming lightning rods for our own delusions, fantasies and fears, the things that "don't fit" should make us strive to better understand ourselves, our universe, and our place within.

The cultural, sociological and mythological implications of UFOs are vast. By identifying the social engineering components to the UFO issue, perhaps we can at least recognize and begin to come to terms with our many vulnerabilities. The real challenge facing us regarding UFOs and the unknown is this: can we then forge a new pathway forward? One thing is certain. We must let go of the idea that we can simply sit back and ask the prison guards for the keys. If we are to ever escape the mythological zone, we must make the escape ourselves.

WHAT'S WRONG WITH
THIS PICTURE?

Curt Collins

The fiasco was indistinguishable from a hoax and couldn't have been more damaging to ufology if it had been sabotage. Photographs of the body of an extraterrestrial being from the Roswell UFO crash were revealed at the National Auditorium in Mexico City on May 5, 2015. Three days later, the story imploded when international news accounts reported it was a fake, just another in a long series of embarrassments to the UFO field. The whole saga is complex and full of branching controversies, but the focus here is on the real investigation that exposed the "Roswell Slides," and why it matters to the serious study of UFOs.

The slides were said to be found in Arizona in 1998. While on a job cleaning out a house scheduled for demolition, Catherine Beason saved a box of slides from being thrown away. It wasn't until 2008 that she noticed two unusual pictures inside that were separated from all the others, two slides of a small alien-looking body laid in a glass case. She didn't know what to do with them, and later gave the collection of slides to her brother, Joseph Beason, an Internet application developer in Chicago. He recognized the potential value in the slides, but needed specialized help. Beason wasn't knowledgeable about UFOs, but the body looked extraterrestrial, and it made him think of the famous 1947 New Mexico flying saucer incident. In early 2012, Beason approached Roswell experts Don Schmitt and Tom Carey.

Schmitt and Carey had been writing and lecturing exclusively together as Roswell UFO investigators since 1998 in a decades-long quest for the "smoking gun," proof that it was the crash of an alien spaceship. In 2011, Carey put together a "Dream Team" to produce the ultimate Roswell book, and recruited Anthony Bragalia and Dr. David Rudiak, both of whom had provided research help on their *Witness to Roswell* book, as well as UFO researchers Kevin Randle and Chris Rutkowski. The book collaboration was side-tracked due to Schmitt and Carey's preoccupation with projects of their own, and it was at around this time that Joseph Beason and the Roswell Slides entered the picture. Beason sent Carey an email with two high-resolution pictures of the slides. Carey said that upon seeing them, "a chill ran down my spine." He thought the body perfectly matched the description of dead aliens from the Roswell UFO crash stories, and instantly he "knew" it was genuine. He and Don Schmitt signed a non-disclosure agreement with Beason and became partners, promoters in the business of bringing the Slides to a public audience.

Adam Dew was recruited by Beason a few months later, in mid-2012. Dew is a Chicago-based filmmaker in the sports video business. Beason showed him the slide collection, and they became partners in control of the slides. Dew took on the role of project manager after Beason moved to the West Coast, and he also had the idea to make a film on the Slides story, one which would also document the investigation into their authenticity. In the following months, Schmitt and Carey brought two of their other Dream Team partners into the group in subordinate roles: Dr. David Rudiak, in July 2012, for his experience in working on the text of the Roswell "Ramey Memo;" and, in 2013, Anthony Bragalia, for his Internet research skills. During 2013, the team obtained an expert opinion that the slide materials themselves were genuine, encouraging the team to move forward towards a public exhibition.

BeWitness was conceived in November 2013, when Schmitt and Carey recruited Mexican ufologist Jaime Maussan to promote and host a spectacular show to exhibit the Slides. Maussan put together a proposal and, later that same month, he, Schmitt and Carey flew to Chicago to meet with Joe Beason and Adam Dew. There the deal was signed, and Maussan said, "I think this is going to change the world... this is going to be the biggest event ever in the history of the UFO." In December, Beason and Dew formed Slidebox Media, LLC to execute their leadership of the enterprise. Dew was the frontman for Slidebox Media while Beason remained offstage, in a confidential role. The group's best-kept secret, however, was the Chicago meeting with Maussan, while most of the other details about the Slides leaked and circulated as gossip and rumors.

The Announcement

On November 12, 2014, the rumors were confirmed at a lecture on UFOs at the American University in Washington, D.C., part of an event titled Alien Contact: Science and Science Fiction. The speaker was Tom Carey, who had an important announcement. "I'm going to break news about a smoking gun... we've been doing due diligence on for two years... We have come into possession of a couple of Kodachrome color slides of an alien being." At the time, he mentioned only the highlights but, in the following months, the key points of the story emerged:

- The two slides showed a small, partially-dissected humanoid.
- The body was distinctly non-human, and couldn't be a deformed child, mummy or a dummy.
- The body lay on a green Army blanket, in a makeshift, hastily-constructed glass case, i.e., could not be a museum.
- On the body was a small sign or placard, but the handwriting could not be read.

- Kodak experts authenticated the slides as genuine and unaltered, from 1947, the year of the Roswell UFO crash.
- The body matched the aliens described by Roswell witnesses, not the popular culture image of aliens from the 1940s (therefore, not a vintage hoax).
- The slides had belonged to a deceased couple, the Rays of Midland, Texas.
- The Rays were VIPs, knew Mamie and General Dwight D. Eisenhower, and were well-connected, and may have had access to top-secret facilities.
- Hilda Blair Ray was a high-powered lawyer with a pilot's license, and possibly involved in military intelligence in World War II.
- Bernerd Ray, was a field geologist who conducted oil exploration expeditions in the Permian Basin, a region that included Roswell.
- The investigators had an endorsement of the Slides from the last living witness to seeing bodies from the Roswell crash.

Tom Carey's university lecture ended with a teaser: "I have been given permission for the *first time* to talk about it here, right now, about this event that's going to take place early next year. So we have a lot more, we're still working the case, but this is big stuff."[1]

The news caught the attention of the UFO community. When I renewed my interest in UFOs in 2011, I joined a few online groups and networked with some UFO researchers through Facebook, starting a private discussion group with a few dissident UFO buffs where we could candidly share our views and blow off steam. The group had been following the Slides rumors for months, but, with Tom Carey's announcement about a public event, we were hooked. In early 2015, when we found out that Jaime Maussan was hosting the event, it was a colossal red flag. Maussan had a reputation for promoting sensational UFO stories, including some spectacular mistakes, frauds and hoaxes.

Jaime Maussan held a two-hour press conference in Mexico City on February 4, 2015 to announce "BeWitness, The Change in History."[2] Maussan said the show would include several experts on the subject and feature former astronaut, Edgar Mitchell. "Edgar will give credibility to this event, he is a hero in American culture, one of the few who walked on the Moon and also he lived in Roswell..." There were short pre-recorded interviews with his experts, Don Schmitt, Tom Carey and Adam Dew. Schmitt said, "It will certainly be the most important event in our lifetimes." Carey talked about the value of the Slides, saying, "I think it's physical evidence. I think we have physical evidence... a picture is worth a thousand words."

Maussan debuted the trailer for Adam Dew's documentary, *Kodachrome*, which gave us the first glimpse of the "alien" slides, but their details were digitally blurred to save them for the reveal. It also showed the slides being examined in a laboratory with an expert calling them genuine and a witness viewing them, saying it resembled the alien body he'd seen at Roswell. It ended with a technician making a "3-D reconstruction of the body" that produced alien features.

Tickets went on sale for BeWitness to be held May 5, 2015 at the National Auditorium in Mexico City, with prices ranging from about $20 to $80 USD. Additionally, it was announced the event would be streamed live worldwide in a pay-per-view basis on the internet for about $20.

Independent Investigation is Initiated

The promoters also launched a Slidebox Media website. With all the new information, our group really had something to sink our teeth into. If even 1/10th of what they'd claimed was real, it would be an amazing discovery. The clock was ticking, and we were in a race against the May 5 deadline. We started digging, checking the story, researching vintage Kodak film and investigating the background on Mr. and Mrs. Ray. This was the moment of conception for the anti-sliders, eventually christened the "Roswell Slides Research Group," or RSRG.

There was an early leak of Slidebox's alien picture. In the *Kodachrome* trailer, a split-second shot of a slide was shown without the digital blurring, and "Narrenschiffer" captured the image.[3] The slide was shown at an angle, and he had to adjust it to restore the correct dimensions. He then posted the image online, where it was widely shared. While an unknown amount of detail and clarity was lost, it was clear enough to show the main features. For the RSRG, Nab Lator produced another version in an attempt to produce a clearer image, but his results were only marginally better. Nab looked at other frames of the video, including those showing the placard.

The RSRG started searching for pictures of objects, like real and fake human oddities, mermaid carcasses and mummies, that could prove a match with the leaked slide. Gilles Fernandez sent Kevin Randle two pictures comparing a child mummy to the leaked slide to show similarities in their feet. Tom Carey dismissed the comparison saying, "(it) isn't a foot at all... the being's feet actually end behind the placard. Yes, we were on to that almost two years ago. Of course, this will not satisfy what's going on out there right now on the blogs, which is insane."[4]

My friend, Spanish UFO researcher José Antonio Caravaca, created a new group on Facebook, called "Roswell Slides," exclusively for the serious investigation of the BeWitness story. We continued to work within that group, sharing information in real time to members who were spread across various time zones and nations. Along with José, the most active members were Isaac Koi, a UK researcher preserving and sharing UFO history, French skeptics Nab Lator, an "armchair researcher of the paranormal," and Gilles Fernandez, who holds a Ph.D. in cognitive psychology. Also active in the group were USA skeptics Lance Moody and Tim Printy (who provided skills including expertise in photography) Roger Glassel of Sweden, Canadian filmmaker Paul Kimball and Texans Ricky Poole and S. Miles Lewis, founder of the Anomaly Archives in Austin.

In a strange twist of fate, our group also included Canadian science writer and ufologist Chris Rutkowski, who had been recruited for Carey's Roswell Dream Team as "someone with an open mind, who would point out where we might have slipped off the rails." Chris found himself shut out when the secrecy over the Slides enterprise caused the dream to die.

Along the way, others were brought into the RSRG group for their specialized talents: Alejandro Espino, Aaron John Gulyas, Philippe Hernandez, Irna Osmanovic, Tim Hebert, Jeff Ritzmann and Shepherd Johnson. The group comprised friends, and friends of friends, UFO researchers and skeptics working together to come to grips with an event that was going to "change the world."

Early on, a possible match for the body in the slides was located. On Feb. 11, Ricky Poole posted a photo, "....showing a child mummy on fabric with a placard." It was from the Smithsonian Museum of Natural History, and it resembled the body in the leaked photo. Shortly afterwards, Roger Glassel located an illustrated article on the mummy by Dr. David Hunt, the Forensic Anthropologist at the Smithsonian Institution.[5] Our team contacted Dr. Hunt, and he found the blurry image of the Slides body to be consistent with the one in his studies, saying, "I feel that even if it is not the same mummy, it is strikingly similar." He also sent us a collection of high resolution photographs of the mummy and CT scan views of its skeleton.

The mummy of the Egyptian boy was catalogued as specimen number 2397; those digits became our name for him. We contacted the Wistar Institute in Pennsylvania, where it was curated prior to its transfer to the Smithsonian in 1958, but they were unable to find a photograph from the era displaying the mummy. We did find one photograph circa 1874 that included the child mummy, but the case it was displayed in was not a match. The size, position, proportions and condition of 2397 were nearly identical to what we could see of the body in the leaked slide. While we could not say it was the same mummy, our findings contested the promoters' claim of "non-human."

The BeWitness team was bound by NDAs, and secrecy. The RSRG methods were in sharp contrast to this, operating more like a classroom of eager students, sharing knowledge and challenged to excellence by each other's efforts. Our early efforts were somewhat unfocused, and we faced the problem of duplication of effort by multiple researchers. For example, I was embarrassed to receive a reply from a specialist indicating that he'd already been contacted, individually, by three other members of our team. To avoid annoying experts who might be reluctant to discuss matters, which they might find frivolous or nutty, we began co-ordinating our contacts with consultants, giving us a simplified and complete record of our correspondence with them.

The group gathered a lot of data, and that presented its own challenges. Tim Printy said, "this is sort of a collective thing. Some of the work has been outstanding and it moves so fast it is sometimes difficult to keep up." Facebook was fast and convenient, but the platform was not designed to support research projects. The constant stream of new material made finding information difficult. Many of us found ourselves missing the organization options available in online message boards, but, by then, we'd gotten in too deep to make a switch.

Isaac Koi took the lead in organizing the data gathered by the RSRG, creating collections of things like photographs of child mummies, sideshow exhibits, human abnormalities, and also museum display cases. As visual data was gathered, I made photo montage collections; with these we could easily show that the BeWitness alien resembled a child's mummified body and that the skeletal proportions matched that of a child aged between two and three years.

Our work showed that the glass case in the Slides was consistent with period museum displays, and it disproved the promoters' claim of temporary, erector set-like construction. The shelving provided another clue in the spacing of the holes, which could be used to measure the length of the body. I visited hardware stores and antique furniture shops where similar glass cases and shelving material could be measured and photographed. In studying the shelving, Tim Printy used the data to demonstrate that the body size was significantly smaller than the "gray-sized" 3.5 to 4 feet figure claimed by the promoters.

Members researched the background of the Rays, but found nothing to support the Eisenhower friendship or "well-connected" claims by the promoters. Tim searched Texas newspapers and found additional articles and photos of Bernerd Ray through the decades, evidence that refuted the promoters' claim he'd become "a ghost in his profession" after 1947.

Publish or Perish

The buzz for BeWitness was building. Roger Glassel said, "If this isn't stopped before the 5th of May, and even if a solid explanation will be at hand on the 6th after seeing the photo slide, I'm afraid that the damage will already be done. With a Mexican event and a documentary, it will be man bites dog in the news media and no time for mummies." Most of the press was within the UFO community, but the story received some publicity on Feb. 18, when Chicago's WGN-TV morning show interviewed Adam Dew and aired his *Kodachrome* trailer. When asked if scientists were consulted, Dew indicated that work was just beginning, saying "We're trying to find people that will look at it and give those opinions." While he talked, the images onscreen were Gilles Fernandez's pictures of mummified bodies compared with the leaked slide, and, apparently, the producer and the hosts were unable to tell the difference. Dew finally noticed and said, "That image has been out on the internet since we released the trailer, people trying to debunk it, which has been really helpful actually, because they have been putting out—doing a lot of research work for me, that I've been trying to do the last couple of years in my free time."[6] Dew's comments raised questions about just who was researching the case, and if it was only a part-time investigation.

We investigated the alien witness shown in the *Kodachrome* trailer, introduced by Adam Dew as "an Army lieutenant at Roswell Air Force base in 1947." That was not true. Eleazar N. Benavides was stationed at Roswell, but held the rank of Private First Class.[7] Benavides had appeared before, under the pseudonym "Eli Benjamin" in Schmitt and Carey's book, and in the UFO shows, *Sci-Fi Investigates and UFOs Declassified*. The mistake in Benavides' rank reflected on credibility, either of the witness or of Dew in reporting it. As a result of the alias being exposed, at the BeWitness event, Benavides' real rank and name was correctly given.

By the end of February, we had enough evidence to make a case that went beyond establishing reasonable doubt towards the credibility of the BeWitness promoters' claims. It was agreed that we should publish something prior to May 5, and we had to decide on what to say. The promoters' case for the Slides was based on nothing more than speculation, and Paul Kimball felt that we needed to counter it with facts, not speculation of our own. In the paranormal and UFO arena, there's often an attempt to reverse the burden of proof, and we were getting trapped into trying to prove a negative. Isaac Koi noted, "While this (discussion) has been perfectly amicable, I think it gives an indication of the difficulties that would be involved in writing an item collectively." Lance Moody was more optimistic, and insisted that it was worth trying.

On March 2, "The Roswell Slides Research Group" website at roswellslides.com was set up by Paul Kimball, and, immediately afterwards, publicly revealed. Blogger Rich Reynolds provided a puffed-up description: "a group of respected UFO researchers, academics, and media professionals, including a former member of the so-called Roswell Dream Team (formed) to investigate further the Kodachrome slides and activity pertaining to them."[8] Even the name came as a surprise to us. I worried if we could live up to the expectations created by the announcement, but it seemed to prompt Lance Moody.

Lance wrote a paper on the group's preliminary findings, with the goal of its being "short, simple and non-dogmatic," and shared it with the group for revisions. His draft was excellent, but there were many differences of opinion over the tone and scope of things, even about the structure itself, whether it should be written as an article for general audiences or more as an academic-style paper. Also, Lance's first draft was pointedly UFO skeptical, and some of the members, myself included, were concerned that a "skeptical" paper would be ignored by the very people who needed to read it. I thought that we should address only issues relating to BeWitness and the Slides, and not get involved with the tar baby of the reality of the Roswell UFO crash story itself. Others persuasively argued that Schmitt and Carey's prior work on the

Roswell case was being grafted on to the Slides, and their credibility and methodology was pertinent. There was an initial flurry of work on the RSRG paper, but, after contributors saw their input revised or erased by one another, work on it dwindled to nothing.

The RSRG worked great as a think-tank, but got bogged down as a committee. José Antonio Caravaca told me, "I think it was a big mistake not to publish anything." With the group's effort to publish a report dead, we decided to allow individual members to use the shared work for articles of their own. On March 16, I published "Roswell Slides or Fraud Prints?," giving a brief recap of the BeWitness story up to that point, and examining the promoters' claims of equating the Slides with physical evidence. We thought that 2397 just might be our ace in the hole, but the group agreed that José could publish an article using our studies, and on March 25, his article included arrays of our photo comparisons, presenting evidence that the body shown in the Roswell Slides matched the anatomy of a child-sized mummy.[9] Gilles Fernandez published a heavily illustrated article the same day, summarizing some of the findings of the RSRG, and showed how features of the Slides body resembled grotesque human specimens in anatomical museums, and child mummies. With those and other photographs, he refuted several of the claims made by the promoters. Regarding the extraordinary narrative they presented, he concluded, "our team has found nothing convincing about this saga."[10]

In early April things were quiet. Paul Kimball withdrew from ufology and left the RSRG to focus on more earthly matters, and later posted, "For anyone wondering where the Other Side of Truth blog has gone, I've put it on hiatus..." Paul was the sole key holder to the RSRG site, and we wondered what that meant about publishing our findings, but decided the first priority was continuing the work. Our real problem was that we'd done as much as possible with the evidence then available. Mid-April saw the promotion for BeWitness ramp up, with advertising, media coverage, interviews, and videos, so we soon had some more information to work with. Names of the expert scientific consultants began to surface.

Don Schmitt and Tom Carey's first North American interview about BeWitness was on *The Conspiracy Show with Richard Syrett*, April 12, 2015. They emphasized their thorough investigation and Schmitt said, "This will be part of the event... all of these analytical reports... analyses... photographic experts..." He named the placard consultants, saying, "everyone from Dr. David Rudiak, to Studio MacBeth, even the Photo

Interpretation Department of the Pentagon, as well as Adobe have all told us... that it cannot be read... we truly feel we have performed due diligence; we have done everything we can to substantiate and prove what is contained within these slides..."[11]

BeWitness and Beyond

Tim Printy's online magazine *SUNlite* May/June issue was published just before the BeWitness event. It featured reports on the characteristics of Kodak film, his experiments in using it at different distances, and an article examining the claims made about the ability to date the film precisely to 1947. His article, "The debut of the Roswell slides," exposed the many inconsistencies and problems in the narrative of the Slides and summarized the findings of the RSRG.[12]

The RSRG had examined the BeWitness claims and found no evidence to support them, and our conclusion was that the body in the photos was the mummified remains of a child. Our criticism had been unsuccessful in stopping the event but had raised the awareness of unscientific claims of the promoters and forced them to furnish an attempt at medical analysis of the Slides during the program.

On May 5, the BeWitness show was held with an audience of about 7,000 people in the auditorium and another 2,000 watching via pay-per-view. Several members of the RSRG watched the streaming broadcast together online, and, during the show, Paul Kimball re-joined our group to participate in a running discussion. We noticed that Schmitt and Carey only spoke on the background of the Roswell UFO case, and it was only Adam Dew that discussed the investigation of the Slides. He presented a video clip and an anonymous document testifying to the authenticity of the slides, but there were no analytical reports on the placard or anything else—only anecdotes. We had expected to see new slides showing the Rays together with the Eisenhowers or with other important military figures, but there were none. Nothing was shown even to connect them to Roswell.

The first slide of the body was shown about halfway through the show, followed by computer-generated animation isolating the skeletal face and fleshing it out with alien features. Later, Maussan presented a moving hologram of an alien "reconstruction" of the body. The Mexican team presenting the scientific analysis had worked only from one-dimensional images—digital copies of the original slides—and Dr.

José de Jesús Zalce Benítez concluded the body pictured was not human, or even a mammal. Canadian anthropologist Richard Doble said, "this is nothing like us... its legs almost look like it's a reptile... like it evolved from something like a gecko." He speculated that its species communicated electromagnetically. Richard Dolan's lecture closed the show, suggesting that the Slides could open the door for Disclosure and bring down the wall of secrecy about UFOs. As a grand finale, Maussan showed the second slide, but more time had been devoted to imaginative artistic alien artwork than to the photos themselves.[13]

The program was over five hours long, and, when it was finished, we noted that it had failed to deliver anything of substance beyond the reveal of the two slides themselves. There were no immediate clues to identity or location beyond the other objects seen in the case and the portion of the room that housed it. The clearer pictures of the mummy conclusively ruled out our leading suspect, 2397, as being the body, so the search was still on.

On May 7, there was a break. José Antonio Caravaca, guaranteeing his source's anonymity, was able to persuade one of parties involved to send him a high-resolution copy of slide #11, the brighter one with the woman standing behind the glass case. José shared it with the rest of the RSRG, and we eagerly began studying it. The next day his source sent him something even more interesting, a scan of slide #9, which gave a close-up isolated view of the blurry placard. José posted the placard image in our group at 1:57 AM. Nab Lator had mentioned months before the possibility of using the program SmartDeblur by Vladimir Yuzhikov on the slides as "a tool for restoration of defocused and blurred images." In the case of the placard, we needed it to "unshake" the motion blur from the camera.

Nab immediately put SmartDeblur to work and experimented with reading the placard. While the software can automatically try to improve a picture, it usually needs to be refined by user input, a process that can require much trial and error. Two hours later he announced his initial findings to the group. The placard featured printed text (not handwriting), it was in English, it was still grainy, but he could read part of the top line. This raised the hope that the entire placard could be read, and he went back to work to push further. Throughout the morning other members joined the discussion, excited at the breakthrough. At 9:29 AM Nab posted the deblur that revealed the top line was a headline in all capitals that read:

"MUMMIFIED BODY OF TWO YEAR OLD BOY."

Jaws dropped. The results were so stunning that members asked, "Are you kidding me?" Nab assured them, "Not kidding." Throughout the day, Nab was still learning how to work with the software, and, bit by bit, progress was made in clarifying the text. Tim Printy, Lance Moody and Isaac Koi joined the effort, also using SmartDeblur, all working together learning how to improve, save, duplicate and share the results.

Chris Rutkowski raised concerns over the provenance of the scan and the fact that we were unable to reveal the confidential source for it. At the time we could only verify that our scan matched all the other published images of the placard, including those shown in Dew's *Kodachrome* trailer and the views we had of it from BeWitness. We couldn't prove what we had was genuine, but all evidence showed that it was as genuine as the Slides themselves. We needed another copy directly from the Slides promotion camp, so Lance Moody emailed David Rudiak asking for a scan of the placard, and Nab emailed Adam Dew, saying, "I've had limited success with the software SmartDeblur 2.2. In case you didn't know already, the body is a mummified two-year-old boy. Can you send me a better scan for analysis?"

Another topic of discussion was how to share our findings, and we agreed that the results needed to be independently verified before publication. We talked about showing the deblurring method in a video, and I began writing an article on the reading of the placard text. Throughout the afternoon and into the evening, the team gradually continued to clarify the text. Finally, at 6:06, Nab posted the near-completed reading of all four lines of the placard, and it left no doubt that the Slides were photos of a mummy on display at a museum. Still the work continued in an effort to get clearer, consistent results that could be duplicated by others before releasing the news.

There was a leak. An early deblurring attempt was posted on Facebook, then eventually re-posted by Richard Dolan, who stated, "I imagine it would be helpful to have more clarification on the process, but this looks definitive." Rumors and questions started swirling. Slides defenders began making accusations that the RSRG had faked the results, and even the most reasonable people wanted to see verification. Unfortunately, at this time, the other members of the RSRG were offline and unavailable and, perhaps hastily, I made the decision to release our results. At 9:18 PM, I published the story about the placard on my blog, Blue Blurry Lines.[14] The complete placard text was eventually determined to be:

MUMMIFIED BODY OF TWO YEAR OLD BOY
At the time of burial the body was clothed in a slip-over cotton
shirt. Burial wrappings consisted of three small cotton blankets.
Loaned by Mr. S. L. Palmer, San Francisco, California.

When the others in the RSRG found out, most were pleased, but some members of the group raised objections to releasing our findings prematurely. Luckily for us all, two hours later Slidebox Media solved our placard provenance problem. In response to the deblurring, Slidebox uploaded an image file of the placard on their web site at 11:12 PM, along with our deblurring, which they labelled a fake. "The 'Roswell Research Group' is a group of internet UFO Trolls, claiming to be searching for the truth but repeatedly spreading lies." They said it was, "...a fake created by taking a low-resolution copy of our scan and editing it in photoshop." [15]

Libel and slander issues aside, we then had a scan of the placard directly from the source. Shortly afterwards, more help arrived. On his blog, Rich Reynolds posted, "Anthony Bragalia has provided these scans of the placard seen on the Kodachrome slides... the scans the Roswell Team worked with."[16] With the additional placard scan versions in hand, the RSRG was able to verify that they all pictured the same source image, they could also be deblurred to show the same text, and it proved that the results of reading the placard were genuine.

The RSRG website finally had a report from the group to publish.[17] We published our press release exposing the truth about the Slides with the placard deblurring. Later updates included additional material on the mummy, along with the YouTube videos demonstrating the deblurring process by Lance Moody and Tim Printy.

In response to lingering controversy, disbelief and charges that the RSRG had faked the deblurring of the placard, Isaac Koi posted directions at the *Above Top Secret* site on how to duplicate the process using SmartDeblur on Slidebox Media's original scan.[18] Around the world, others independently duplicated the results, including Frank Warren, Alejandro Rojas, Whitley Strieber, David Rudiak and even Vladimir Yuzhikov, the creator of SmartDeblur. In the following weeks, Nab Lator published an article on his blog to explain the deblurring process.[19] Meanwhile, a few others duplicated the placard text using different commercially available software such as Blurity, Photoshop CC and InFocus, making the promoters' claim of multiple expert attempts to read the placard less credible.

BeWitness team member Anthony Bragalia was initially in denial and disbelief, but on May 10 admitted he'd been wrong. He still insisted, however, that "The data points and the narrative of the slide(s) are all true." The text of the placard matched the mummy's description in the September 1938 booklet from Mesa Verde National Park, and he conceded that the "interpretation of the text was correct... that definitively solves the mystery of the 'Roswell Slides.'"[20]

On May 12, Tom Carey published a defiant rebuttal to the RSRG deblurring. "We believe that the recently released 'reading' of the placard by the so-called 'Roswell Slides Research Group' was faked." He could not believe that, "...a cast of characters... is somehow able to 'read' it when (experts with) more sophisticated equipment and techniques at their disposal, could not. I ask you, what's wrong with this picture?" He concluded by saying that they were getting third parties to run Smart-DeBlur on the placard and they were "prepared to abide by their findings, wherever the chips fall."

Two days later, on May 14, his partner, Don Schmitt, issued another statement. "I now realize that the image in the slides is a mummy as specified by the display placard." He asked for understanding, "Still, if I have offended or hurt anyone through my participation in this event, you have my deepest apology and have every right to hold it against me."[21]

One of the Slides story's key "data points" had been the Rays' friendship with the Eisenhowers. On May 20, 2015, Shepherd Johnson received a reply from the Eisenhower Presidential Library stating, "We have not found any mention of the Rays in either the papers of Dwight or Mamie Eisenhower. It... does not appear that the couples knew each other."[22]

One big thing was still missing. No one had located another picture of the body. On May 13, Shepherd Johnson filed a Freedom of Information Act request for the photograph of the mummified boy's body that was mentioned in National Park Service documents. On June 9, Jorge Peredo of Mexico found another tourist's picture of the mummified child in an online photo album, a color slide, taken in December 1956 by Frank Hadl at Montezuma Castle National Monument.[23] Three days later, on June 12, the NPS released a 186-page file as a result of Shepherd Johnson's FOIA. It contained thorough documentation of the 1896 excavation of the boy's grave in Arizona at Montezuma Castle by S. L. Palmer, the transfer of the remains between museums, and also two photographs of the body, one at the grave site, and a clearer one from 1939 picturing it with burial artifacts.[24] The photographs and documents provided the final proof. The promoters of the Roswell Slides had it all wrong.

Aftermath

In the aftermath of the placard deblurring, the team promoting BeWitness folded, leaving only Jaime Maussan to defend it. He set up the site "The Face of Roswell," and held another event, "Mesa De Análisis De Un Cuerpo No Humano," to refute the debunking of BeWitness. Even with the documentation from the NPS, Maussan and his experts refused to believe it was a mummified boy. While they conceded the reading of the placard, they rejected its value, saying that it did not describe the non-human body it was placed on. Throughout the rest of 2015, Maussan continued to support the Slides in interviews and at his appearances at UFO conferences, including the annual MUFON Symposium.[25] In May of 2016, Maussan hosted a two-hour special on Tercer Milenio TV on the first anniversary of BeWitness, still promoting it as genuine. In November 2016, Maussan was honored at the StarworksUSA UFO Symposium with their "Award for Excellence In Investigative Journalism."

In 2016, Don Schmitt and Tom Carey released a new book on Roswell, but it made no mention of the BeWitness fiasco. In interviews to promote it they were sometimes asked about the Roswell Slides, but their incredible (and unsubstantiated) revised position was that they had not seen the Slides prior to BeWitness. They claimed Beason and Dew had "snookered" them by sending only cropped versions of the slides in order to conceal the museum setting and that there was digital manipulation, "hocus pocus," to prevent them from reading the placard. While they grudgingly accepted the deblurring as genuine, they still thought the body pictured was somehow unusual.[26]

Slidebox Media, LLC went dark. Joe Beason stayed hidden, but Adam Dew resurfaced in 2016, attempting to film interviews to complete his *Kodachrome* documentary since the ending had to be changed.

The UFO community's reaction to the Roswell Slides fiasco was mixed, but most were left wondering if it was all a big mistake or if we had been hoaxed. There were many who felt it was just another embarrassment and wanted it quickly forgiven and forgotten. That's not enough. Forgetting such problems is a passive invitation for future fakes. When you get bad product from a shopkeeper, it may be his supplier's fault. What matters is how the problem is resolved to restore good faith. In the case of the Slides, all the merchant offered was excuses.

The secrecy of the BeWitness promoters with their NDAs prevented a thorough investigation and thwarted the true due diligence they had sought. Instead it was show business. We were told that the evidence had been subjected to expert analysis, but the promoters themselves were the ones deciding which experts were qualified, only presenting findings supporting their existing beliefs that the body in the Slides was something non-human. The fatal problem was not in mistaking the body in the Slides for an alien, but in allowing an elaborate narrative to be built around that mistake like a house of cards. What the Roswell Slides episode did was to expose the serious flaws common in standard ufology research practices. The BeWitness fiasco was just a by-product.

Some commenters expected the RSRG to become a UFO truth squad and wondered what we would tackle next. It was largely by chance the group came together on this project—we all enjoyed working on it and shared the drive to pursue a common goal. That said, it's unlikely lightning would strike twice. The truth is, most UFO cases can't be satisfactorily solved. Usually we have only witness testimony; when there is actually something tangible, it's often ambiguous physical traces, a photo or a recording of some sort, and the evidence itself is puzzling. There are often enough questions remaining for UFO mystery mavens to claim even the flimsiest cases are unsolved and anomalous. In the BeWitness story, the evidence itself provided the solution. The placard the Slides pictured not only told us exactly what the body was, its text led to further documentation and proof beyond any reasonable doubt. Without the placard, the promoters would all still be on the UFO lecture circuit touting the Roswell Slides as genuine alien photos, the extraterrestrial "smoking gun" that changed history.

Could the Roswell Slides Research Group serve as a model for future research and investigation of UFO cases? I've provided an inside look at the strengths and weaknesses of our group's methodology... now you can make your own decision. By pooling our resources, we each had the best available data, access to the counsel of our peers, and the inspiration and encouragement to keep trying to find the truth. Groups can be great tools, but they have their limitations. Each of us must remain objective, seek the best evidence and ask challenging questions, whether as part of a team or as individuals.

TRUFO VS. **UFAUX:** PLANETARY POLTERGEISTS & **WEAPONS OF MASS ENCHANTMENT**

SMiles Lewis

The following transcript is a condensed excerpt from a two-part lecture titled "UFOs and Consciousness: The Fantastic Facts About UFOs, Altered States of Consciousness, and Mind-at-Large." The lecture sought to highlight the literature supporting areas of research I think could be most useful in moving UFO investigations forward and which support some of the speculative hypotheses that I find the most compelling. It has been edited to focus solely upon the probable use of the UFO for Covert Folklore Warfare by all too human actors.

∼

In this talk, I'll give you an overview of what I call ParaCryptoU-FOlogy—the alternative theories of the UFO phenomenon that suggest a covert socio-cultural control system of earth lights and ball-of-light phenomena that interact with human consciousness in parapsychological ways. It may also interface with the collective unconscious of humanity and other species as well as some sort of a planetary mind, or Gaian consciousness, that some have described as a GeoPsyche and Planetary Poltergeist.

We'll also discuss the potential misuse of these mechanisms for "Grand Deception" stratagems that manipulate the phenomenon and we'll reconsider classic strange encounters in light of known government mind control programs. Finally, we'll discuss the probable fake, false, faux UFO campaigns and concocted contact narratives being created by certain human agencies for reasons that have to do with socio-cultural control rather than extraterrestrial aliens.

I must stress that I am not trying to convince you that my perspective is the right one. That, to me, is the hallmark of somebody from whom you should run screaming. I am here tonight to tell you about the many different areas of exploration I've come across that I think point to something more interesting and more complicated than simple extraterrestrials in nuts-and-bolts vehicles whose tires you can kick physically. That is not to say that there are not these types of encounters happening. In fact, many of the ideas I'm going to talk about would provide the perfect cover for such traditional extraterrestrial encounters.

This is the problem I have with most people who claim to have an answer to the UFO phenomenon: they pick a theory, but it only fits part of the data. That's also why I advocate for a multi-theory interpretation of the UFO phenomenon. I don't think there is any one explanation that accounts for all the data. I think there is a number of things going on simultaneously.

My obsessive search for information about UFOs occurred during the height of the 1990s "Zine Scene" as desktop PC-enabled publishing was expanding upon the photocopied Samizdat networks. Great magazines like *Crash Collusion*, from here in Austin, *Excluded Middle Magazine* in California, *Arcturus Books* catalog in Georgia, inspired my own foray into self-publishing. Those were great heady times, which led me to publish my first issue in the summer of 1994. It was called *E.L.F. Infested Spaces*, after Terence McKenna's phrase, "Elf Infested Spaces;" E.L.F. because of the ubiquitous stories of mind control I kept coming across and research about the psychoactivity of electromagnetic fields, and how these various psychotronic mind-influencing technologies could be used to manipulate people, and theories of E.L.F. waves serving as the conduit for psychic information.

Over the years, I reprinted in *ELFIS* a number of really important UFO studies that speak to these alternative theories of UFOs: "UFOs: The Pineal Connection" by Serena Roney Dougal,[2] "Topographic Brain Mapping of UFO Experiencers,"[3] and, one of my favorites, "A Testable Theory of UFOs, ESP, Aliens, and Bigfoot"[4] by *Synchronicity* author Alan Vaughan looking at correlations between geomagnetic activity and reports of various types of phenomena.

Another is the "Bibliography on the Psychoactivity of Electromagnetic Fields,"[5] which is an incredible resource. It is page-after-page listing scientific papers about the effects of ELF and other electromagnetic radiation on physical and psychological responses. A number of the research projects were at military bases near where, gee, there's been a lot of UFO activity. See also, "ELF Magnetic Fields and EEG Entrainment: A Psychotronic Warfare Possibility?" by Robert C. Beck.[6]

It was likely Whitley Strieber's first book, *Communion,* that got me thinking about psychotronic effects and the role of the earth. He wrote that the human brain and various body parts give off electromagnetic fields and that perhaps these could be manipulated: "A more acute technology than our own might be able to mediate mental and physical function to a great degree."[7] His intimations of an interplay between these energies and a planetary consciousness inspired the romantic animist in me.

Terence McKenna also encouraged that notion when he said, "one possible view of the flying saucers is that it is a kind of projection from the consciousness of the planet, that is Gaia," and "I think in that sense, Jung was really onto something when he saw it as coming from the unconscious ... almost as though the UFO is a manifestation of Gaia as mother goddess."[8]

In his "Five Arguments against the Extraterrestrial Theory" paper, Jacques Vallée said that "... it could be Gaia." He provided two variants on this idea. "An alien intelligence, possibly earth based, could be training us towards a new type of behavior. It could represent the visitor phenomena of Strieber or some form of super nature," like Lyle Watson talked about, "possibly along the lines of a Gaia hypothesis."[9]

It is, perhaps, Paul Devereux's research that has most influenced my romanticized thinking of UFOs as organelles in a Gaian ecosystem. For years he's researched these weird earth lights phenomena—luminous lights that are generated by the earth due to earthquakes and tectonic stress. In 1995 he wrote a passionate article called "Beyond UFOlogy: Meeting With the Alien"[10] in which he talked about the importance of altered states of consciousness, the DMT research of Rick Strassman, and Terence McKenna's perspectives that this is some kind of history-haunting phantasm that is somehow tied to the earth. He also cites Dr. Kenneth Ring's work,[11] and includes many other little known bits of data regarding the effects of these electromagnetic fields on human physiology and consciousness.

The environmental issues related to "fracking" have made headlines in recent years. Did you know it may be relatively easy to trigger such luminous phenomena? There's been research into this since at least 1992 with fluid injection causing luminous phenomena.[12] It seems highly likely that various human agencies have noticed this and may be using this to their advantage.

Another researcher whose books I've been really fascinated by and who cites all the medical and electromagnetic literature on the physiological and consciousness effects of such EM fields is Albert Budden. His book is called *Allergies and Aliens: The Electromagnetic Indictment*. You may have heard about people who are hypersensitive to chemicals: they can't get near the fumes of gas, or various other types of chemicals cause them extreme reactions. Well, there are also people who are electromagnetically hypersensitive who can't wear a watch, can't be near computers, can't be under 60 Hz frequency fluorescent lighting. His contention is that the phenomena represent the collective unconscious trying to, as several other people have suggested, make us believe in them but that it's a result of electro pollution. Another aspect of his "Electro-Staging" hypothesis is the phenomenon's ability, like a poltergeist, to manipulate telekinetically the physical environment and use everything from water vapor to dust particles to larger size physical objects to cobble together a physical form through which to interact with the witness. He says, "the unconscious responds to external geo-generated EM fields during altered states of consciousness and presents perceptions and realities that are dramatizations of alien contact in order to establish an acceptance of the unconscious within society."[13]

Paul Devereux speaks of humanity's Shamanism technology—lost techniques for accessing the world around us. He and others have documented the worldwide belief that Balls-Of-Light represent disembodied consciousness and spirits. Certain classes of BOL accounts are closely associated with miners and the earth's interior. Within all the UFO-lore and the contactee stories, whether it's belief in some kind of ascended masters under Mount Shasta or ideas about Shambhala or the Vril, or even in the science fiction pulp of Shaver and Ray Palmer, there is this consistent imagery of inner earth mythology. I believe this and other Gaian overtones are due to the probable source—the earth herself.

The buzzing sounds associated with UFO close encounters and the hive mindedness of the beings reminds me of ancient traditions that deal with the oracular, the dispensation of prophecy and wisdom from the gods.[14] Their messengers were often heard in association with the buzzing of bees. I think it's not just the electromagnetic technological aspect of the sound but that there is obvious symbolism there that points to this idea of the hive, like the bees, and this hive mindedness; this hierarchy that is so often evident in the Theosophical traditions of so many esoteric groups, whether it's the Ashtar Command and the various levels of their command structure and ascended masters and white lodges. I think, perhaps, these are reflections of the onion-like layers of Jung's collective unconscious and more than merely analogous to the hierarchical taxonomy of biological classification.

One of the most important things that abduction researcher Karla Turner added to the dialog on UFO abduction reports was the idea of the Virtual Reality Scenario.[15] She talked about this a lot in her lectures and gave examples where the abductee, the experiencer, would see and experience one thing, but nearby witnesses would see something quite different but still anomalous and weird.

There are a few examples of this in the literature where the researcher followed the abductee as they drove somewhere and watched them sit and never leave their car, but later on the experiencer would relate that, "Oh, the UFO came down, and I had this experience." It's not that these people are necessarily lying. They seem to have had some sort of fugue-like state, some kind of Out-of-Body-Experience. So many of the descriptions of these close encounters have the quality of OBEs. Karla Turner also believed that "abductees report alien-controlled information" and this alien Other force controls the perceptions of the experiencer.

Back in the 1990s, Rupert Sheldrake's book, *A New Science of Life*, was declared by *Nature* as "the best candidate for burning there has been for many years."[16] More recently his lecture was initially banned from the TED-Talks YouTube channel. I find a lot of the ideas that Sheldrake has espoused really important in trying to understand UFOs and related phenomena. His ideas about fields (not the physical electromagnetic fields that we've been talking about) involves looking at them more as an abstract idea. I think that they have relevance to the realms of Psi and remote viewing, Jung's Collective Unconscious, and Aldous

Huxley's Mind-at-Large. I've often tried to put it this way: To me, morphic fields and morphic resonance theory are akin to the various esoteric ideas about the Akashic records and the collective unconscious. I suspect that pretty much any idea can be its own field and that such fields can be accessed non-locally by consciousness. I'm reminded of the famous incident where former military remote viewer of much ill repute, Ed Dames, was fooled into remote viewing a mythical character, but thought it was a Soviet missile attack because, well, he perceived that there was some metal object rocketing across the North Pole. It was red, and it was heading to the United States so of course, he saw it as a Soviet missile attack. But what had he been tasked with remote viewing? Santa Claus! If something as unreal or as quasi-real as Santa Claus can be remote viewed, well, then that pretty much means to me that these Akashic fields can be tapped, and I suspect that may be one way of communicating across vast distances in a way that we think of SETI doing but without the electromagnetic radio waves. Vallée suggested as much in his 1992 book, *UFO Chronicles of the Soviet Union: A Cosmic Samizdat*, when he spoke of the Soviet technique of "biolocation," or biological-field dowsing.[17]

British UFOlogist Jenny Randles coined the phrase the "Oz Factor," which is "a sort of inner tuning, as the percipient's mind blocks out attention to all external sounds in order to note the message that is about to bombard his or her consciousness." Again, I think this has relevance to Sheldrake's species field. Within at least two of her books, *Mind Monsters*[18] and *Beyond Explanation*,[19] and within her UFO newsletter,[20] she put forth this idea of Synchronistic Reality Mode and the ability for the human mind to take in this anomalous information in a parapsychological way and create a virtual reality telepresence experience.

We're now moving into a time when we've got this technology ourselves, in our pockets. Here is an artist's rendering of someone wearing eyeglasses like Google Glass [not pictured in this essay, but described as follows]. In this example the person is getting information about somebody who is buried in a cemetery in the form of a "hologram" standing in front of them that looks rather like a ghost, but it's simply them interacting with some kind of informational field, and it's projecting information into an augmented reality, a virtual reality created by the glasses they are wearing. There's an App for that! You can get an app for your smartphone that will use your phone's GPS coordinate data with other databases to see if somebody has tagged the area where you are located with metadata. Then your app can extract that, and it can be displayed as an overlay with your phone's camera display. Perhaps this is the same way that people, when they go into haunted houses, may be tapping into some kind of informational field that's present and accessing past experiences embedded in that field.

I think that the phenomena can be interacted with in a way that's more akin to that portrayed in Carl Sagan's book and movie *Contact* where Jodie Foster's character experiences a very vividly real feeling of meeting with an extraterrestrial, except that it appears to her in the form of something that she can more easily comprehend. Instead of using radio waves, there is some other kind of biological field that can be tapped into and we can experience these things as perceptually real, and they may be from real beings somewhere else, or they could be right here just one dimension over. Or perhaps they are undetectable to us because they are part of a mirror world left-handed molecular ecosystem.[21]

I suspect that the UFO phenomenon represents a transpersonal virtual reality communications channel. These various altered states of consciousness facilitate anomalous information transfer, facilitate telepathy, remote viewing, and other forms of ESP. They are the interface mechanism for us to receive and transmit messages from not just our own collective unconscious and the archetypes, but to experience the collective consciousness of other beings and other intelligences, other species on this planet and elsewhere.

Jenny Randles expressed that very possibility as a thought experiment on the UFO UpDates email list back in 2000:

> Aliens are in contact but not actually coming to earth. They are only capable of long range probes that treat abductees like receiving radio telescopes. These 'psychic' people are used to communicate, extract information about us and engage in inter-species relationships at a deep level of our inner selves. As such the aliens are real, the contact with them not physical, the experience of contact subjective, but reflective in a psycho-social sense of the 'mental rape' being conducted (hence the extent to which these experiences are visualized and dramatized in this way).[22]

Dennis Stillings edited one of my favorite UFO books that has the greatest title ever, *Cyberbiological Studies of the Imaginal Component in the UFO Contact Experience.*[23] Cyberbiology is defined as "consciousness-related aspects of relations to ourselves, and to other systems, including the environment." This idea that somehow we are in a biofeedback type relationship with the phenomenon led me several years ago to write:

> The UFO phenomenon exists in a synergistic cybernetic interface with humanity. Whatever the true nature of UFOs, they interact with us within several different milieus, all of which are influenced by the media and culture. This media and culture in turn feeds back into the phenomena in a continuous cycle.[24]

Through his editorial choice of essays, Stillings is supporting this idea that we're dealing with some sort of cyberbiological planetary poltergeist.

Another writer/researcher is retired colonel Thomas Bearden, who wrote a really fascinating book called *The Excalibur Briefing*.[25] He, too, describes the onion-like aspect of the collective unconscious or the Akashic records and this idea that we could be interacting through this phenomenon—through the transpersonal channel that I've been trying to describe here—with various aspects of our own individual unconscious, the collective unconscious of the entire species or, as he breaks it down, to family, city, state, creed, nation, race, geographical area, species, biosphere, and the universal. Bearden expounds on the intricate physics he believes scientifically prove the Tulpoidal mechanism of this planetary poltergeist idea; that our collective anxieties are psychically manifesting in a worldwide type of poltergeist activity that causes physical manifestations.

I think that there are these hierarchies and at any of those levels there could be a variety of independently operating consciousnesses that we could be interacting with. I really think that it's quite possible that the reason we experience these apparent alien others as insectoid is because their ultimate origin could be the collective species unconscious of the insect kingdom. I mean, my God, we are committing insecticide every day. It would seem to be in their best interest to try to convince us to stop damaging the ecology of the planet.

Another area relevant to the connection between humanity's collective anxieties and UFO contact phenomena is the work done by courageous ethnologists and anthropologists on UFO encounter and alien abduction narratives. There has been a number of theses and dissertations done on this that deal with the idea that what we're seeing in the narratives is not so much a reflection of physical, real encounters but that they are a reflection of societal problems that are going on. Anthropologist and Adjunct Lecturer at Florida International University, Dr. Steven Mizrach, wrote a very controversial article back in the 1990s called *UFO Abductions and Race Fear*.[26] He was expounding upon the work of James Pontolillo: *Demons, Doctors, and Aliens: An Exploration Into the Relationships Among Witch Trial Evidence, Sexual-Medical Traditions, and Alien Abductions*, which was put out by the International Fortean Organization in 1993. Susan Lepselter, Associate Professor within Indiana University's Anthropology Department, did her dissertation here in Austin, Texas on *The Poetics of the Uncanny*. It is a fascinating read and has just been published by Michigan University Press as *The Resonance of Unseen Things: Poetics, Power, Captivity, and UFOs in the American Uncanny*. Also of relevance to issues of race, captivity narratives and power role reversal is the dissertation, *Taken: Constructions of race, biology, and Colonialism Informing the Alien Abduction Narrative in the United States* by Carol Suzanne Matthews, University of Kansas (2001).

If there is such a worldwide phenomenon of earth energies that is tied into some sort of GeoPsyche and that is connected to our collective anxieties, could that channel (and the earth energy organelle programs of socio-cultural control flowing through it) have been hijacked by human agencies for nefarious purposes?

Another classic quote from Vallée:

> I believe there is a machinery of mass manipulation behind the UFO phenomenon. It aims at social and political goals by diverting attention from some human problems and by providing a potential release for tensions caused by others.

> UFOs are real. They are an application of psychotronic technology. That is they are physical devices used to affect consciousness. They may not be from outer space. They may, in fact, be terrestrial based manipulating devices. Their purpose may be to achieve social change on this planet.[27]

Several years ago, Greg Bishop interviewed parapsychologist Dean Radin and they spoke about this idea of psychotronic devices and how they could affect the local geomagnetic environment in ways that affect people's consciousness, perhaps as an unintended by-product of whatever the device is intended to do:

... exotic military hardware—experimental gizmos—most of which is mistaken for UFOs. Some of which can indirectly (not intentionally) cause people to perceive things. You can imagine that having this gigantic electromagnetic thing hovering in the air, it changes the local environment in ways that makes people's brains go funny. That sort of stuff apparently really does go on.[28]

Michael Persinger of Laurentian University in Sudbury, Ontario, Canada, is the researcher who proposed the Tectonic Strain Theory that is akin to Paul Devereux's Earth Lights Hypothesis. Whereas Devereux is very much a Gaia kind of guy, Persinger is a much more materialist reductionist, hard science guy. While there are claims that his research has yet to be replicated, he's developed what's come to be called the God helmet, which is a series of magnets in a head-mounted device that can induce experiences similar to Out-of-Body-Experiences, as well as a sense of a felt presence similar to that described in abductions, hauntings, and close encounter-type phenomena.

Persinger doesn't believe there is any alien Other within these phenomena. Yet, in 1977, he and Gyslaine F. Lafrenière also put forth the idea of the GeoPsyche that, "essentially involves the interaction between large numbers of biological systems and the geomagnetic environment within which they are immersed."[29]

I should add that Persinger's and Devereux's earth-generated luminous phenomena ideas are not widely accepted. Another of my favorite Canadian researchers, Chris Rutkowski, has written several highly critical counter arguments to Persinger's and Devereux's theories that are worth considering.[30]

When researching UFOs, one inevitably comes into contact with stories of mind control: tales of close encounters, telepathic contact and control, stories of electronic harassment, gaslighting, and gang stalking, etc. You'd have to have been living under a rock to have never heard of the CIA's MKUltra project. All of these stories of alien ESP, military RV (Remote Viewing), unwitting human experimentation by government, earth energies influencing perception, led me to dig deeper into MKUltra and related projects.

It continues to blow my mind every time I read about just how widespread these programs were and how our government became as bad as our enemies. If you've never heard of Operation Paper Clip, it involved the importation of Nazi scientists from Germany after World War II. More than 1,500 of these engineers, scientists, and technicians were seeded throughout the United States educational system, across universities from one coast to the other.

The best book I've found on these mind control projects is Hank Albarelli, Jr.'s, *A Terrible Mistake: The Murder of Frank Olson and the CIA's Secret Cold War Experiments*.[31] That book is huge, and is filled with facts about the CIA's MKUltra program. There were many sub-programs—MKNAOMI, MKDELTA, Blue Bird and others. Of course, there are also the rumors that have yet to be substantiated of Project Monarch, but all of these projects had as their aim things like a truth serum, enhanced interrogation techniques, and Manchurian candidate style mind-controlled assassins.

Albarelli also writes about how MKUltra employed magician John Mulholland to investigate psychic researcher Andrija Puharich and the famous Kelly Hopkinsville case. Which makes me wonder, were they just trying to get his assessment of cases and people that they felt were not trustworthy, or were they having him follow-up on their own mind control experiments?

What does this have to do with UFOs? Several researchers have suggested, over the years, that some or all UFO close encounters and alien abduction experiences might be the result of continued MKUltra type research. Vallée was talking about these issues in interviews with other leading ufologists like Jerome Clark (for *FATE* magazine) back in 1978:

> "What we do know is that you can make people hallucinate using either lights or microwave or electromagnetic energy. You can also make them pass out; you can cause them to behave strangely, put them into shock, make them hear voices or even kill them."[32]

However, nothing ignited the mind control conspiracy sub-genre within the ufological scene as much as Martin Cannon's important paper, "The Controllers: A new hypothesis of Alien Abduction," first published in the pages of the *MUFON UFO Journal* in 1989.[33] Jim Keith's *Mind Control, World Control: The Encyclopedia of Mind Control* (1997) and *Mass Control: Engineering Human Consciousness* (1999), Helmut and Marion Lammer's *MILABS: Military Mind Control and Alien Abduction* (2000) and others signalled that the mind control interpretation of Close Encounters had successfully carved out its own niche within the UFO scene.

The level of paranoia within the UFO community has only grown since then. These days, just about everyone eventually gets labeled as an agent provocateur—even ol' Carl Jung, whose ideas on the collective unconscious and the archetypes I incorporate so deeply into my ideas about UFOs. It is, apparently, not widely known but is well established that Jung worked with the founder of the CIA (when it was the OSS) Allen Dulles, in his psychological profiling of Hitler and the German people during the war.

It's been suggested by others that this may be where Dulles got the idea to use people's belief in the paranormal and specifically UFOs for psychological warfare purposes. In fact, a former chemist and researcher on the Manhattan Project, Leon Davidson, as far back as the 1950s and into the 1970s, was talking about this idea that the UFO phenomenon was being manipulated by the CIA specifically as part of a Cold War tool to disinform the Soviets and for various other purposes:

> Dulles also adopted a concept from his old friend Carl Jung and co-opted the myth that benign aliens have visited Earth for millennia. He used magicians' illusions, tricks, and showmanship to blend in sightings, landings, and contacts with the legitimate military test sightings... Later, Dulles found the saucer believers and their clubs an ideal propaganda vehicle.[34]

MKUltra has had a lasting legacy. There are a lot of different cases during the 1970s of these apparent mind control assassins. H.P. Albarelli and others before him have found dramatic connections between the people surrounding Oswald, the MKUltra mind control research community, and individuals at the birth of the modern UFO era.[35] Both Kenn Thomas[36] and Peter Levenda[37] have written books and/or lectured on these very bizarre links between the formation of the Flying Saucer Era, Post-WWII American Nazism, and MKUltra activities.

Did you know that Ted Kaczynski participated in one of the CIA's MKUltra programs? He wasn't dosed with LSD, and he volunteered willingly. He was not, like so many others, one of the unwitting experimentees in the MKUltra programs.[38]

What about Whitey Bulger, the Mafioso? Like the alleged killers of Frank Olson—the subject of that book I cited earlier, *A Terrible Mistake*—Olson's assassins and Whitey Bulger were active in organized crime and willingly participated in MKUltra prison experiments.[39] Afterwards they were used by the CIA and FBI for their own nefarious purposes.

There has been a number of different attempts over the years to get the truth out about these experiments. The first were the Church Committee hearings in the 1970s, the US House of Representatives Select Committee on Assassinations (HSCA) in 1978, and the Advisory Committee on Human Radiation Experiments in the 1990s. The Canadian government had to create "The Allan Memorial Institute Depatterned Persons Assistance Plan," and provided $100,000 to each former patient of Dr. Ewen Cameron's MKUltra experiments.[40] Cameron served as President of the American Psychiatric Association, Canadian Psychiatric Association, American Psychopathological Association, Society of Biological Psychiatry, and World Psychiatric Association.

I've described the many different classic cases that I grew up loving as a kid. Let's briefly look at them again "through a glass, darkly," through the lens of covert-ops and deception.

The Flatwoods Monster in 1952 was one of those classic flying saucer monster cases I grew up on. I'm not saying this is an explanation for it, but Nick Redfern has reported[41] on a RAND document called "The Exploitation of Superstitions for Purposes of Psychological Warfare" that was written for the Air Force back in 1950.[42] In it there is a description of a particular psychological operation that was done in Italy to spook the locals, and it involves the creation of a simple robotic scarecrow that they would wheel into town and scare the natives, supposedly. He noticed the similarity in the description to this 12-foot being that was described in the Flatwoods case and wonders if the two may be related.

One of the first abduction cases before the Betty Hill abduction case has also come under scrutiny. Antonio Vilas Boas was out tilling his field. The tractor began to stall. He saw a UFO. It landed. Occupants came out. They gassed him, dragged him onboard, and forced him to have sex with a very peculiar naked humanoid that barked like a dog and then, after they'd had sex, she pointed at her belly and then to the sky as if to imply, "Your children are coming with us up there."

One has to wonder if maybe this was the test-bedding of new human technology. In 1978, an individual by the name of Bosco Nedelcovic, who was an interpreter and translator at the Inter-American Defense College, started talking to UFO researchers in the states about his participation in various projects that, he says, were the ones perpetrating at least some UFO incidents, specifically the Vilas Boas abduction. According to researcher Philip Coppens, Nedelcovic claimed that he was, "part of a nine-man helicopter team that abducted civilians and conducted both psychological warfare experiments and hallucinogenic drug tests, specifically in the Minas Gerais region of Brazil. The team included a doctor, CIA and Navy personnel, while the helicopter was equipped with a metal cubicle, about five feet long and three feet wide, used—somehow—in the psychological warfare operations."[43]

I'll tell you what that 5x3 box reminds me of—it's the isolation coffins that were used by the psychiatrist Ewen Cameron in Canada, as part of his MKUltra sensory deprivation and psychic driving experiments where they abused hapless Canadians who were just looking for a little psychological relief.[44]

Let's move on to the first publicized "alien" abduction in North America. Again, I'm not suggesting that this is the definitive explanation, but it's always struck me as significant that the description Barney Hill gave of the lead alien (besides his other description of a "red-headed Irishman" that doesn't quite fit with the rest of it). He said, "He looks like a German Nazi. He's a Nazi. He had a black scarf around his neck that was dangling over his shoulder." The drawing Barney sketched under hypnosis, with the little cap on its head, and the scarf on the shoulder,[45] always reminded me more of French fashion than German. Over time, his description became more in line with that of his wife and more in line with the standard grey alien with big eyes. There are other aspects of this case, like the strange beeping noise that they heard right before the experience, and descriptions of strange marks on the hood of the car that always struck me as where somebody could've placed one of these psychotronic mind control devices.

Nick Redfern has also reported on the famous army reserve helicopter encounter that brings us again to the connection between UFOs and Out-of-Body-Experiences. He writes:

> Captain Coyne [the pilot and witness] received telephone calls from people identifying themselves as representatives of the Department of the Army, Surgeon General's Office, asking if he, Coyne, had experienced any 'unusual dreams' subsequent to the UFO incident. As it happened, not long before the Army's call, Coyne had undergone a very vivid out-of-body experience.
>
> Sgt. John Healey also reported ... 'the Pentagon would call us up and ask ... have I ever dreamed of body separation? And I have. I dreamed that I was dead in bed and that my spirit or whatever was floating, looking down at me lying dead in bed.[46]

Another famous case is the Pascagoula, Mississippi Clawmen from 1973. I always found this case fascinating—probably because it involved alien entities who were radically different from the classic short, big-headed, black-eyed aliens. This case involves tall clawmen with elephant-like skin and pinchers for hands that floated over the pier where the two witnesses were fishing and is very different from other types of close encounters.

According to Hank Albarelli and Zoe Martell, they've talked to researchers who were chemists at Fort Detrick, which was the testing ground of so much of the chemical warfare research that was part of MKUltra, and they make the claim that this was somehow part of that experimentation. They say that "former Fort Detrick researchers... revealed an odd experiment that took place in Pascagoula, Mississippi, and produced one of the most puzzling UFO and strange entity cases on record in America." They go on to state, "that the pier was not far away from a former Fort Detrick research site, Horn Island." They continue:

> Detrick microbiologists conducted intensive experiments on the islands "involving human research subjects" and a number "of natural hallucinogens as well as advanced neuroscience techniques" aimed at the objection of producing "previously unexplored and unique psychological warfare methods.[47]

There are many more threads we could tug on to discuss this weaponization of folklore and governmental, military, and intelligence communities misuse of the UFO community's belief systems as weapons of mass enchantment for psychological warfare. Quickly, here are just a few.

In his 1991 book, *Revelations: Alien Contact and Human Deception*, Vallée pondered the possibility that the reason for the numerous sightings of UFOs over sensitive military installations may be due to hoaxes performed to test the security of these bases and the reaction of the personnel when confronted by a UFO. In that book he writes, "antiterrorist exercises in which the attackers disguised their craft as a flying saucer have actually been run more than once."[48] He was discussing this in the context of the Bentwaters/Rendlesham base encounters. Jacques seems to have been convinced of this in the 1980s by former CIA analyst Dr. Christopher "Kit" Green.[49] Both men are alleged members of the infamous ufological "Aviary" of intelligence community spooks.[50] More recently, researcher Sacha Christie has continued this line of inquiry.[51]

Jacques Vallée, Gerald K. Haines and others have stressed the idea that UFOs have been used as cover for exotic military R&D tech, helping protect projects like the U2 spy planes and stealth aircraft before they are made public. Haines asserts that the Air Force's Project Blue Book knowingly misattributed sightings of the CIA's U-2 and OXCART planes as UFOs.[52] Other UFO researchers, such as Bruce Maccabee, vehemently disagree that this could be true except in a few rare cases.[53]

There is also the classic Paul Bennewitz case where AFOSI agent Richard Doty used a variety of unethical tactics in the name of protecting National Security—there are rumors that J. Allen Hynek delivered one of the computers to poor ol' Paul that was loaded with software installed on the part of the Air Force or NSA to convince Bennewitz that he was intercepting communications from aliens. Of course, that claim comes via disgraced but intriguing UFO researcher Bill Moore, who, admittedly, was also doing AFOSI agent Dick Doty's bidding in driving his friend Paul further into madness.[54]

Former head of MUFON, James Carrion, before stepping down from the job, moved in the direction of interpreting UFOs as a psychological warfare technique. He went so far as to suggest that the Roswell incident was a disinfo ploy to cover up research about the United States' efforts at creating a tsunami bomb,[55] and continues researching his claim that the Ghost Rockets were one of the earliest examples of UFOs being used for strategic deception operations.[56]

What's the purpose? Is there an attempt to manipulate human consciousness? Does this go beyond the simple use of UFO stories as laughter-curtain-cover for exotic aircraft and technology testing? A recurring theme is the idea of uniting humanity through a common enemy by manufacturing a counterfeit foe.

There are many important historical figures suggesting this unification in the face of an extraterrestrial threat, like John Dewey in 1917:

> Someone remarked that the best way to unite all the nations on this globe would be an attack from some other planet. In the face of such an alien enemy, people would respond with a sense of their unity of interest and purpose.[57]

I know this sounds familiar to you because you've probably heard it from various other people. It was said by Sir Anthony Eden in 1947:

It seems to be an unfortunate fact that the nations of the world were only really united when they were facing a common menace. What we really needed was an attack from Mars.[58]

Sir Anthony's quote inspired the 1947 book, *Flying Saucer*, by Bernard Newman, which proposed the idea that is mirrored in the 1963 *Outer Limits* episode, "Architects of Fear," the idea of scientists creating a Chimera, a fake alien threat and staging events to unite humanity against a common but counterfeit foe: Uniting us against the UFaux, the false, counterfeit UFOs.

This is one you've got to remember, old "Ronnie RayGun" [President Reagan] saying, no less than three times that:

Perhaps we need some outside, universal threat to make us realize this common bond. I occasionally think how quickly our differences would vanish if we were facing an alien threat from outside this world.[59]

He made nearly identical statements to this, first in 1985 in front of a high school student body and faculty,[60] then at the general assembly of the U.N. in 1987, and again at the Grand Ballroom for the National Strategy Forum in 1988.[61]

In Vallée's seminal 1979 book, *Messengers of Deception*, he talked about what had just become declassified in 1978 (as reported in the book *Bodyguard of Lies* by Anthony Cave Brown) and that was the LCS (London Controlling Section), and what he called the "Martian Conspiracy." The Brits called their psychological warfare experts the "Martians." Vallée suggests that at the end of World War II there was, within this joint deception campaign between the Americans and the British, a sense of, "well, we've managed to unite our intelligence agencies and use these engines of deception. Could these same techniques be used to prevent another world war?"

More recently, economist and Nobel Prize laureate Paul Krugman went so far as to say that we need a fake alien invasion to stimulate the economy. He said this on CNN,[62] and then went on Real Time with Bill Maher, echoing the theme of the infamous, allegedly satirical, *Report from Iron Mountain* (1967) with "a serious proposal" suggesting we need a fake alien threat to boost the economy.[63]

There is this history of notable people warning about this possibility. I mentioned previously Manhattan Project scientist Leon Davidson who wrote about the CIA using ECM, electronic countermeasures, to fake UFO sightings. One such technology platform was called Palladium. Apparently, we've had this technology to spoof objects on radar for quite some time. The Holy Grail, for most UFO researchers, is when we have witnesses *and* radar. But now we find that these radar blips can be faked. Apparently this was used widely in harassing the Cubans and the Soviets to try to ascertain the abilities of their electronic countermeasures and radar stations. Gene Poteat talks about Project Palladium in his 1998 essay, "Stealth, Countermeasures, and ELINT, 1960-1975" and elsewhere.[64]

The idea of spooking the natives, so to speak, has been around for quite a long time. Peter Watson talks in his 1978 book *War on the Mind* about projecting images on clouds and using loud speakers as psychological warfare to convince people of various things. Then there are the infamous plans of Major General Edward Geary Lansdale to stage a Second-Coming-Coup against Castro using a submarine projecting images of Jesus Christ off the Cuban coast.[65]

On September 11, 2001, there were a lot of UFOs in the form of unidentified blips on radars along the Eastern Seaboard of North America. This reminds us of Palladium and technology for spoofing aircraft. There are reports, both military and mainstream, about their ability to inject into the radar screens these false radar returns. This may have confused the air traffic controllers and aided the perpetrators of that day's events.[66]

In May of 2001, alien disclosure zealot Steven Greer held a well-attended event at the Press Club in Washington D.C. At that press conference, Dr. Carol Rosin told of her mentor Dr. Wernher von Braun warning her that the powers-that-be were going to stage an escalation of threats from terrorism to asteroids to extraterrestrial invasion, and that this was going to be used to justify space weapons.[67] Remember, von Braun was one of those more than 1,500 German researchers embedded in America after World War II.

Over the last several years, UFOs have seemed to become a little more mainstream—from childhood educational systems to adult global economic policy discussion. I've said for some time that UFOs are a great way of educating people to think critically and rationally to investigate the world around them. Well, between 2008 and 2013, UFO crashes and alien abductions have repeatedly been staged for little kids at primary and middle schools in the UK. It's all part of a creative writing program. There is a non-governmental organization called the National Literacy Trust which is funded by the Department for Children, Schools, and Families. The program is called "Everybody Writes."[68]

There was the Davos World Economic Forum in 2004. They had a panel titled, "The Conspiracy Behind Conspiracy Theories: Have Extraterrestrials Made Contact With Government Leaders?" Dick Cheney was one of the people on the panel for that discussion, and the moderator was Chief Executive Ian Much from the international corporation that "prints the money," De La Rue.[69]

At the 2011 Global Competitiveness Forum on "Global Challenges and Solutions 2020" Conference in Riyadh, Saudi Arabia, there were several UFO researchers speaking, including Nick Pope, Jacques Vallée, and Stanton Friedman. Bill Clinton gave the keynote address and said "I don't have to tell you what the implications of that would be, if it turned out to be true," alluding to the potential discovery of earth-like planets.[70]

Whether the UFO phenomenon is considered simply as the result of human misperception of mundane stimulus or something more exotic such as a transpersonal virtual reality communications mechanism, or planetary poltergeist (with or without its own consciousness or self-directing autonomy), human belief in alien Others creates cults, religions, and social movements of significance. Even in the absence of specific documentation declaring and funding UFO deception programs, it is clear that a wide variety of human agencies have manipulated the superstitions and myths surrounding stories of contact with non-human entities—folklore has been weaponized as a means to various ends.

We know that, despite there being "no evidence of a direct threat to national security," the infamous CIA-sponsored Scientific Advisory Panel on UFOs (the Robertson Panel) formally suggested debunking the phenomenon to "reduce the current gullibility of the public and consequently their susceptibility to clever hostile propaganda,"[71] going so far as to suggest the Disney corporation be involved in such public re-education. This is especially intriguing considering Disney animator Ward Kimball worked with Von Braun, was an original founding board member of the Fund for UFO Research, and claimed that the Air Force approached Disney to produce alien acclimatization films.[72] And what about Walt Disney Studios Director of Educational Research, Robert S. Carr, whom Vallée claims worked for Disney on classified projects[73] and later became a regional director for NICAP?

One of the other outcomes of the Robertson Panel was the CIA memo from H. Marshall Chadwell to the Director of Central Intelligence urging "the psychological strategy board immediately investigate possible offensive or defensive utilization of the phenomena for psychological warfare purposes both for and against the United States."

Certainly, we have evidence of several human agencies attempting such manipulation through popular culture, as reported in *Silver Screen Saucers*, in which Robbie Graham documents the Robertson Panel's debunking influence more than a dozen years later on the 1966 CBS TV broadcast of *UFOs: Friend, Foe, or Fantasy?* (narrated by Walter Cronkite), and Pentagon employee Chief Master Sgt. Mike Gasparetto's recognition of the 2007 Spielberg production of *Transformers* as "a great recruiting tool." Graham also documents the history of U.S. government and military bait and switch operations in which filmmakers are offered tantalizing evidence of UFOs and alien reality as part of apparent acclimatization efforts, only to renege at the last moment.[74]

More recently we have pop-punk singer turned UFO disclosure spokesperson Tom DeLonge claiming contact with military sources feeding him information verifying a wide variety of UFO myths. However, thanks to the WikiLeaks release of John Podesta's emails, we have record of DeLonge perhaps giving us a truer hint at what his military mentors are really after. DeLonge says in an email to Podesta, "This project is about changing the cynical views of youth towards government."[75]

We have over 15 years of evidence of elaborate campaigns conducted by both corporate and non-governmental organizations utilizing people's interest in UFOs, the paranormal, and conspiracies for viral/stealth marketing and alternative reality gaming, from the Majestic ARG[76] in 2001 to the *Fourth Kind* movie (resulting in Universal Pictures paying out $22,500 to the Alaska Press Club and Calista Scholarship Fund for its use of 'fake news' and websites promoting the false storyline)[77] to the MacMillan Space Centre's viral marketing UFO drone hoax[78] in 2013 and the faked green fireball video and crashed alien-craft site for a FutureLife smart-drink ad campaign in South Africa[79] in December 2015.

Tension surrounding any subject can lead to very negative behavior and outcomes. Within the UFO literature there are obvious tensions surrounding the issues of race, ridicule, and sovereignty of nation states and individuals, not to mention the potential domination and subjugation resulting from encountering a technologically superior species. The manipulation of such tensions is the domain of public relations, both commercial and political.

Researchers Wendt and Duvall point out in their 2008 paper, "Sovereignty and the UFO," that state institutions are inherently threatened by the very possibility of such potential otherworldly political actors due to the anthropocentric structure of modern rule. Such alien interlopers violate our airspace and populations at will and call into question the relevance of individual state sovereignty in favor of potential global governance in the face of potential off-world visitors. Thus the governing structures have had to ignore the phenomena and enforce the "UFO taboo."

In the face of such empires of ignorance, Wendt and Duvall rightly advocate for (while acknowledging the dangers of) a militant agnostic resistance to the UFO taboo:

> ... resistance must also be militant, by which we mean public and strategic, or else it will indeed be futile... Modern rule and its metaphysics are extraordinarily resilient, so the difficulties of such resistance cannot be overstated. Those who attempt it will have difficulty funding and publishing their work, and their reputations will suffer. UFO resistance might not be futile but it is certainly dangerous, because it is resistance to modern sovereignty itself. In this respect, militant UFO agnosticism is akin to other forms of resistance to governmentality.[80]

In our attempts at understanding UFOs and possible contact with Alien Others, let us recognize the challenge of resisting and overcoming such taboos so that we may be free of both the cultural overlays imposed by our faulty perceptions, and the perception management programs being waged against us, whether in furtherance of global governance or nationalistic independence and xenophobic tribalism. We, as stewards of spaceship earth, must no longer be ruled by false fears of counterfeit foes, nor the manufactured machinations and stratagems of empires that seek to undermine our ability to truly see and understand whatever lies behind the UFO phenomenon.

UFOS AND MODERN CAPITALISM: DISSENT, **DISENFRANCHISEMENT,** AND **THE FRINGE**

MJ Banias

"It is easier to imagine the end of the world than the end of capitalism."

—FREDRIC JAMESON, OR SO SOME PEOPLE SAY.

UFO discourse exists upon the fringes of mainstream social reality. It has been *othered* by the mechanisms of popular culture and relegated to the taboo fringe. This is not the result of some government conspiracy, nor some hidden cabalistic agenda; rather, it is the constructs of modern ideological capitalism that have entrenched ufology into the outer limits of contemporary society and culture. This essay will establish the ideological illusions generated by modern capitalism, and how and why the general sciences work against UFO discourse, in order to outline the ways in which UFO discourse is opposed to the capitalist ideological establishment. I will argue that it is due to this conflict between capitalism and UFO discourse that ufology is forever trapped in a marginalized state.

As I was drafting this essay, I was reminded of John Carpenter's satirical sci-fi film, *They Live* (1988), in which drifter John Nada, played by Roddy Piper, stumbles upon sunglasses that allow him to "see" the world for what it truly is. When he first puts them on, the advertisements on billboards change from their usual imagery to words such as "CONSUME" and "CONFORM." All money, instead of bearing the usual American symbolism, is simply a white piece of paper stamped with the word "OBEY." Everyday modes of consumption, advertisements, objects, and capitalism itself, shed their *normal* exterior, and become "clear" for what they are—mechanisms to control humanity.

Nada learns that certain people are not what they seem. The sunglasses give him the *power* to visually differentiate actual humans from the film's antagonists, skeletal-faced aliens who are infiltrating Earth. These aliens are in positions of corporate and political leadership; they manipulate world economic markets, the media, and government in an attempt to deplete Earth of its natural resources for their own personal gain. They are the *perfect* capitalists.

Nada realises that the constructs of our reality, the ideological messages that exist in the media or in everyday economic exchange, are false and have no basis in *True reality*. Rather, they are illusions, constructed by those in power, to control. In the film, Nada is able openly to resist once he learns the truth.

As an audience, we are not so lucky. That *power* to understand *True reality* is inaccessible because all human understanding is shaped by ideological constructs—value and belief systems established in our minds by our social and cultural upbringing. There is only the universe we have constructed ourselves; an objective reality is forever out of reach; all attempted understanding and communication about such a reality would be hindered by our social and cultural illusions, languages, and mechanisms. We are, in essence, entrenched in an ideological illusion. There is no place we can "stand" to view or know, unfiltered, an unadulterated reality; our perception of the objective truth is fundamentally based upon human social and cultural conditions.

In *They Live*, Nada is forced to experience the crumbling of his ideological world. When the modes and mechanisms of economic production and consumption shed their ideological exteriors, Nada realizes the entire Capitalist system is nothing more than an insidious fantasy to control the human race. To Nada, the differences between a homeless drifter and an elite banker disappear. Poverty and wealth, even producer and consumer, become meaningless once Nada finds the sunglasses in a dumpster—there is only humanity (the oppressed), and the alien invaders (the oppressors).

For those of us who live outside of the film, there are no such sunglasses. However, by attempting to deconstruct our ideologies, we might be able, at least, to get a *Nada-esque* peek into these mechanisms of social control. To establish why UFO discourse has been pushed to the fringes of the social world, much like the homeless drifter Nada, we need to sort out who or what is controlling the ideological illusion, from where does the power come that constrains ufological debate to the realm of the oppressed, and who or what is the oppressor?

Going Down the Rabbit Hole

Many in the UFO subculture claim that a secret cabal, shadow government, or similar group of individuals is responsible for the purposeful relegation of the UFO to the lunatic fringe. This, unfortunately, is a dogmatic conspiracy theory based upon belief. There is no secret society that has imprisoned UFO discourse; rather, it is our collective social reality, governed by the mechanisms of modern capitalist ideology, that has done so. There is no conspiracy. There does not need to be one. Capitalism is, in simple terms, an ideology designed to control. Ideological capitalism permeates and drives our culture; it is what relegates ufology beyond the fringes of acceptable social discourse.

In order to discuss ufology and its place within our cultural discourse, we must first understand capitalism and its insidious operation within our society. The elite and wealthy 1% control the physical and economic representations of capitalism, such as banks, big oil and pharmaceuticals, weapons manufacturing, and various other multinational corporate entities. The physical economic structures of capitalism are maintained by groups of people who have their own agenda: to line their pockets and maintain the economic status quo. We can see why some in the UFO subculture have concluded that a secret society is running the planet. In very simplistic terms, maybe they are—but it's not a secret, nor is it hidden, and we, the people, have given our consent for those physical capitalist structures to exist and flourish. More importantly, these physical manifestations of modern capital are simply a piece of the puzzle. Modern capital has moved beyond being controlled by those in elite positions of power.

Capitalism, which we generally define as the hegemonic global economic system, has ultimately been established as the only economic system. No country in the world exists free of the capitalist model. It is more than simple economics; it is a system that generates ideology. It has grown beyond money and trade—it has become a way of thinking. Our social consciousness revolves around it. Our daily existence and experience, our shared cultural ideology, our collective reality, *is* modern capitalism. By hook or by crook, you and I have allowed no knowable reality to exist outside of it.

The economic crash of 2008 serves as an example of how modern capital functions beyond physical economics and maintains ideological illusion. The American government, which is supposedly designed to serve the people and the public good, openly protects the physical and ideological mechanisms of capitalism. When the big banks caused the financial crash of 2008, and the government sponsored a bailout, the government allocated more than 12 trillion public tax dollars[1] to pay for the mistakes (or crimes) of privately owned banking institutions. While there was an initial public outcry, nothing was, or has, changed. No serious enforceable regulations to protect the public were put in place to ensure this could not happen again. With the exception of one investment trader, none of the high-level bankers who caused this crash went to prison, somehow circumventing the legal system designed to protect the people. As of 2015, only $4.8 trillion of the bailout package has been given to the banks.[2] It is interesting that the American news media does not discuss the $8 trillion public dollars (at the time of writing) still being paid out to private corporations, when funding for education and other public services are being cut. No conspiracy, no secrets. All of this is public knowledge reported to the people by mainstream media. Modern capitalism is not only an economic system, it is also an information system that generates public perception and awareness. In effect, it is the ideological structure of our contemporary world, inescapable and omnipresent.

If modern capitalism is responsible for the relegation of UFO discourse to the fringe, the first question we need to ask is: why? To get to an answer, we must "look awry" at UFO discourse, and the systems of power that repress it. We must chip away at the "symbolic order" of modern capital.[3] We must understand that capitalist ideology permeates our cultural reality, and that it uses the bastion of objective truth we call Science to force its ideological agenda.

Science, The Rebel Who Sold Out

When asked about the scientific tracking of UFO sightings and reports during an interview on the Open Minds podcast in 2015, UFO researcher and author Chris Rutkowski responded by saying:

> [This data] is the foundation upon which all the speculation is based. The whole constituent of ufology is based on these reports from the average person... this is what is really being seen. When you strip away all the other stuff, we know these cases are real. Let's try to build on this basis... go from the data outwards rather than from the outside into the data.[4]

The general sciences discredit ufology due to its speculative nature, primarily regarding hypotheses suggesting the existence of an *intelligent Other* visiting Earth. While the scientific community's objection to ufology may be legitimate, good ufologists, like Rutkowski, do not "cry aliens" when a well-documented/credible UFO sighting occurs. Rather, they cry, "What was that? We probably should look into it ..." It is interesting that the same cry was the basis for the birth of the sciences as a social enterprise. The sciences established themselves upon a principle of counter-culture, a revolt against mainstream ideological thinking—people, primarily men, wanted to escape the ancient religious stranglehold on knowledge, and to develop an enlightened observable method by which to understand the world. Today, science is no longer counter cultural, but is now the arbiter of mainstream culture, the self-proclaimed hub by which all knowledge *is*. Ironically, science has become what it rebelled against.

Science has adopted an ideological illusion that it is the only road to "the Truth." Academia has entrenched science into the social worldview as the harbinger of destruction for religion and, if one reads Neil deGrasse Tyson,[5] the destroyer of philosophy. Interestingly, we collectively understand, scientists included, that science does not have all the answers right now. We also understand that future developments will undoubtedly change many of the scientific rules, laws and theories we now "know." However, science, in some strange ironic twist of ideology, is also able to convince people that some ideas are not worth studying. It is a curious phenomenon. Scientists, and people in general, accept the present limitations of the sciences, and its future potential to grow and change, yet, in the same breath, they are able to dismiss other ideas, such as UFOs, as apparent nonsense.

We accept the ideological myths told by the sciences; they "make sense" to us. However, significant scientific "facts" have been proven, and later disproven as human knowledge expands, grows and shifts. As our cultural and social landscape changes, so too does current scientific knowledge. Take Phrenology, for example, a cutting-edge science in the 19th century that attempted to prove the size and shape of one's skull was a measure of intelligence. Obviously, this is nothing more than a debunked pseudoscience today, as all evidence currently contradicts it—but, in the 19th century, brain scientists taught this theory in universities and colleges. From an economic and political standpoint, it was used to justify racism, slavery and colonization. Science was used to justify an economic agenda: the subjugation of a group based upon "scientific facts." Today, the sciences continue to support the power of the corporate elite. While it may not be used openly to dehumanize, as it did centuries ago, it does create a simulated sense of truth, the illusion of objective reality which, actually, is ideology.

That being said, the UFO phenomenon has not been relegated to the sidelines because of scientists themselves. In actuality, scientists do not usually oppose UFO discourse; indeed, like most people, undoubtedly they do not even think about it. It is simply a non-issue for them. They really don't care about it. However, the few scientists who are interested in ufological phenomena are looked at with curiosity. Any scientist who pursues an interest in the subject has a choice to make: they can shut up about their fascination with UFOs and work on the projects that fit within established parameters, or, they will choose option one but continue to work privately on their ufological research. Unfortunately, this work will be slower, as they will have to use their spare time and their own resources. Also they do not have the aid of their peers to review the work. A third option is to "go rogue." They leave their employer and dedicate their life to the study of the UFO phenomenon. There is almost no outside funding for this type of work; the scientists will be ostracized and targeted by the scientific establishment for going "loony." There is simply no organization that works within the mainstream official scientific community that will fund scientific research into UFOs. Why?

According to a report released for the Scientific Integrity Program by the Union of Concerned Scientists:

> Using their vast financial resources, corporations attempt to exert
> influence at every step of both the scientific and policy-making

processes, often to shape decisions in their favor, or to avoid regulation and monitoring of their products. In so doing they often attempt to fundamentally alter the decision-making process.[6]

Between 2005 and 2011, over five thousand scientists were surveyed at nine American federal agencies, including the Food and Drug Administration, the Environmental Protection Agency, and the Department of Agriculture. The results of the survey proved that hundreds of scientists experienced direct interference in their work that "stemmed from corporate influence."[7] The report provides many examples of large pharmaceutical companies, energy companies and various other multinational corporations pressuring scientists, and, more importantly, government regulators, such as the FDA, to be complicit in altering and even hiding scientific findings in order to bring various products and methods to market.

Large multinational corporations make up over 65% of all scientific research and development in the United States alone.[8] Science is controlled by those in already established positions of power, primarily major corporations whose only fiduciary responsibility is to their shareholders and to the promotion of deregulated free market capitalism. It begs the question as to what (or whose) ideologies are being preserved, maintained, or developed, and for what purpose?

We have given "science" a sort of anthropomorphic consciousness, but science is not a literal "thing," rather, it is a collection of socially accepted ideological constructs, methods and mechanisms, financially controlled by economic and political forces. Scientists do not work in a vacuum, able to explore any project they wish, such as UFOs; instead, they are bound to work for various established organizations, which have a wide range of agendas. First of these agendas is the promotion of modern capital, or, at the very least, maintaining the economic and ideological status quo. The sciences, without a doubt, have become the tool of multinational corporations.

We, typically, do not question the scientific establishment, and with good reason. Science is, for the most part, a good thing. It saves lives, creates vaccines, and advances humanity towards a better and easier future. We cannot call for some revolution against science because it is ideological, nor that it promotes a primarily capitalist agenda. All human endeavours are ideological, and all ideologies change over time. More importantly, capitalism itself is undoubtedly here to stay with no perceivable reality outside of the ideology it establishes. There is simply no place "outside" of our social reality from which to revolt.

There is no grand conspiracy or agenda within the scientific or corporate communities to raze UFO discourse. Within the physical economic realm of modern capitalism, ufology and the UFO subculture is irrelevant, at least right now. The elites within the corridors of economic and political power generally have little interest in the UFO subject. It is the ideological constructs and mechanisms established by modern capitalism that constrain the discourse.

The only question we can ask then is, *why do the ideological mechanisms of modern capitalism, which science supports, reject ufology and UFO discourse?*

(Anti-)Capitalism and the UFO

UFO discourse is the antithesis to modern capitalist ideology. While ufologists, and members of the subculture, function within the physical capitalist economic system along with the rest of the planet, there is a sort of hypocrisy to it. To the UFO community, the ideological mechanisms of capitalism are present but not permanent; this is where ideological capital must draw the line and reduce UFO discourse, to attempt to oppress and control it. Capitalism, much like a living organism, deems its own self-preservation as fundamental. However, capitalism is not a predator. It does not hunt down an opposing discourse and destroy it. Instead, it is a survivor. Any discourse or ideology that opposes it will be negotiated back into capitalist ideology, that is, sanitized and marketed, and/or alienated to the fringe as taboo if renegotiation is currently impossible.

Ultimately, UFO discourse has little economic value. Ufology is not a large-scale producer or consumer in the economy. While some aspects of the discourse have been negotiated into capitalist structures, such as television shows, books, magazines, conferences, and other consumable goods, the majority have not. More importantly, the consumable aspects created by UFO discourse are economically inconsequential. Most UFO discourse exists in a free format, such as blogs, websites, and social media platforms. While these formats do generate some economic benefit, via advertisements or subscriptions, the actual dollar amount is miniscule and allows for very few members of the UFO subculture to live off their ufological work.

This is really no surprise to anyone involved in UFO community. Economics is only one piece of the capitalist puzzle and, in our modern world, a very small piece indeed. While someone can explore the actual financial impacts that ufology has on the economy, it is ultimately unimportant here. We need to explore the ideological aspects of UFO discourse and how it is in opposition to modern capitalism.

The UFO discourse opposes modern capitalist ideology in three key ways.

1. *Predisposition for Dissent:*

If we examine UFO literature, as well as the vast collection of websites, blogs, YouTube videos, and other discursive media that comes from the United States, it all generally carries with it a tone of dissent. The UFO subculture has a certain feeling towards the government, the military-industrial complex, and the establishments of authority, such as the corporate and scientific communities: it is that they are not worthy of trust. Conspiracy theories, alleged whistleblowers, and leaked top secret documents all lend to this ideological build-up of opposition to elite power structures. While much of this opposition is misguided, conspiratorial, and even ridiculous, the culture of the discourse is problematic for the general ideology of modern capitalism.

It is not the overt dissention which is problematic, as ideological capitalism merely negotiates dissenting ideologies into itself, as it has done with Civil Rights, Punk rock, and many other similar "anti-establishment" movements. Rather, it is the rate at which the dissent moves, shifts and readjusts. While certain aspects of government, or other powerful corporations and institutions, are perpetually under scrutiny from the UFO subculture, the "flavor of the week" changes so often that the dissenting ideology is essentially non-negotiable. The constant shifting of who can and cannot be trusted is chaotic and seemingly follows no rhyme or reason. In simple terms, the tendrils of dissent move and spread so quickly in varying directions, with no discernible pattern, that modern capitalism is impotent in its continuous endeavor to subjugate dissenting ideologies into itself. Since it has no way of containing the dissent, it must make it unpalatable; it must ensure the dissent is relegated to the fringes. However, this has become increasingly difficult, especially since Wikileaks and Edward Snowden have muddied the playing field with regard to trusting authorities. According to polls conducted in 2015, roughly 50% of the American population believes in at least one major conspiracy.[9]

2. *Culture of the Disenfranchised:*

Capitalism fundamentally requires an alienated and disenfranchised group—the poor—since economic capital cannot be distributed evenly. Capitalism ensures that certain groups remain economically disenfranchised; however, for this situation to be maintained, the disenfranchised themselves must believe in the ideological illusions generated by capitalism. During the *Occupy* protests of 2011, there was a surge of anti-capitalist sentiment, so much so that there was significant potential for a major disruption of capitalist ideologies. However, because much of "the 99%" were unable to envision a reality outside of the capitalist illusion, the *Occupy* movement's wave broke on the ideological rocks.

Dissidents of mainstream ideologies, by default, exist upon the fringes, alienated by the mechanisms of power. This distrust of established social order has forced many members of the UFO subculture into a dual state—they function within physical economic capitalism, but work against it ideologically, often unknowingly. The illusion is more important than the economics: if people cease to engage in the ideological illusion, then there is a major upheaval to the status quo. The upheaval will not necessarily end capitalism, but will force it to undergo a significant adjustment, the most damaging of aspect of which is a democratization of power.

While many in UFO discourse view Disclosure, exopolitics or the channeling phenomenon as purely speculative, these are key examples of movements within UFO discourse that attempt to democratize power. While many disclosurists, 'exopoliticians,' and channelers are simply con-artists, the ideological perception of the phenomenon by the subculture generates a call of equality, free of production and consumption. In essence, the Disclosure and exopolitics movements and the channeling phenomenon "promise" to reshape the world into one free of wealth or poverty, where all are equal and consumerism is no longer necessary. They attempt to create a worldview free of capitalism itself. While a *deus ex machina* style visitation from an *intelligent Other* would potentially shatter modern capital, that has yet to occur. Rather, mainstream ideologies are in contention with a subculture which is attempting to envision an end to capitalism. The picture is unclear, but even considering that such a picture may exist is unacceptable. The magician, who uses gaudy trinkets and mesmerizing lights to distract, cannot have the audience thinking about how he performs the trick, lest they understand the mechanisms used to dupe them.

    3. Democratization of Power:

    The final method in which the UFO discourse subverts modern capital is via ideological democratization. Many philosophers and critics plainly suggest that real democracy cannot exist under the capitalist system. There are many reasons for this, but Noam Chomsky states it here:

> If we mean by Democracy, citizens having an equal share in participating and determining decisions that affect the society, then capitalism, in any form, is inconsistent with Democracy... any form of capitalism that is likely to exist will have sharp inequalities because it's based on hierarchy, domination, production for profit and not need, accumulation of capital, deprivation of others, subordination of people who have to sell their labor in order to survive. Of course that is going to translate automatically into any political arrangement...[10]

    In the previous two methods by which UFO discourse subverts capitalist ideologies, we see a subculture that functions upon dissent and is therefore disenfranchised by that dissent. Much like Nada in *They Live*, UFO culture looks upon the world differently. While participants in the discourse may not be aware of their opposing ideology, it exists, nonetheless, and modern capital is unable fully to negotiate that threat into something it can fundamentally control as it has before; it ensures, then, that the UFO discourse exists in the taboo fringe. However, by doing so, the subculture has gained a pseudo-freedom—it can function unhindered and establish its own set of ideologies.

    One of these ideological principles is that within UFO discourse and subculture, there exists no hierarchy, domination, or subordination. It is a discourse with no locus of control, no elites, and no ivory tower that establishes *ideological truth*. There is no established power in the discourse, therefore power moves openly between constant shifts in ideas. The sciences, and any other academic or mainstream discourse, have visible establishments which govern. They establish rules, hierarchies, and systems to control who is a member of the discourse, and what the discursive ideologies are. The UFO discourse has no such mechanism; it is democratized, with members of the subculture able freely to express their own ideologies, which vary from reasoned logic to utter speculative hokum. While this may be a key reason as to why ufology, as a field of study, has made little productive and objective progress, the discourse itself has functioned in this state since its inception. It is, in simple terms, a field of study which is completely democratized. It is an example of a living and functioning discourse that counters modern ideological capital—it creates a pseudo-reality that does not require mainstream official ideologies in order to exist; it is in this democratic state where modern ideological capital is impotent, unable to entrench itself and establish ideological order.

Into a *Terra Obscura*

Ideological capitalism is not some beast that needs to be slayed by "free thinkers." We, the free thinkers included, are the beast. In the act of destroying the illusions of our reality, we would destroy ourselves. There is no perceivable line between the ideology of modern capital and our reality. The two are intertwined because we, as a society, have forced them to be so. The UFO discourse is not an agent of change, destined to end the illusion of capitalist forces; rather, it is a world view, which calls those illusionary forces into question. UFO discourse does not fit into the ideological reality of the mainstream. It is by virtue of the discourse's chaotic nature that ideological capitalism has no choice but to relegate it into the taboo fringe, and negotiate it into mainstream consumption when it can.

Ufology, then, as a field of study, and the subculture that subscribes to its tenants, are at a crossroads. It will require more than UFO investigators, researchers, and scientists to continue progressing forward. It will also require a critical theory, a philosophical approach, that will continue to examine not only the discourse itself, but the reality in which the discourse exists. The ideological reality of modern capital, as well as other social mechanisms and structures, will continue to shift, and, with those shifts, the UFO discourse is affected. We must begin to explore that ebb and flow, to perceive the illusion of the ideology and, thereby, resist and change it. Ufology must continue to push towards democratization, towards a shared body of knowledge and ideas that cut against the grain of mainstream official culture.

How then can UFO discourse thrive in the capitalist ideological reality currently predisposed to ensure its relegation to the cultural edge? In simple terms, it cannot and it will not. There is no future for ufology, and UFO discourse as a whole, in the mainstream. If a grandiose extraterrestrial contact event occurred tomorrow, and the UFO question was forced into mainstream ideology, ufology would die an instant death as the entire subject would quickly become negotiated into the general sciences and, therefore, into capitalist ideological structures. If we assume that the status quo is maintained, and there is no public announcement regarding extraterrestrials, ufology will remain where it is. What can only occur then is a grassroots movement, which always operates against the current ideological reality. It will take scientists, researchers, investigators, philosophers and critics who exist in the fringe, open to a continuous shaking and fragmenting of socio-cultural order. The UFO discourse will continue to function in an authentic state, completely democratized, with all of the issues that come with such a relativism. The mainstream scientific establishment will never adopt ufology; rather, ufology must adopt the scientists. It must do the same with theorists, philosophers and other academics who are able to thrive within the fringe, instead of shy away from it. Many of my colleagues in ufological circles would argue that it is essential for UFO discourse to move away from the theological, and towards the scientific method. I would agree with them; however, the razor cuts both ways, and the ideological mechanisms of the sciences can be as dogmatic as the religious tenets of the UFO believers.

The next generation of ufologists are beginning to accept the fact that the lack of ufological progress is evidence enough to show that change is required and, ultimately, unstoppable. Mainstream capitalist culture has no choice but to resist UFO discourse, as it calls into question the ideological illusion, which capitalism must maintain. The future of ufology is a *terra obscura*, an unknown land, which has yet to be trod. Much like the drifter in *They Live*, we wander through the shadows, blinded by the illusion, but aware that there is a path laid for us by the strange UFO phenomenon.

ANARCHY IN THE UFO!

Red Pill Junkie

"Introduce a little anarchy. Upset the established order, and everything becomes chaos. I'm an agent of chaos."

—*Batman: The Dark Knight* (2008)

Let us start with a somewhat impertinent question: Why are you *doing* this? I mean, why do you find yourself presently with your hands on this book, reading these words at this particular moment? Don't you have anything better to do with your time? Friends to meet, bills to pay, a lawn to mow, or a TV show to binge-watch? If the answer lies in the fact that you are interested in the topic of this volume—the UFO phenomenon—well *hooray*, and good for you, fellow weirdo. But is that it?

Have you ever bothered to pry *deeper* into the origin of this odd interest of yours? Tried to understand the fuel driving your passion for a subject perceived as an absurdity by most of humanity and our social institutions?

One of the reasons you're reading this essay is because I, its author, have too held a lifelong fascination—nay, *obsession* really—with UFOs. Like most people lured by the hypnotic power of those bright, multi-colored objects, throughout the years I consumed claim after claim of encounters between witnesses and this *Other* reality, as if the pages of those books now gathering dust in my library had been laced with an addictive substance.

I took my fix of reports and believed the theories proposed by the so-called experts in the field, only to throw them away and replace them with *other* solutions to the mystery submitted by charismatic mavericks once they had succeeded their predecessors. Accounts, which I first regarded as genuine evidence of otherworldly visitation, were eventually discarded as crude frauds, whereas new cases were hailed by newcomers as proof that Contact was *just* around the corner. If all this sounds familiar to you, dear reader, is because it is the typical cycle into which all UFO enthusiasts eventually fall.

Sadly, most of them never do find a way out of it ...

Unlike most aficionados, I decided to stop pedalling the wheel for a moment and approach the problem from a different perspective: I took Jacques Vallée's speculations to task and shifted my focus not onto what UFOs *are*, per se, but rather onto what they reportedly *do*, and the effect of their presence (whether real or imagined) in the affairs of men. Suddenly, the disc once presumed to serve as a vehicle for traversing outer space became a mirror for surveying inner space. And, thus, I finally caught a glimpse of Truth—if not about the nature of UFOs, at least about the nature of me.

For you see, dear reader, the self-truth UFOs taught me some time ago is that I'm an anarchist. And if you keep reading these pages, that proves deep down you're one too—whether you want to admit it or not.

So, *do what thou wilt*, friend, and read on... or not.

~

"Uuuugh. Somebody please tell me what I'm doing here..."

"Doing? You're doing what any sane man in your appalling circumstances would do.

You're going mad."

—ALAN MOORE, *THE KILLING JOKE* (1988)

For an adult, there's no easier way to recapture the feelings of early childhood than by contemplating the night sky. Children are not only constantly exploring the world that's new to them, they are also learning to recognize and control the fiery impulses fuelling their young bodies, which is why most of their experiences are a mixture of conflicting emotions: Sadness combined with happiness, curiosity blended with repulsion, wonder tinged with fear.

Gazing at the stars brings forth the inner kid in all of us, because that cosmic vastness not only gives humans an incredibly disproportionate sense of scale against which to compare our fleeting existence, but it also serves as an unsympathetic reminder that all those energies unfolding before our eyes are *totally* beyond our control. Measured by the stellar yardstick, we're but a bunch of helpless rugrats.

To understand a thing, though, is to begin slowly to have power over that thing. Our species has come a long way since those nights sitting by the campfire, when our nomadic ancestors played to connect those distant dots to create gods and monsters suited for their idiosyncratic mythologies; now we realize those points are suns like our own, so distant that many of them are but a ghostly echo of their former self. And even though those celestial bodies won't bow to our will (not in the way we've already started to tame other formidable forces of nature) they have, nonetheless, yielded to the might of our reason, and we learned to calculate their goings and comings over the horizon with startling accuracy. Predictability begets familiarity, and regularity is an antidote to anxiety.

Other more random phenomena, which were universally considered bad omens by ancient cultures all around the globe, such as the passing of lonely comets or meteor strikes, have also started to fall into the cycle of regularity. Yes, we know sooner or later some vagrant space boulder will challenge our title as the dominant species of Earth—a challenge the dinosaurs failed—but at least we now know it's not a question of *If*, but of *When*.

In his globally acclaimed TV series, *Cosmos*,[1] Carl Sagan tells his audience how, during the age of Copernicus and Kepler, astronomy became the first *true* modern science by way of supplanting superstition with logic. Glimpsing into the exquisite machinery of the universal clockwork with brand-new mechanical extensions to our senses (telescopes) and applying the principles which became the backbone of the Scientific Method, gave those early natural philosophers enough confidence that there was nothing in Creation which could remain forever hidden from Man's comprehension; the world we inhabit today is the direct result of said confidence. By first mapping the charts of the heavens, we eventually moulded the face of the Earth.

And yet there remain portents and apparitions still haunting our skies. They have proven so unruly and resistant to reassuringly conventional explanations that they've become the biggest threat to our trust in the dominion of Reason—to the point that the vast edifice that modern science has erected, since the days of Galileo, could seemingly come crashing down, were its stewards merely to entertain the existence of these visions and grant a crumb of credence to those who have borne witness to them: "Return to the age of chimeras haunting the nights of our forefathers? Never!" Thus, the logical route of the stewards of this vital scaffolding is the path of denial and ridicule. A method which inevitably backfired in the most unsettling ways ...

Psychedelic raconteur Terence McKenna (1946—2000) was someone who had as much respect for the arrogant orthodoxy of academia as for the naive obtuseness of most UFO advocates, who seem unable to conceive of the phenomenon outside the imaginings of a 1950s pulp sci-fi novel. During his presentation for the "Angels, Aliens & Archetypes" conference held in San Francisco in November of 1987, titled *Shamanic Approaches to the UFO*, McKenna posited that the phenomenon's primordial task seemed to be neither charting the flora and fauna of our planet, like some space-age version of Charles Darwin, nor establishing a foothold for an impending colonization fleet. What UFOs were *really* doing, in his eyes, was something far more subtle and pernicious: eroding our faith in science, and acting as an antidote to a scientific paradigm spawned by the ideas of Copernicus, Galileo and Kepler, which ultimately has brought us to the brink of total collapse:

> Rationalism [and] scientific technology which began and came out of the scholasticism of the Middle Ages, and the quite legitimate wish to glorify God through appreciation of His natural world, turned into a kind of demonic pact, a kind of descent into the underworld, the Nekya, if you will, leading to the present cultural and political impasse that involves massive stockpiles of atomic weapons, huge propagandized populations cut off of to any knowledge of their real histories, male-dominated organizations plying their message of lethal destruction and inevitable historical advance. And into this situation comes suddenly an anomaly, something which cannot be explained. I believe that is the purpose to the UFO, to inject uncertainty into the male-dominated, paternalistic, rational, solar myth under which we are suffering ... The UFO is nothing more than an assertion of herself by the Goddess into history, saying to science and paternalistically-governed and driven organizations: 'You have gone far enough! We are going to turn the world upside down. Your science is going to be shown up for what it is: nothing more than a pleasant metaphor, usefully extrapolated into the production of toys for wealthy children.[2]

Had Robert Anton Wilson, Pope of Discordianism[3] (the philosophical movement centered around the exaltation of chaos and disorder over conformity and order), been seated among the audience that day, I imagine he would have risen up at that very moment shouting "Hail Eris!!" In Greek mythology, Eris was the goddess of Discord, responsible, according to some legends, of the famous war of Troy, for giving the hero Paris a golden apple and instructing him to present it as a prize to "the most beautiful" of the female deities—a task without hope of a happy resolution, given how the Greek pantheon was famous for being subject to the same base emotions as their human creatures, like vanity and jealousy. It almost feels as if the flying saucer is the modern version of Eris' golden apple, thrown into the skies just to anger her cousin Athena, goddess of Wisdom and Philosophy. We mortals seem to be trapped inside a cosmic game whose rules and stakes we may never comprehend—yet that does not mean we all can't get a kick out of it, like Discordians do.

Just what is it about the UFO that makes it so revolting to the classical tenets of science, anyway? I believe that, ultimately, the antagonism is more ideological than theoretical: if we disregard the usual refutations proposed by the inheritors of Carl Sagan's legacy—i.e. the inconceivable gulfs between observable stellar islands, the massive amounts of energy required to traverse them, and the sheer richness of the cosmic archipelago compounding the irrelevance of our own little reef of the Milky Way—there remains the one element which, ironically, joins both believers and skeptics in their rejection of the high strangeness emanating from shunned close encounter reports: The nonsensical, non-regimented nature of those alleged interactions, which can be classified only as "Trickstery."

We've mentioned the 1950s pulp fiction which helped popularize the stereotype of interstellar visitation during the post-war years, and, even though some of those same publications also assisted in disseminating the earliest sightings and the nascent flying saucer myths,[4] the record shows most that "serious" sci-fi authors of that era viewed the UFO subject with contempt: Asimov, Clarke and Bradbury always scorned the phenomenon and paved the way for the modern atheist-based skeptic movement still championed by the likes of Richard Dawkins and Michael Shermer.

But why would liberal freethinkers, who tried to make a living out of conjuring tales of a universe pulsating with sentient life, made accessible through the same scientific ingenuity which helped defeat fascism in our own world, be so against the notion of non-human interlopers? Their rejections are better understood when we consider the oblique modus operandi of these entities, which flies in the face of the popular vision of how interstellar ambassadors *should* conduct themselves when crossing our planetary borders. The clichéd "saucer on the White House lawn, take me to your leader" scenario clearly holds no appeal for the UFO intelligences. Instead they give cardboard-tasting 'pancakes' to a lonely chicken farmer in Wisconsin. Instead of gathering genetic samples from the most prominent members of our species, such as Albert Einstein or Stephen Hawking, these space veterinarians rely on medieval methods to conduct husbandry with Brazilian farmers (Antonio Vilas Boas) while collecting sperm and ova from post office employees (Barney Hill), Christian housewives (Betty Andreasson) and horror novelists (Whitley Strieber), to name a few of the most prominent abductees. These darn aliens will simply *not* follow the proper channels!

Furthermore, rather than hailing to our complex, mathematically-coded salutes sent through the electromagnetic spectrum—the "*logical*" way to conduct a productive exchange with an alien intelligence—the UFO phenomenon appears to shun the need for expensive (read, *exclusive*) interfaces, and resorts instead to tricksterish displays of arcane symbolism seemingly intended to bypass the waking mind and subliminally to affect the human Id in such a way that it seeks to shake the consciousness off any previously-held orthodox preconceptions. One example of these symbolically-charged stagings is the eschatological visions Betty Andreasson was subjected to after she was taken by Gray-like entities to what was seemingly another world: An enormous, glowing eagle reduced to ash in phoenix-like fashion, reborn into a hideous gray worm.[4] The oneiric quality of these fringe cases is what has driven many investigators to relegate them to the realm of dreams and nightmares; but is that the sensible thing to do when facing a phenomenon which constantly defies our boundaries of rationality?

Yet another example of the unorthodox semiology surrounding this mystery can be found in the controversial crop circles. Opinion is fiercely divided in the UFO community on whether the seasonal agro-glyphs appearing in the fields of England and other countries are the result of direct non-human intervention or simply anonymous human artwork. But even the few "croppies" who have come forward to claim circle ownership—for example, Matthew Williams, the only person ever convicted under British law for making a circle[5]—allude to a high strangeness surrounding the formations, implying even the man-made circles are the result of a "psychic" collaboration between the artists and an undisclosed agency. The result of this covert collusion are the strikingly beautiful symbols and mandalas, which seem to employ geometry to impart lessons of a primordially spiritual nature, even though the angry owners of the fields in which they keep cropping up (no pun intended) regard them not as art or high forms of spiritual expression, but as pranks threatening their livelihood. Whatever the reason behind these transgressional formations, they are NOT the prime number sets Sagan and his colleagues would expect to receive from a sensible civilization.[6] And perhaps therein lies the problem ...

What keeps hard-nosed UFO investigators awake at night isn't that the records are littered with numerous cases which defy a clear-cut "rational" explanation with their unnecessary absurdity—poltergeist activity after a close encounter, cryptid sightings surrounding an alleged landing, cattle mutilations and bizarre apparitions inside the infamous

Skinwalker ranch property,[7] synchronicities and precognition, etc. No, the truly unsettling thing is entertaining the possibility that these cases are *not* the outliers, but proof that the phenomenon is absurd by design.

Arthur C. Clarke once wrote that any sufficiently advanced technology would be indistinguishable from magic. Perhaps he forgot to consider how any sufficiently advanced mentality would equally be indistinguishable from *Madness*. In the search for the *Other* by which to gauge our own self, what we're really hoping for is a mirror depiction of our own expectations only *slightly* ahead of us such that it may still be comprehensible. Yet a truly *alien* mind would be from our earthly perspective, and by the very definition of the word, *crazy*. The reflection would be like a twisted image in a carnivalesque hall of mirrors—we gaze in fear, unprepared for the bizarre impression.

For there are cases which even the people open to the possibility of an alien presence in our world find deeply unsettling. The attacks suffered by the victims of Spring Heeled Jack in the 19th century, the Mad Gasser of Mattoon of the 1930s, the panicked teenagers pursued by Mothman in the 1960s, and even the odd encounter that Woodrow Derenberger had with an enigmatic individual who identified himself with the nonsensical name of Indrid Cold,[8] an innocuous human-looking being unable able to assuage Derenberger's understandable fear despite flashing him a large smile. Here we find yet another powerful right-brain symbol in the form of the grinning man archetype, which made its first literary appearance in Victor Hugo's *The Man Who Laughs*, and eventually morphed into the modern icon of *Batman*'s The Joker.

It's not hard to make a case that, of all comic book characters to have emerged from the pages of pop culture, The Joker is by far the one powerful enough to cross into our reality. Paranormal investigator and cryptozoologist Loren Coleman, author of *The Copycat Effect*, has studied the effects of The Joker icon in real-life criminal cases, such as the Aurora mass shooting of 2012.[9] James Eagan Holmes, the only perpetrator accused by the authorities for the crime, had dyed his hair red and purportedly called himself "The Joker" when he was finally detained by the police. In 2015 Holmes was given 12 consecutive life sentences, one for each life he took. Sadly, Coleman has records of more felonies allegedly inspired by the fictional killer clown in his online blog, Twilight Language.

"I'm an agent of chaos," Heath Ledger's Joker confesses to a horribly disfigured Harvey Dent (Aaron Eckhart) in an iconic scene in *The Dark Knight*.[10] In that regard, Batman's maniacal nemesis may have more in common with the UFO phenomenon than we dare to admit. The UFO mystery seems to stem from a liminal realm in between normal life and total madness: a twilight space where light and dark can give way to either our most wondrous fantasies, or our most horrible nightmares.

~

"I'm not a schemer. I try to show the schemers how, pathetic, their attempts to control things really are."

—BATMAN, *THE DARK KNIGHT* (2008)

The UFO disruption is not only a threat to the authority of scientific orthodoxy, it fundamentally defies every conceivable paradigm that human society is built upon, in almost every sphere one can envision: religion, economics, communication, and state politics, to name but a few. The latter is particularly vulnerable to a phenomenon that seems to delight in displaying how pathetic our attempts are to paint human authority as an ostensibly superior force. There's no better example of this than the numerous cases of rogue objects trespassing into nuclear silos, terrorizing the personnel in charge of safeguarding the most important defensive link in the US national security chain, and "adversely affecting"—to paraphrase retired Col. Charles Halt, key witness in the famous Rendlesham case[11]—the functionality of the atomic arsenal threatening human continuity in this biosphere.

If the UFO intelligence(s) have been trying to establish contact, then clearly it is not a top-down type of contact meant to involve appointed representatives of government institutions. The reports we've gathered tell us it is far more egalitarian: a grass-roots type of contact involving individuals from all walks of life, which only seems to make sense if we accept two propositions: 1. The intelligence(s) have little use for traditional social structure; and 2. it or they are possibly not bound by the constraints of space and time the way we are. If time is no issue, then perhaps the best way to establish a dialog with humankind is on an individual basis.

Of course, such a non-protocolary development would never sit well with governing authorities. The CIA-sponsored Robertson panel of 1953 concluded that reports of Unidentified Flying Objects were themselves *more* threatening to the stability of the country than the *actual* possibility of an extraterrestrial intervention. It recommended a smear campaign to minimize or ridicule close encounters in the press, and the monitoring of UFO groups for fear that they could easily be manipulated by Soviet agents. The same approach was taken with self-proclaimed "contactees"—individuals from all walks of American society claiming direct contact with the flying saucer occupants, whom they fondly regarded as our "space brothers." In his 2010 book, *Contactees*,[12] Nick Redfern writes how the most prominent figures in the contactee movement were closely monitored by FBI operatives who attended their lectures and made reports on what the speakers said to their audience. Imagine the consternation of J. Edgar Hoover when reading that George Adamski's Venusian friends regarded socialism as the most perfect form of human government. It is my opinion the Cosmic Love propagandized by the Contactees of the 1950s paved the way to the Free Love counterculture of the 1960s, and the governmental authorities viewed both grassroots movements in the same manner: as a threat, graver and more insidious than an open confrontation with the communist bloc.

But what of the other side of the former Iron Curtain? Most historians would agree in naming the fall of the Berlin Wall (which started in June 13, 1990) as marking the beginning of the Soviet Union's collapse. My own personal calendar, however, identifies September 21, 1989 as the true date when the winds of change started blowing. This date corresponds with the commencement of remarkable UFO activity in the small city of Voronezh, involving the apparent landing of craft, sightings of enormous humanoid creatures, terrifying interactions with local boys, and more astounding accounts which would have made even the most trashy pulp fiction writer of the 1950s think twice before submitting such stories to his publisher.[13] It is a remarkable case in the modern annals of ufology, more so for the fact it was able to trespass the traditional boundaries of censorship erected by the Kremlin decades ago which used to stop UFO accounts dead in their tracks. For many decades, this imbalance of reporting gave the impression the UFO phenomenon was exclusive to Western nations; the dissemination of the Voronezh case is, thus, another testament to Gorbachev's Perestroika reforms. Empires bloom and crumble, and yet the mystery of the UFO remains, but the fact that a once-mighty empire was willing to acknowledge its powerlessness over a mysterious, external influence is truly remarkable.

That which is a nuisance to the governing authority becomes appealing to those with a distaste for orders and regulation, and the unruliness of UFOs seems to stir something in the core of the most marginalized layers of society. This is by no means a modern trend. In his seminal book, *Passport to Magonia*, Jacques Vallée puts this into perspective:

Celestial phenomena seem to have been so commonplace in the Japanese skies during the Middle Ages that they influenced human events in a direct way. Panics, riots and disruptive social movements were often linked to celestial apparitions. The Japanese peasants had the disagreeable tendency to interpret the "signs from heaven" as strong indications that their revolts and demands against the feudal system or against foreign invaders were just, and as assurance that their rebellions would be crowned with success.[14]

Rebellion, revolt, and social unrest. I first mused about their possible link to UFOs in the summer of 2011,[15] when the streets of London were besieged by riots which had originally erupted in Tottenham. It was during that time that Mike Sewell, a BBC Radio 5 sports reporter, begrudgingly made public his own sighting of a large disc-shaped object on the morning of August 4, while he was driving to Stansted airport. Looking at the distance between these two London locations through applications like Google Maps yields a relative proximity, but finding a direct correlation between UFO activity and social unrest in the same geographical area throughout history is a tricky proposition at best. In his entry on "UFO waves" for *The Mammoth Encyclopedia of Extraterrestrial Encounters*,[16] Martin S. Kottmeyer points to the high levels of UFO activity in the United States, coinciding with times of deep disturbances in American society during the mid-1960s, as possible indicators for the validity of the "Paranoia Theory" as a psychological explanation to the UFO phenomenon. The paranoia theory extrapolates from the work of behavioral psychologists like Dr. Norman Cameron of the University of Wisconsin, and interprets UFOs as a form of "paranoid ideation," possibly triggered by moments of "deep national shame and humiliation." While the anti-war protests and the Watts riots occurring simultaneously with the UFO wave of 1965 seems to fit the bill, other periods of social instability and general anxiety won't align so easily to this theory, such as the low level of UFO activity registered by Blue Book during the Cuban missile crisis of 1962.

Still, given how several countries famous for their high levels of UFO activity in past decades also suffered periods of social repression and political authoritarianism—e.g. Brazil, Argentina, Chile, Mexico, etc.—looking for a possible link between this non-terrestrial phenomenon and episodes of earthly unrest is not without appeal. Of course, if a statistical and reliable link *were* to be corroborated, and we eschew the simplistic interpretation of UFOs as psychological delusions induced by mass hysteria, we'd still be left with the insurmountable task of finding an explanation for the activity, not unlike the metaphorical "chicken and egg" conundrum: are UFOs somehow attracted or conductive to manifestations of profound social change, or is the phenomenon directly or indirectly responsible for such events?

Investigators like Mack Maloney[17] have written extensively about the proliferation of UFO sightings during times of war, and yet extrapolating further than what the reports inform us of—i.e. that strange unconventional activity has often been observed in the theater of war throughout history—propels us to speculate as to whether the UFOs are merely observing our exploits of tribal combat as dispassionate witnesses, or if they are somehow intervening in the balance of those battles, the way Homer depicted it in his narration of the classic war which would give reference to all human conflagrations past, present and future—the Iliad. Do these entities give enough of a damn about the welfare and prospect of our species that they feel the need to foster the erosion and upending of stagnant structures of power from time to time?

Or, do they just delight in inspiring mischief in our world for their own personal and inscrutable amusement?

We've briefly explored periods of externalized turmoil, but what about *internalized* turmoil? Delving into the problem of UFOs one must, eventually, approach it from the point of view of human perception: its limitations and susceptibility through different factors, which can either distort, numb or sometimes even enhance it according to the given circumstances and particulars of the individual. Seriah Az-kath, host of the weekly radio show *Where Did the Road Go?*[18] which delves with all sorts of fringe and paranormal topics, has personally experienced a high degree of strangeness bumping into his daily life, which has left him with more questions than answers, along with a passion to pursue this topic from unconventional perspectives. One of Askath's experiences happened back in the year 2000. As he was driving to his radio station one night at around 11pm, he observed what seemed to be a gigantic, brightly-lit object hovering over Cayuga lake, New York.[19] He pulled over and rolled down the window, yet, despite its apparent massiveness, the object was completely silent. The eerie encounter stopped as unexpectedly as it had begun when the bright lights dropped below the tree line and were out of sight. Seriah asked around and searched for UFO reports the next day but, as of the time of this writing, he seems to have been the sole experiencer of this close encounter, which might be explained by the sparse population around that area and how late it was.

Years later, when author and researcher Mike Clelland[20] astutely asked about his state of mind around that time, Seriah conceded his life was "a complete chaos" back then, going through several upsetting changes and developments. A fact which raises the question on whether his internal mood was an influential factor conducive to the sighting, and makes one wonder if a hypothetical passenger riding with him would have been able to perceive the same thing... if anything at all.

Are UFOs, then, akin to "crisis apparitions" or poltergeist activity, which parapsychologists have tried to link to the unruly "psychic" energy unconsciously released by troubled pubescent children? Paranormal researchers have sought for a "Unified Theory" capable of linking disparate phenomena, which some suspect have more in common than we'd care to realize—PSI, ghostly manifestations, cryptid sightings and UFO encounters. While many still find such propositions absurd and do all they can to keep their ufological peas from touching their cryptozoology carrots or phantasmagorical potatoes on their paranormal plate, others have come to the realization that consciousness plays a significant role in all of these phenomena. In all of these manifestations, whatever the triggering input (internal, external or a convoluted combination of both), it is human consciousness which is perceiving said input and parsing it through a finely tuned "cultural filter;" and while geographical location and chronological factors will surely play a role in the precipitation of UFO encounters, proposing that some individuals seem more "sensitive" or "attractive" to such anomalies (even if only transitorily due to temporal circumstances) seems not too unreasonable.

Internal turmoil and lack of rigidity are not just the earmarks of adolescence: they are also intrinsic to the creativity-prone, which is possibly the reason why artistic types tend to show a higher interest in the UFO phenomenon than people who choose a more conventional (read "conformist") lifestyle; or, at least, they are more outspoken about it. From John Lennon's famous observation of a UFO over New York on August 23rd, 1974[21]—and let's not forget Lennon had left Yoko Ono and was staying with his secretary-turned-lover May Pang, as possible indication of his state of mind at the time—to David Bowie's reported sightings and life-long interest in extraterrestrial life and mysticism, it hints not only to the allure which the subject has for people with iconoclastic tendencies, but it also gives reason to speculate how such attitudes might yield a better understanding of the phenomenon than those who observe it from a more fixed paradigm. Consider Bowie's astute hindsight about a sighting he had while traveling through the English countryside with a friend:

> I believe that what I saw was not the actual object, but a projection of my own mind trying to make sense of this quantum topological doorway into dimensions beyond our own. It's as if our dimension is but one among an infinite number of others. [22]

A finer, more elegant, and more sophisticated explanation to this mind-boggling mystery, I feel, than of those who are certain these craft hail from Zeta Reticuli II.

~

"Noise is relative to the silence preceding it. The more absolute the hush, the more shocking the thunderclap."

—ALAN MOORE, *V FOR VENDETTA*.

In his case to show the modern UFO phenomenon as being the same as the belief in the Faerie realm from old Europe or other folkloric customs around the world—only now clothed with the appropriate veneer of space visitation suited for 20th-century sensibilities—Vallée reminds us of how interaction with non-human intelligences has always been dissuaded by the Status Quo... to the point, even, of using the penalty of death as the ultimate deterrent, stereotypically portrayed by the effigy of the witch's pyre. The result of this suppression was to force this body of knowledge to find refuge underground, spawning hermeticism in the Middle Ages. In seeking communion with these entities, one can delineate a tradition beginning with alchemists Facius Cardan and Paracelsus, going all the way to the George Adamski and the contactees from the "golden age" of the modern flying saucer era. Many modern students of the phenomenon would point to Aleister Crowley as a bridge between the early alchemists, summoning sylphs with arcane rituals, and the common citizens who claimed to be ambassadors of the Space Brothers. Indeed, Crowley sought conference with metaphysical beings through various (and sometimes devious) means, and claimed to have succeeded. One of those beings is popularly identified with the monosyllabic name of "Lam," and, while Crowley's pictorial depiction of it is interpreted by some as a psychic self-portrait,[23] others see a striking resemblance to the archetypal Gray alien.[24] Another "transmundane" entity that Crowley purportedly contacted was Aiwass, who passed along the anarchic commandment upon which the law of Thelema was structured: "Do what thou wilt shall be the whole of the law."

What does "Do what thou wilt" really mean, anyway? According to students of Thelema, Crowley didn't simply mean to satisfy one's petty whims and desires, but finding one's true path or purpose in life, the "true will" or higher purpose. In children's literature The magical land of do-as-you-please—accessible by befriending denizens of the fairy-kind, according to British author Enid Blyton in her book series *The Faraway Tree*—inspired comic book writer and Chaos magician Alan Moore when he created his own treatise on modern anarchy, *V for Vendetta*, arguably the most influential piece of popular culture in the last three decades;[25] a testament to its relevance is simply the ubiquitousness of Guy Fawkes' smirking facade in any form of modern civil protest—the grinning man archetype emerges again.

V, the superhuman terrorist hellbent on overthrowing the fascistic regime ruling over a disturbingly familiar dystopian England, explains to secondary character *Evey* how do-as-you-please needs not be interpreted in the same violent manner embraced by the Manson family, who slit the throat of the '60s psychedelic revolution to the tune of Helter Skelter. "Anarchy [means] without leaders, not without order," says V. True order, for Moore, comes from voluntary acceptance of personal boundaries, without the need of a regulatory body imposing any limitations upon individuals.

But anarchy, according to Moore, must be preceded by a chaotic stage in which all the obsolete structures upholding the status quo must be disrupted and obliterated. Those structures can be either tangible symbols, as in the case of the old parliament building destroyed by V in Moore's graphic novel, or abstract ones like the respectability and trust in mainstream media.

After the Condon Report, issued by the University of Colorado, gave the U.S. Air Force the long-sought justification to stop paying attention publicly to the UFO phenomenon, the press was also given permission no longer to take the issue seriously—a process that had already started with the Robertson panel. Ironically, the giggle factor imposed on the topic by mainstream media is one of the reasons that newspapers and TV news have become almost irrelevant in the 21st Century. The early Internet bloomed with online forums and chat rooms devoted to fringe topics never discussed by traditional media—alien abductions, Area 51 and the assassination of JFK—and has now turned into the preferred medium by which Millennials absorb the news. The veneer of officialdom is no longer a valuable asset in an era when lack of confidence in official channels has become almost second nature to the populace; much to the contrary, the smear campaign adopted by traditional journalism on fringe topics has completely backfired and triggered its rejection by an ever-expanding portion of a distrusting public, whose rationale is something like: "If they have lied to us for so long about something as transcendent as an alien presence in our midst, then why should we trust them on ANYTHING at all?"

In a post-*X Files* age when pop culture needs not remind us that "government denies knowledge," it's the three Lone Gunmen, incarnated in a thousand alt-news blogs and websites, who get the last laugh.

In such an upside-down state of affairs, what should we say about ufology's obsessive appeal for "Disclosure"? Truly it would seem that, as we observe the events unfolding in the second decade of the 21st Century, the eventual disappearance of the Nation/State, as we currently know it, seems a more likely scenario than for those entities to recognize an anomaly over which they have no control whatsoever; an anomaly that refuses to conform to our 'sensible' expectations and seems hell bent on throwing into question everything we take for granted—even the nature of reality itself.[26]

Preposterous? It would have been equally preposterous to suggest, in the 1970s, that the mighty Soviet Union would come crashing down in less than two decades. It was also preposterous to think Britain would vote to leave the European union, or that the American people would choose to elect a former reality TV celebrity to the highest office in the Free World. Empires bloom and crumble to dust, and yet the mystery of the UFO lingers still—for it, perhaps, is not a puzzle meant to be unlocked by a consensus, but confronted and dealt with by each and every one of us when the proper time comes.

When will ufology stop yearning for official respectability, dare we ask? It seems as foolhardy and hopeless a pursuit as expecting street graffiti one day to be accepted as a fine art by ivory-towered academicians; not because there is always the occasional Banksy to serve as an exception to the rule, but because it is precisely the TRANSGRESSIONAL nature of these countercultural forces that endows them with their true power. For if history teaches us anything, it is that the most effective way to shape a society without disrupting it entirely is not from the inside, but from the *outside*.

Change the Consciousness, and the culture will change in tow.

Vallée saw, in the UFO phenomenon, a *cultural thermostat* occasionally nudging human affairs to a given, unforeseeable outcome. My rebellious nature prefers to regard it as a *chaotic catalyst*, ever turning human society up on its toes with its farcical displays of power. From an alchemical perspective, perhaps what this catalyst seems to be seeking is to create an appropriate state of *Nigredo*,[27] a necessary stage of general decomposition which must be followed through if one is to reach the desired outcome of *Albedo*, in which the Great Work is complete and the final transmutation of crude matter into divine substance is finally achieved.

Observed in such a way, perhaps the confounding trickery of these "Cosmic Jokers" is intended to shake us out of our collective stagnation, and force us to see a way out of our "dark (k)night of the soul" into a sunnier morrow.

Maybe.

For even if there's no humanly comprehensible solution to this mystery, it doesn't mean one can't utilize these ultimate symbols of anarchy—which even dare to defy the law of *gravity*—for personal empowerment. I have successfully turned my lifelong obsession for UFOs into *my* personal alchemy, encouraging myself to pursue questions I know full well are without easy answers, and to grow both intellectually and spiritually for it. To assume one is certain of the phenomenon's true origins and intentions at this stage is beyond arrogant—it is childishly naive. But if there's one thing I'm certain of here, it is this: if you let your curiosity guide you through uncharted territories seeking not fame, nor selfish gain or dulling self-reaffirmation; if you seek NOT to conform to other people's facile theories and answers, then I guarantee you this passion will propel you on a lifelong journey of childlike wonder for which there is no path of return.

That the journey is not without perils is a given, for no quest worth undertaking is devoid of them. John Keel used to warn parents not to let their children be interested in UFOs, since he saw in the phenomenon a realm of deceitful monsters threatening to drive even the most down-to-earth among us insane.

But catalysts are meant to boost what's already in the solution. If LSD has the potential to give the world the gift of a Ram Dass or a Steve Jobs, it can also spawn a Charles Manson. Same substance, different outcomes.

Thus, I say to you that, with any luck, not only may the UFO catalyst turn you utterly mad, but *entirely bonkers*. Alice told me a long time ago, the best people in this world are usually labelled as such by those who haven't the spine to imagine they can change it—it's easy if you only try, I'm told...

Solve et Coagula, fellow anarchist. And FUCK 'EM ALL!

"Are you ready? Are you ready to jump right off the edge of everything?"

—Grant Morrison, *The Invisibles, Vol. 3: Entropy in the U.K.*

MAKING MOUNTAINS OUT OF MASHED POTATOES: UFOS AS A PARAPSYCHOLOGICAL EVENT

Susan Demeter-St. Clair

In August 2010, I was contacted by an Aboriginal family who live near the Bruce Peninsula at Cape Croker, Ontario. Some members of their extended family had been invited to visit and camp out in their yard so that they could all attend the community's annual Pow Wow together. It was late in the evening when the UFO incident occurred. Five of the family members had gathered around a bonfire to talk, catch up, and enjoy the star-filled sky. The witness stated, "We first noticed what we thought was a satellite and then it started to move strangely. It started getting bigger and bigger by the second. It looked like a star at first, it was that high up. Then we all heard strange voices inside and outside of our heads that said, 'look up.'"

The family encountered a large inexplicable ball of light that seemingly descended from some distant point in the night sky. When asked to guess the duration of the experience, one of the witnesses remarked, "I do not know how long it was there, but it lit up my sister's entire yard, and we could see the forest as if it was daylight. It made no sound and I almost feel like I lost some time. I don't know what it could have been?"[1]

All family members present that night were willing to discuss what happened with me, all acknowledged hearing an external voice urging them to look at the UFO, and all of them felt in some way profoundly affected by their UFO encounter. This is one example from dozens of cases, which I have personally investigated in the Canadian province of Ontario, that demonstrates a certain degree of what is known in UFO studies as 'high strangeness.' The term is a catch-all for the often absurd and paranormal features of UFO encounters.

In his ground-breaking book, *The Hyperspace of Consciousness*, astrophysicist and UFO scholar Massimo Teodorani describes the importance of such reports, and the need to study them in a meaningful way:

> In reality, the witnessed cases gravitating around such light phenomena are even more intriguing than the phenomenology deduced by scientific investigation described so far. Many persons claim to feel suddenly attracted by such lights. Some even induced into telepathic contact by the light balls themselves. Of course, there are no scientific demonstrations yet of such claims, but certainly the witness statistics of such happenings is quite rich and valuable, especially when people reporting these facts are reserved and divulge their experiences privately. I have been meeting personally with such people wherever these phenomena occur.[2]

Telepathy, disembodied voices, and other psychic experiences have been scientifically explored for more than a century via psychical research and parapsychology.

This essay will argue that high strangeness UFO reports that include various types of psychic phenomena may be the key to a greater understanding of the UFO enigma, or, at the very least, trigger more meaningful questions in our ongoing efforts to understand it.

I am not attempting to reinvent the wheel here. These ideas have been explored previously, most famously by psychoanalyst and father of Depth Psychology, Carl Jung—the first to examine UFOs seriously as a paranormal event. In his 1958 book, *Flying Saucers: A Modern Myth*, Jung looked at UFO cases through the lens of social psychology, and he suggested they were the result of shared mental images triggered by social anxieties.

The foundation for paranormal-based hypotheses for UFO encounters was well laid many decades ago by some of the greatest minds who took the time to investigate it. This was informatively discussed by scientists such as Drs. J Allen Hynek and Jacques Vallée in the 1970s. Moving onwards, beginning in the late-1980s, ufology took a free-fall off an intellectual cliff and landed where it is splayed today—in a mess of Disclosure and conspiracy theories, and characterized by a lack of neutrality.

I will here attempt to show the value of the parapsychological hypothesis as an approach to UFO case studies despite its being neglected or swept under the rug by most ufologists. By ignoring the paranormal in UFO cases, we have been left with little more than incomplete and unsatisfying attempts at explanations.

Pop Culture Succeeds Where Ufology Has Failed

One of the greater problems I see within modern UFO circles is the outright dismissal of high strangeness reports by investigators who subscribe to the Extraterrestrial Hypothesis (ETH) as the default explanation for cases that challenge conventional science. Terms like "woo woo" to describe witnesses are freely thrown about in online UFO forums and social media, including by those UFO researchers who proclaim to take a more scientific or neutral look at UFO events.

While I can appreciate and respect a "nuts and bolts" approach to the phenomenon, the one clearly tangible vehicle central to any UFO story is the human witness. To ignore certain aspects of the experience, that are described as "paranormal" by the people who witness them, is an act of folly. It is the paranormal, or, in my view, exceptional *human* features of these experiences where parapsychology can play a strong role. What I am referring to here are things such as telepathy, or ESP, synchronicity, and the apparition-like appearances and behavior of the "aliens" that are sometimes reported along with the UFO experience or sighting of what appears to the witness to be an alien craft or spaceship. This is high strangeness.

The general public is actually far better acquainted with cases of high strangeness or paranormal UFO encounters through pop-culture than it is through the efforts of UFO study groups or investigative organizations. It is cinema, in particular, that has given us a greater appreciation of this experience.

From my own perspective as a UFO researcher, *Close Encounters of the Third Kind* (1977) is the seminal cinematic work for the portrayal of some of the more unusual aspects of the UFO phenomenon. Much like the witnesses I interviewed in 2010, who felt compelled to look at the UFO by disembodied voices, characters in Spielberg's film also felt an unusual compulsion to look for the UFOs that was coupled with paranormal or psychic phenomena. In this respect, the film gives us a much richer appreciation and understanding of the UFO experience, and of its impact on the lives of the witnesses, than does much of what is being offered to us today in the way of nonfiction UFO books. Most of the current popular UFO literature offers us little to no meaningful analysis of cases or innovative ideas towards attempting to resolve the mystery.

Commentary within UFO websites and forums is not much better. Online UFO discussions, when not just an echo chamber for the prevailing viewpoint of the online post's creator, often descend into heated and circular arguments. These do not engage anyone beyond those who might enjoy watching virtual shouting matches.

I have, occasionally, participated in UFO study discussions through social media, and the wide-held and incorrect assumption is that if you do not agree that UFOs are spaceships, then you must not believe they exist at all—a prevalent view among the ETH crowd. Their belief that UFOs must be the result of aliens is as firmly entrenched as any religious fundamentalist faith. It is all rather disappointing.

High Strangeness and the Scientist

Spielberg's *Close Encounters* was strongly influenced by the research of the late Dr. J. Allen Hynek, who was a scientific advisor to the study of Unidentified Flying Objects that was conducted by the United States Air Force and named Project Blue Book.

It is to Dr. Hynek that we can attribute the term "high strangeness," which he coined in a technical paper he presented to the American Association for the Advancement of Science in December 1969. Almost a decade later, he addressed the United Nations on the subject of UFOs, describing them as:

> ... a global phenomenon... so strange and foreign to our daily terrestrial mode of thought... it carries with it many implications of the existence of intelligences other than our own ... [It] bespeaks the action of some form of intelligence... but whence this intelligence

springs, whether it is truly extra-terrestrial, or bespeaks a higher reality not yet recognized by science, or even if it be in some way or another a strange psychic manifestation of our own intelligence, is much the question.[3]

Considering these remarks, it is of no surprise that paranormal or psychic events were included in Spielberg's film, for which Hynek served as a technical advisor on the UFO phenomenon.

Poltergeist phenomena, electrical disturbances, telepathy, synchronicity, and other paranormal occurrences are experienced by multiple characters across parallel storylines in the film, all of which converge at the meeting point with an otherworldly intelligence.

Popular Ufology Needs Shaking Up

Forty years have passed since Hynek delivered his speech to the U.N. and Spielberg released his classic UFO film. A handful of researchers, most notably J. Allen Hynek, Jacques Vallée, Jenny Randles, and John Keel, continued to examine the paranormal within UFO reports, but their ideas have been continually drowned out in favor of the ETH, conspiracy theories, and the Disclosure movement.

Currently, the testimonies of UFO witnesses that describe corresponding high-strange and paranormal events are often either ignored or met with ridicule from ufologists who would rather not deal with the more bizarre aspects of UFO reports, and by the professional skeptic organizations who are openly hostile to anything other than the Null hypothesis, i.e.: it's all just swamp gas and Venus.

This, in my opinion, is a big mistake.

Dr. Hynek's friend and colleague, Jacque Vallée, who, incidentally, was the inspiration for the French scientist in Spielberg's film (played by Francois Truffaut), has noted this error on the part of UFO investigators by stating:

UFOlogists have consistently ignored or minimized reports of seemingly absurd behaviors that contradict the ETH by selectively extracting data that best fits their agenda or version of the theory. Thus, the ETH—just like the skeptical argument—is based on anthropocentric self-selection.[4]

By cherry-picking reports and ignoring or being unsympathetic towards cases of high strangeness, researchers are losing valuable pieces of information and data that could work towards a greater understanding of the experience as a whole.

UFOs: Physical and Psychic

UFOs, much like ghosts and other similar manifestations, are elusive. The late anomalies scholar Hilary Evans noted this within his comparative study of entity cases. UFO pilots, religious visions, and ghostly visitors have much in common in terms of how they appear, the circumstances in which they are experienced, and the overall effects they have on their witnesses.

UFOs are occasionally measurable via radar signatures or leave physical traces. The idea that they are at least partially psychic has therefore been loudly denounced by the mainstream UFO crowd. This is a false assumption because the same state of being physical and psychic has also been noted in experiences perceived as ghosts of the dead, visions of the Holy Mother, and more complex paranormal manifestations such as the poltergeist. Like UFOs, these phenomena also occasionally produce physically measurable effects. These have been documented within the literature of scientific parapsychology.

In 1952, a twelve-year-old girl who was living with her family in Port Dalhousie, Ontario, was woken up in the middle of the night by an odd humming noise. She got out of her bed with a strong compulsion to go to the window. Looking out, she saw a sky filled with strange lights and disc-shaped UFOs.

The next morning, she told her family about what she had seen, and her brother instructed her to wake him should that ever happen again. And it did. That very next evening. Again there was the humming, again the urgent feeling to go to the window, and again the UFOs appeared. This time she did run out of her room to alert her family, but, mysteriously, hard as she tried, she could not awaken them. The odd hum she recalls having clearly heard externally on both nights (denoting a physical sound) was never to reoccur, nor has it ever adequately been explained.

I interviewed the above witness, who is now a retired professional, in 2014, and she recounted other UFO experiences that had occurred throughout her life, which included synchronicity and other psychic elements. She believes what happened at the age of twelve set the stage for later events in her life and that her inability to wake her family signifies that the experience was meant for her alone.

This continuation of various types of paranormal encounters is not unusual among UFO witnesses. "Throughout my life, I have had one foot here, and another foot over there," this same witness told me—"over there" being Magonia, another realm or dimension connected to UFOs and faerie lore by Jacques Vallée in his 1969 book, *Passport to Magonia*, which recounts many high strangeness cases.[5]

In a letter dated August 24, 1977, Allen Hynek wrote to Iris Owen who, along with her husband, Dr. George Owen, founded The Toronto Society for Psychical Research, later to become New Horizons Research Foundation. Hynek had expressed a keen interest in an experiment in Psychokinesis, which became known as the Phillip Experiment.

From his letter:

> Your work at the Foundation has certainly shown that the mind can influence physical matter—Phillip, table-tipping, poltergeist phenomena—all attest to this. I am being driven, somewhat reluctantly to the feeling that many UFOs are caused by our own psychic energy interacting with matter somehow.[6]

If we consider this from a parapsychological perspective and apply it to the Port Dalhousie case from 1952, we can speculate on the paranormal aspects of the experience as being centered in the mind of the twelve-year-old witness as opposed to what was seen in the sky, much like a poltergeist focus, which has been well studied within parapsychology.

The focus person of a poltergeist is an individual, within the literature usually but not always a teenager, who is going through some emotional turmoil, and who is unable to express this due to the social dynamics they find themselves in. To explore this idea further we would need to conduct a deeper examination of the witness, preferably at the time of the event, and her family, and the circumstances of her life at the time of her UFO experience.

Were the UFOs she witnessed a psychic manifestation and a cry for attention or help, which was unanswered by the family she was unable to awaken? Is this a case of a poltergeist manifesting itself as a UFO event, and possible precognition at the very dawn of the space race?

Two decades after Hynek originally wrote to the Psychical Research Society in Toronto, Jacques Vallée co-authored a paper with Eric Davis, which expanded Hynek's idea.

An excerpt from their paper: *Incommensurability, Orthodoxy and the Physics of High Strangeness; A 6-layer Model for Anomalous Phenomena*:

> Everything works as if UAPs [unidentified aerospace phenomenon] were the products of a technology that integrates physical and psychic phenomena and primarily affects cultural variables in our society through manipulation of physiological and psychological parameters in the witnesses.[7]

Furthermore, in discussing the challenges of high strangeness, the authors express the following:

> The rational study of reported cases of Unidentified Aerospace Phenomena (UAP) is currently at an impasse. This situation has as much to do with the incomplete state of our models of physical reality as it does with the complexity of the data. A primary objection to the reality of UAP events among scientists is that witnesses consistently report objects whose seemingly absurd behavior "cannot possibly" be related to actual phenomena, even under extreme conditions.

> Skeptics insist that intelligent extraterrestrial (ETI) visitors simply would not perpetrate such antics as are reported in the literature. This argument can be criticized as an anthropocentric, self-selected observation resulting from our own limited viewpoint as 21st century Homo sapiens trying to draw conclusions about the nature of the universe. Nonetheless, the high strangeness of many reports must be acknowledged.[8]

By acknowledging the high strangeness factor there is no doubt that UFO cases involving paranormal elements would be well served in utilizing parapsychology models for analysis.

Here, Davis and Vallée make the strong argument for new and more innovative hypotheses as part of a multidisciplinary approach to studying UFOs:

> In the view of the authors, the current hypotheses are not strange enough to explain the facts of the phenomenon, and the debate suffers from a lack of scientific information."[9]

This statement echoes the sentiments of Massimo Teodorani that I quoted earlier. They also argue that UAP (UFOs) can be thought of both as physical and as psychic:

> We hope that it will prove stimulating as a unified approach to a puzzling phenomenon that presents both undeniable physical effects suggesting a technological device or craft and psychic effects reminiscent of the literature on poltergeists and psychokinetic phenomena.[10]

"Nuts and bolts" ufologists pride themselves on having a scientific mindset. With this in mind, I would challenge them to consider what some professional scientists who have looked into UFOs have had to say in regards to high strangeness. One of the first scientific field investigations of UFOs was known as Project Identification, conducted by Dr. Harley Rutledge, and it has been well documented that several synchronicities were noted throughout the study. Astrophysicist Massimo Teodorani comments on Rutledge's work and shares a similar experience of his own while musing on the possibility of a "mind-matter creation," i.e.: a parapsychological event:

> Another point of great interest, which has been often experienced, is a synchronicity phenomenon between an observer and the apparition of anomalous light forms in the sky. This occurred to scientists, too.
>
> Rutledge himself experienced synchronic events many times, and if I must be honest and sincere this happened to me, too, 15 years ago. It happens that we suddenly turn our sight to a specific point of the sky and there see the (generally star-like) light.
>
> This is a clear example of synchronicity, and sometimes (as it has been already mentioned) of telepathy too.
>
> The question is who or what triggers this and why? Or is the light created as an archetypal form from our own consciousness due to reasons we don't know yet, but where, once more, mind-matter coalescence occurs suddenly as a micro-creation effect? Therefore, this is a topic we should consider deeply, because it might be the signature of something extremely important that opens many doors to a supernal knowledge, and technology too.[11]

Parapsychology and UFOs

Parapsychology has a lengthy history in studying phenomena both physical and psychic, and this can be extended to the examination of the UFO experience. Having been immersed in the study both of UFO encounters and paranormal phenomena such as poltergeists, I can confidently say there are parallels to both, and this is currently being overlooked by most of ufology.

This was also Scott Rogo's conclusion. Rogo was one of the only parapsychologists actively to examine UFO encounters and he noted several commonalities between the UFO experience and poltergeist outbreaks. One example would be that UFO witnesses have reported that they have both thought of or talked about UFOs and then later go on to see one. Sometimes they feel a strong urge to look in a certain direction and it is at that moment they experience a UFO. This can be interpreted as precognition or synchronicity in action. Rogo went on to publish his findings in the book entitled *The Haunted Universe*:[12]

> In the spring of 1966 a young couple who were renting a small house in a semi-forested area of Woodstock in New York State noticed six greenish lights of about 6 feet in diameter in a nearby field. On another occasion, they saw something flying close to their car and move towards a wooded area while making a high-pitch sound like a vacuum cleaner droning. They heard these sounds many times over a period of several months. Then, one afternoon, the sound seemed to stop moving and stayed stationary over the house. The woman looked at all the electrical equipment in the house and could not find a source. It seemed to be located in one of the house's walls. The couple verified that from outside of the house they could not see anything strange on the wall. But when they looked around at a nearby field they saw a green light and a smaller red one moving away from each other until they disappeared. They were frightened by the experience, but that was not all that was going to happen. They also heard a man's voice and the sounds of someone walking. They were really panicked at that point, but the noise and sound eventually stopped. The next day, they noticed that the grass near their house was flat and scorched, and it did not improve much during the entire summer.[13]

Was this a UFO encounter or was it a poltergeist? It appeared to be both.

UFO accounts, much like dreams, seem to contain symbolic messages that are not necessarily reflective of what their content conveys. These experiences of precognition, synchronicity, and the expressing of one's thoughts in absurd ways have also been noted during poltergeist disturbances. "For example, someone who wants to leave the house after having enough of the disturbance finds his shoes in the freezer."[14]

Within my own research, I have noted that the falling leaf motion is seen in both unidentified objects in the sky and experienced during poltergeist manifestations of objects that appear to be pushed or dropped by unseen hands.[15] Considering these similarities, it is unfortunate that the subject of UFOs remains highly contentious among parapsychologists. The website for the professional association for parapsychology quite clearly states that they do not intake or investigate UFO reports.

Part of this reluctance can certainly be laid at the doorstep of more outlandish UFO groups that maintain, without any scientific evidence, that the ETH is the only explanation for UFOs and that, any minute, now governments of the world will confirm this for them, or the aliens themselves will make their presence globally known. The lack of intellectual discourse within popular ufology and the steadfastness held to beliefs will understandably serve as a deterrent to most professionals.

A Haunted Sky: Social PSI and UFOs

Eric Ouellet, the Canadian liaison for the Parapsychological Association, is one of the few exceptions within the study that is chipping away at this. Eric has created the social scientific discipline known as Parasociology, and he is primarily focussed on exploring how societies interact with telepathy, precognition, and psychokinesis or PSI. His first book on the subject, *Illuminations: The UFO Experience as a Parapsychological Event*, gives us fresher ideas to examine by asking: are UFO encounters, including UFO waves, a direct result of Social PSI?

PSI is the anomalous phenomenon studied by parapsychology and generally falls into two categories: Extrasensory Perception (ESP), and Psychokinesis (PK). Social PSI includes the social dynamics for which the experience takes place.[15]

When applied to individual cases and different UFO flaps, some interesting insights and patterns begin to emerge. This premise builds on the ideas of Jung, and it works well with Jacque Vallée and Scott Rogo's findings that UFO witnesses tend to see what they are culturally conditioned to expect, and do so in a precognitive way that occasionally seems to anticipate future technology.

Ouellet writes:

> People saw airships in the skies of North America at the end of the 19th century a few years before they were flown; Scandinavians saw many ghost rockets in the sky just after the end of World War II and before much more powerful rockets were available to reach Scandinavia; a few years before the launch of the space age with the Soviet Sputnik satellite, many people saw things in the sky that were interpreted as spaceships.[16]

Could these UFOs have been apparitions of future events?

One of the strongest cases for Social PSI as an explanation for a UFO wave is the Belgium flap that began on November 29, 1989 and lasted until March 1991. This UFO flap is very well defined in its time frame, and it was thoroughly documented in real-time by both military and civilian authorities, including UFO researchers, all of whom displayed an unprecedented level of cooperation in investigation efforts.

There were numerous multi-witness reports that included various shapes and sizes of both UFOs and humanoid "aliens," but the most commonly reported UFO was a dark triangular shape with a very bright white light in each corner and a weaker red light in the middle of the triangle.

On November 9, 1989, the Berlin Wall came down; this set the stage for the ensuing rapid collapse of Communism in Central and Eastern Europe. While mostly non-violent, there was no way for people living through it to predict the turn these events could take, and it should not be difficult to imagine the anxiety, fear, and uncertainty they were experiencing.

If we consider the turbulence of that time throughout Europe, and include the USSR, which was experiencing a similar concurrent UFO wave, the hypothesis that the UFOs were born of social upheaval becomes tangible. Instead of an individual poltergeist focus person, we have entire societies contributing to a psychic manifestation in the sky that mirrors, in a very symbolic way, the political and military unrest occurring on the ground.

When considering the Belgium wave and the Social PSI hypothesis put forward by Ouellet, UFO scholar David Halperin asks:

Can it be coincidence that Belgium, so singularly favored by the UFOs of 1989-90—sightings that seemed to stop at the German and French borders—housed the headquarters of NATO in its capital Brussels? That the NATO symbol was (and is) a white star, while the red star was a symbol of Communism? That the most common type of Belgian UFO displayed a Jungian-style quaternity of three bright white stars (lights) surrounding a faint red star?[17]

In my opinion, this adds a dimension of synchronicity or a meaningful coincidence to these UFO events, and this, in the scholarly literature, plays a strong role in the overall UFO experience.

Could the Belgium wave have been a societal cry for help to NATO by a population that had been living under Communist rule and experiencing very uncertain times? Like individual poltergeist cases where the focus person is unable to express their anxiety in a more conventional sense, we can, through the lenses of parasociology, speculate as to the effect this historic time had on people collectively and how it may, in turn, have manifested as a UFO wave over NATO headquarters.

Summary

To reframe the UFO debate we need to formulate new models for analysing existing and incoming data, and introduce innovative hypotheses by asking better questions than have thus far been asked.

I have given examples from scientists and scholars of varied disciplines, who, like Allen Hynek before them, have studied UFOs and drawn similar conclusions of the phenomenon. Their findings encompass the totality of the UFO experience and strengthen the need for parapsychological and parasociological models as part of a multi-disciplinary approach to the further study of UFO events.

The steadfast adherence to the ETH among many UFO enthusiasts is akin to religious faith. To a degree, the same can be said of those UFO skeptics who apply the Null hypothesis as the only possible explanation for unresolved cases. Such dogmatic stances are harmful to the subject, and certainly they do nothing to further the progress of our understanding. More importantly, by wilfully ignoring high strangeness cases or, worse, dismissing them as "woo woo," we do a disservice to the UFO witnesses who have shared their experiences with those of us who study the phenomenon.

Parapsychological hypotheses and models can more fully address the complex human and social dynamics of this rich and enigmatic experience. They can do so in a more flexible way than any of the dominant hypotheses, including the ETH, because they allow for the objective and the subjective to have influence over one another while incorporating the very well established physical and psychic nature of UFO events.

By acknowledging the high strangeness and absurdity of UFO encounters and viewing them through these lenses we can finally begin a forward momentum. The Parapsychological Hypothesis is not a solution to the UFO enigma, but it opens and encourages exciting new research avenues within the field.

* All UFO witness interviews cited within this essay were conducted in confidentiality. Names of interviewees are withheld by agreement.

FRANKENSTEIN & **FLYING SAUCERS:**
CREATING, DESTROYING, AND
RE-ANIMATING A PHENOMENAL
MONSTER

Ryan Sprague

n November 17, 2012, the Association for the Scientific Study of Anomalous Phenomena (ASSAP), held a summit in England to determine if ufology was a dead field. It was based on the notion that UFO sightings were in steep decline. Directly following the summit, Chairman of ASSAP, Dave Wood, told the UK Telegraph: "We look at these things on the balance of possibilities and this area of study has been ongoing for many decades. The lack of compelling evidence beyond the pure anecdotal suggests that on the balance of probabilities, nothing is out there. It is certainly a possibility that in ten years' time, it will be a dead subject.";

These were sobering words, and they made international headlines. The true believers simply shrugged off Wood's statement as nothing more than aggressive UFO debunkery, and perhaps rightfully so. Similar words had been spoken many times before. In an article for *Saucers* magazine, Max Miller stated:

... much of the enthusiasm over UFOs has vanished in recent years due to a lack of sightings and important developments. Also, the unimaginable quantity of material, almost wholly devoid of a new approach or even new data, has flooded the UFO field in recent years, and has done little more than to deluge a respectable subject with wholesale garbage.[2]

The above quote by Miller was written in 1959, some five decades prior to the 2012 UK summit—essentially same discussion of the same issue separated by more than fifty years. As technology has evolved, anomalous objects in the sky have become increasingly identifiable. Year after year, the heartrate of ufology seems to weaken. Some would argue it's already flatlined. But the phenomenon itself seems always to find a way to resuscitate the field.

In a paper titled, *Ufology: Is There Life After Death?*, researcher and author Jenny Randles states, "Eventually, something will spark human-ity's desire to know about these things, which any prolonged absence of wide public reporting will fuel."[3] This spark of interest has taken many forms throughout the history of ufology—a mass sighting of a boo-merang craft over the skies of Phoenix, Arizona in 1997, for example, or a disc-shaped object piercing the clouds over Gate C-17 of Chicago's O'Hare Airport in 2006. More recently, the spark has come from the outer reaches of space with the discovery in 2016 of a habitable planet orbiting Earth's closest star, Proxima Centauri. It is such events and discoveries that converge into a desire to learn more, and to *know* more about UFOs. Why, then, do some feel it necessary to hang a toe tag on ufology every time it hits a brick wall? We often fear that which we don't understand, and, if the history of UFO study has taught us any-thing, it's that we understand very little about these phenomena. Yet, even if we did, would we not fear that knowledge as well?

In 1818 England, at the age of twenty, Mary Shelley brought her now iconic monster to literary life. It wouldn't be until 1823 that her name would appear on the second edition in France. The novel, *Frankenstein*, is arguably one of the first examples of science fiction; the protagonist, Dr. Victor Frankenstein, making a decision to create life using science, alchemy, and technology. He achieves this divine goal with results both fantastic and terrifying. The manifestation is the monster we've grown to fear and love.

So how, exactly, does this brilliantly grotesque story relate to ufol-ogy? We can start with a sharp distinction between Shelley's original

novel and the classic 1931 film directed by James Whale. Near the beginning of the film, Dr. Frankenstein's assistant breaks into a university to steal a brain for his master's experiment. He swipes a jar marked
"normal brain" but is startled by a noise. This causes him to drop the
jar, damaging the brain and rendering it useless. He then takes a second jar, labeled "abnormal brain." This would subsequently be implanted into the monster with disastrous results. Interestingly, this entire
scene had no part in the original novel. Regardless, in the film version,
the monster's consciousness was explored and the primitive creature
found itself aware of its reality, causing it to lash out in a frenzy of emotions it could neither process nor control. Had the monster any understanding of *who* or *what* it was, perhaps the story would have unfolded
differently. Or perhaps not. But the role of consciousness in the film
narrative was not just valuable, it was essential. For me, this brings to
mind ufology. We can look at the blood of the monster—seek to study
its physical matter—or we can seek to understand its consciousness.
To do this, we might start by turning the microscope on ourselves to
understand better how our own consciousness (individual and collective) interacts with phenomenal stimuli.

Reality, in its simplest of definitions, is the quality or state of being
actual or *true*. However, when we look at the definitions of *actual* and
true, we find both words defined as: consistent *with* reality. The definitions not only contradict one another, they circle around in a whirlpool of unverifiable factors. Therefore, we find ourselves relying on
something a bit more cerebral. In addition to taste, sight, touch, smell,
and hearing, we have a sense of *awareness*. We are aware of a reality,
which we've believed into existence. This theme was explored by the
late Jim Keith, co-author of *The Octopus*, and publisher of various alternative magazines. In November of 1995, Keith gave a talk in Atlanta,
Georgia, where he went into a deep deconstruction of reality through
the lens of human perception. In a published 1997 version of his talk
in *Paranoia Magazine*, titled *UFOs at the Edge of Reality*, Keith stated:

> Awareness is potentially a creator, and it can create freedoms and it
> can create limitations. The fact that ten people or a thousand people
> believe the same thing, does not render said thing any more real in
> an absolute sense. But it does point out the structural underpinning
> of the determinant of this illusion called reality. What people believe
> deep down is what they consider reality.[4]

Can we then extrapolate that the existence of UFO phenomena rests solely on our *belief in them*? Jim Keith noted:

> I think that their existence challenges the tightly-formulated definitions of reality and imagination, and points up the limitations of those definitions. It seems to me that UFOs sometimes happily cross these lines of demarcation, and defy the definitions. The way they do this gives us some clues to the something else, to the nature of reality, what is real and what is possible, in terms of the understanding and potential expansion of awareness.[5]

This expansion of awareness needs also to be explored. Even to scratch the surface of the UFO enigma, we must move past the mentality that we are dealing purely with nuts and bolts, past the notion that the key to the UFO phenomenon lies in physical analysis. Jacques Vallée once stated that "Human beings are under the control of a strange force that bends them in absurd ways, forcing them to play a role in a bizarre game of deception."[6] Could this deception relate to human perception? The mind has perceptual limits—a filtering mechanism that, based on our awareness, shows us only what we can process in a manageable format. It works under restraints that have been carefully constructed throughout an individual's life and throughout the long history of our species. Are those who witness UFOs breaking those perceptual restraints?

Awareness and perception are the heart of reality. We perceive things on a scale of either filtering that which we see, or widening our scope to accommodate more. When the scope is broadened, we are aware of our newly-enhanced perception, thus altering our former perception of reality. We have, in essence, *created* a new reality for ourselves. This could be the very reason the UFO phenomenon exists in the first place. Could it be possible that we have created a phenomenon that stretches the limits of our perceptual reality? It may be that our established modes of logic limit us so greatly that we can't fully comprehend the monster *we* created. We must ultimately face the fact that, at some point, the awareness of that monster is going to shape and mold our consciousness completely, moving forward.

In a 2014 article titled *Consciousness Inside-Out*, science writer and anthropologist Eric Wargo states:

> We are at a crux in our science and our culture when a new model is desperately needed to think about the relationship between

consciousness and material reality. Much as I'm sympathetic with those who privilege consciousness against materialistic reductionism, I think a more nuanced and non-hierarchical relationship between mind and matter must be possible.[7]

The majority of witnesses I've spoken with, who've encountered UFOs, have described feeling as though their reality was somehow altered in the moment. Time seems to slow down, and the air around them seems different. Their senses seem either to heighten or to disappear altogether. It is as if their perception is fundamentally challenged and they are left with only a hazy memory of what they'd actually seen, having no meaningful frame of reference in which to place it. Whether or not this is partly due to whatever is in control of the UFO is speculative. It could very well be the tuner or limitation of the current awareness and perception of the individual. And, as Wargo points out above, we are left wondering if the materialistic make-up of the UFO is actually there in front of us to feel, smell, and hear, or if it is something "bending," as Vallée puts it, into a contorted reality. While many UFO researchers argue that the question is no longer *if* UFOs exist, I argue that this *still is* in question. It's a matter of how one views existence. Wargo goes on to say:

The word 'exist' comes from the Greek *eksistere*, 'to stand forth.' As mystics from time immemorial have insisted, the material world is a manifestation of consciousness—the self-world continuum experienced passively, as observed, rather than actively, as observing. These two aspects pass from one to the other at certain mysterious boundaries— in dreams, at death, and in paranormal phenomena (such as UFOs) that turn our outside into an inside (or vice versa) without our quite being aware how we made the passage.

This passage between established and newfound realities is where UFOs seem to float, hover, zip, coast, appear and disappear in and out of ambiguity. But even more interesting is the theory that that UFOs, as physical objects we perceive, have been created and manifested through our own pre-existing awareness of the UFO phenomenon to begin with. We believe that UFOs are coming to *us* under their own volition. But what if we were subconscious initiators, pulling UFOs in? This could explain why, even in the case of a mass sighting, individuals see the same object slightly different from one another, their previous

awareness shaping and molding the object from their own set of reduction valves and evolving perception.

While the manifestation may begin with an individual source, what
happens when hundreds, if not thousands of those individuals have
the same thought? We call this *collective consciousness*. The term was
introduced by the French sociologist, Émile Durkheim in 1893, and
has since sparked much debate amongst sociologists, psychologists,
and scientists, but it may very well tell us more about UFOs than any
sighting report or radar tracking ever could. Let's theorize for a moment that an extraterrestrial intelligence is responsible in part for some
UFO phenomena. Given that we now live in an age where privatized
space travel is possible on a grand scale, ambitions expand with every
manned or unmanned journey. As more time progresses and our reach
beyond the stars stretches further, we are collectively accepting that
traveling to other planets is within reach. And so is the possibility of
discovering other lifeforms. Because of this expansion in the collective
consciousness, we may in fact be manifesting the extraterrestrial presence in more ways than we think. Keeping in mind that many claim
and believe we have already been visited by non-human intelligences, is it possible that, as we journey outward into the cosmos, we are
pulling this alien phenomenon closer to us in a convergence of sorts?
They've accepted us into their reality, having presumably been monitoring us for decades, if not centuries or millennia. Is it now our turn
to meet them halfway?

In his best-selling book, *Passport to Magonia: From Folklore to Flying Saucers*, Vallée postulates:

> There exists a natural phenomenon whose manifestations border on
> both the physical and the mental. There is a medium in which human
> dreams can be implemented, and this is the mechanism by which UFO
> events are generated, needing no superior intelligence to trigger them.
> This would explain the fugitivity of UFO manifestations, the alleged
> contact with friendly occupants, and the fact that the objects appear
> to keep pace with human technology and to use current symbols.[8]

It is possible, in Vallée's opinion, that there may be no other half
to the non-human equation. We may quite possibly be manifesting
these events all on our own in a dream-like state and through alien-in-
spired interpretations. But why do we deny this possibility that we are
in control? This Semmelweis reflex of sorts may depend on the lack

of evidence, whether scientifically, philosophically, psychologically, or physically. But, to the contrary, what stark irrefutable evidence do we have otherwise of purely physical, nuts-and-bolts phenomena controlled solely by non-human intelligences? While many scoff at the idea of a metaphysical approach to the UFO phenomenon, which conjures images of "new agers" and "space brothers/sisters," it very well could lead us to a new path. But is it a path worth taking?

When I learned of what several colleagues were to write about in this collection of essays, I noticed strikingly similar ideas and concepts to my own in terms of human manifestation of these phenomena. At first, this made me hesitate, fearing a stalemate in terms of bringing forth new contributions to the debate. But, pushing that small whisper of pride aside, I realized this is exactly the point—I wasn't alone in my ideas. Not only did it excite me to find others researching this, but it made me feel that I was indeed on a path worth taking. A notable addition to this debate is that of UFO researcher and author Greg Bishop, who also theorizes that we may be manifesting UFO events unknowingly somewhere deep in the subconscious, and that perhaps some UFO experiences may be co-created in the moment by the observer and some anomalous intelligent stimulus. In conversation with me about this, Bishop explained that, "Our subconscious picks up many things of which our conscious minds are unaware. The fact that some people can suffer head trauma and suddenly become amazing artists or mathematicians, or speak a completely foreign language, means that either we somehow all have this ability anyway or we are constantly ingesting far more information than we can possibly use." Could we then theorize that UFO experiences, which are often traumatic in nature, unlock these doors in the mind?

One of the biggest issues with looking at these phenomena is the investigator's approach. Greg Bishop suggests that, "Investigators should start with *no* preconceptions about what they are seeking. The goal should be only to gather information from witnesses. They should also begin to ask questions about subjective impressions, such as "how did it make you feel?" Employing the skills of qualified mental health professionals should be a priority, with an idea towards helping the witness integrate the experience on their own terms, rather than those of UFO investigators on the one hand or scientists who wish to tell them that they were mistaken or that is was 'nothing but' on the other."

So, while multiple contributors to this volume are peering into the consciousness aspects of UFO phenomena, the majority of researchers remain steadfast on a nuts-and-bolts approach to ufology. This is all fine and good. Perhaps the issue doesn't even lie in the divergence between hard data and a mind-based deconstruction, but in the question of whether the UFO phenomenon can convincingly be linked to something extraterrestrial to begin with. Carl Jung once stated: "I'm puzzled to death about these phenomena, because I haven't been able yet to make out with sufficient certainty whether the whole thing is a rumor with concomitant singular and mass hallucination, or a downright fact. Either case would be highly interesting." This idea of mass hallucination can arguably be traced back to the inception of the modern UFO era. In 1947, Kenneth Arnold, an amateur pilot from Idaho, witnessed nine bright objects coasting along Mount Rainer in the southeast of Seattle, Washington. When interviewed by a local newspaper, he described the objects' movement like that of a saucer skipping across water. Either lazy editing or a desperate attempt at a gripping headline, the newspaper mistakenly stated that Arnold had witnessed "flying saucers" in the air. Thus, the term had been coined, and thousands of reports began to trickle in of saucer-shaped objects plaguing the skies. Was this merely a case of hysteria, or were people truly seeing saucer-shaped objects? And, if so, were those saucers being piloted or controlled by non-human intelligences?

In his 2015 book, *How UFOs Conquered the World*, Dr. David Clarke explains that a hysteria of sorts could play a pivotal role in the entire phenomenal conjecture. What he has coined "The UFO Syndrome" weaves in and out of a mythological stance on UFOs and their possible occupants. Clarke believes that culture itself feeds the phenomenon, or the perception of it, in an endless feedback loop between stories passed down through media and genuine experiences. While Kenneth Arnold may indeed have seen something in the skies over Washington in 1947, it was a quote misconstrued that ushered in the entire flying saucer phenomenon (or syndrome) thereafter. Now, this is not to say that UFOs were not flying through our skies prior to Arnold's sighting. But what we have now engrained so deeply into our minds as mechanisms piloted by non-human intelligences will forever hold a place in both cultural and individual experience. With the elusiveness of the UFO and the complexity of its study ebbing and flowing between believers and skeptics, Clarke mirrors some of the words of Bishop above, stating that the UFO syndrome "... is fueled not only by the vagaries of human perception, but also by a strong psychological and cultural attachment to the theory and the protective efforts of a community of advocates: the ufologists."[10]

We can explore new paths all we want. What this comes down to are the ufologists, no matter how grounded in scientific method or how metaphysical or cerebral they choose to be. It comes down to those who decide to spend their time, knowledge, and resources studying the phenomenon. But instead of watching a phantom war between realists and dreamers, perhaps we might benefit from standing, if only for a little while, with one foot in each camp. Perhaps, in seeking to bridge the divide between the two approaches, we can bring new life to a field that dies time and again by our own hand and through our own blinkered perspectives. We must look beyond the strictures we've helped create, and bring life to a monster we want neither to destroy nor resurrect ever again. We must let it live on its own terms and in its own image. We may even look to James Whale's brilliant 1931 film for inspiration, where the naive yet passionate Dr. Frankenstein asks: "Have you never wanted to do anything that was dangerous? Where should we be if no one tried to find out what lies beyond? Have you never wanted to look beyond the clouds and the stars, or to know what causes the trees to bud? And what changes the darkness into light? But if you talk like that, people call you crazy. Well, if I could discover just one of these things, what eternity is, for example, I wouldn't care if they did think I was crazy."

Crazy or not, we must look at ourselves in a mirror so clear that the reflection staring back will lead us forward in ways we can only imagine. The reality of UFOs may bring us closer together than we ever thought possible, both here on Earth, and perhaps somewhere in the cosmos we've only begun to explore.

THE **CO-CREATION** HYPOTHESIS: HUMAN PERCEPTION, THE **INFORMATIONAL UNIVERSE,** AND THE OVERHAUL OF **UFO** RESEARCH

Greg Bishop

"If you look for the saucers deep within yourself, that is where you will find them."[1]

—GRAY BARKER

In the first 60 years of looking at UFOs and many thousands of reports, we have not moved any closer to a provable theory of their origin. It appears that the goal of most UFO researchers and advocates at present is to make more people take the subject seriously, or at least consider that UFOs are not just the product of misidentifications, hoaxes, or hysteria. The problem is that most UFO enthusiasts seem to want to answer critics by using an idea (aliens from other planets) that doesn't adhere to our classic standards for proof. The argument is at cross-purposes. The experience is not available on demand, nor is it amenable to normal scientific scrutiny. There is also the existential issue of a supposed extra-human intelligence and if it is connected to the phenomenon or even within our realm of comprehension.

For decades, the pursuit of so-called "respectability" and the nagging idea that the "perfect case," well-documented by video, radar returns, and physical traces will convince doubters has been the holy grail of UFO study. There is already enough evidence in this regard and it has not made much difference to those whom the researcher hopes to impress. Perhaps a quest for a deeper and wider understanding of relevant and previously overlooked issues and their implications is what is called for at this time, and not the need to be believed or accepted.

The late UFO theorist Bruce Duensing wrote that there is really no apparent reason for non-humans to be visiting us, at least not in any way that makes rational sense, and that there may be an intention on the part of supposed "aliens" of presenting images and feelings that are specifically designed to be inscrutable to us.[2] In this scenario, the option to choose our own meaning and intent may be forced on us for some unknown purpose. Is some intelligence communicating with us by holding up a mirror whenever we try to look too closely? If we subtract our own innate bias, cultural cueing, and psychology from the history of UFO reports, what is left? How much of the experience comes from the observer? The answer could range from "None at all" to "Everything." There are many places where a UFO sighting (or any extraordinary experience) could fall on this spectrum.

The existence of an extra-human consciousness is assumed to be a possibility for the purposes of this discussion. We will also work from the premise that at least some reported interaction with apparent non-humans are genuine attempts at describing what witnesses have seen, and are not misidentifications, hallucinations, or hoaxes, although there is a case to be made for the blurring of these lines.

In 2008, I suggested a thought experiment that considered anomalistic encounters with supposed unknowns as a radical form of art which forces the viewer or witness to experience "art" that engages not only their senses, but, more importantly, their inner life. What if a hypothetical artist was so talented that the viewer's life was changed deeply and permanently? What if this change was so insidious that even the artist didn't consciously intend it and the effects varied with the individual, based on the witness' culture, psychology, upbringing, genetics, etc.? This artist would become famous not for what they were trying to communicate in their work, but for what was pulled out of each person's individual makeup as a result of the experience. This may be what is happening during UFO close encounters. There is a massive backlog of apparent craft and beings seen, as well as a wide spectrum of individual reactions. This suggests either that countless types of strange entities are visiting us, or that the brain has some kind of creative control over what is experienced.

In 1952, Albert K. Bender convened the International Flying Saucer Bureau, which was one of the first civilian UFO research groups. In the premiere issue of his house newsletter, *Space Review*, Bender asked for members' theories about the origin of the UFOs. Every last one of them stated something to the effect of, "I think the saucers come from other planets." UFO research has been saddled with this idea ever since. With the background of fantasy and science-fiction and other cultural precedents, this is not surprising. As early as 1732, Voltaire's fictional story *Micromégas* described ETs from Saturn as well as a planet orbiting the star Sirius, and pulp fiction of the early 20th century was rife with evil aliens. Even early U.S. government studies like Project Sign's classified *Estimate of the Situation* in 1948 supposedly touted an interplanetary origin.

We labor under this heavy legacy, but it does not have to be so. A conscious effort should be made not to assign any origin or meaning to these encounters, because we may have been fooling ourselves for so long about what they are that we have backed ourselves into a corner. Although routinely ignored by the majority of researchers and other interested parties, the fields of psychology, physiology, and even the emerging discipline of information theory should be vitally important to anyone who is interested in the subject.

For most of the modern era, the majority of UFO investigators believed that the main objective in interviewing a witness was to shore up the idea of aliens visiting us from other planets. The easy tunnel vision we have built up for ourselves over the decades seemingly ignores the witness in the equation. Many other issues may be very important: What was the UFO percipient doing in the months, days, or hours leading up to the encounter? What happened afterwards? Did the percipient's life change in any way? Did their beliefs and outlook change as a result? These issues and others are only sporadically recorded in the literature, but may actually be far more important than what is supposedly an effort at a statistical or "scientific" documentation and any answers that may be derived.

The terms of the search may need to be changed. If we are looking for an "answer" to the enigma, this assumes that there is an easy or understandable one waiting in the wings for just the right researcher who gets lucky or is amazingly smart. Perhaps the process should be referred to as a quest for understanding rather than any search for a specific truth. This may serve to keep the question open, and direct thought processes and models. The search may be aided by mimicking the obliqueness of its subject.

To this end, perhaps large UFO groups should be disbanded in favor of smaller, autonomous groups with a narrow research focus. Or, the big organizations should concentrate on collecting and cataloguing data rather than pushing a specific theory or becoming the subjects of breathless reality shows. "Mainstream" abduction study may also benefit from a hiatus of 5 to 10 years in favor of small support groups, and then resumed with no assumptions and no use of hypnosis and see what transpires. The suggestion here is that since we haven't really gotten anywhere with anything that can be proven to the greater public and, more importantly, the arbiters of popular reality, such as the media and academia, then, perhaps, different methods and ideas could be more fruitful. No one should fear what could be learned. A serious shift in focus and methodology could change many ideas completely, and that would be a good thing. The answer is encoded in the question.

The phenomenon has not proven to be anything that can be reconciled by our current standards of proof. Therefore, UFO researchers and enthusiasts would best be served by making no firm judgments on any of the data—at least on its existential origins. The Greek philosophy of Pyrrhonism is a good model of inquiry in this regard:

> "Nothing can be known, not even this." Pyrrhonian skeptics withhold assent with regard to non-evident propositions and remain in a state of perpetual inquiry. For example, Pyrrhonians might assert that a lack of proof cannot constitute disproof, and that a lack of belief is vastly different from a state of active disbelief... Pyrrhonians recognize that we cannot be certain that new evidence won't turn up in the future, and so they intentionally remain tentative and continue their inquiry. Pyrrhonians also question accepted knowledge, and view dogmatism as a disease of the mind.[3]

This method prevents the investigator and researcher from falling into the trap of a belief system from which there is a need to entrench and defend opinions since, seemingly, any viewpoint on this weird subject does not cover all the bases.

An example of a sane attitude towards UFO study can probably be summed up as something like "total interest combined with complete agnosticism." Investigators should listen and log everything that that seems interesting and relevant, but try to make no value judgments on them. Keep notes and store the information away for later when it may make more sense or significant connections can be made. The first step is to formulate new questions, rather than to work backwards from an answer. In this regard, the most information-rich reports seem to occur when the phenomenon is closer to the percipient.

The close encounter witness is at first blindsided by something for which he or she has no previous framework, and which the mind tries furiously to stuff into a mental "filing box" during and soon after the event. Later, the aftermath of trying to find some sort of context and meaning is readily available in literature, popular culture, the internet, and from UFO researchers, who are, for the most part, notoriously wedded to an extraterrestrial explanation.

What many fail to realize is that most UFO witnesses have had an experience for which they have no benchmark. They are thrown into an alternative reality where something that they ignored, or perhaps even derided, has been forcefully presented to them. Descriptions of colors, speeds, distances, time frames, "what the aliens looked like" and similar concerns are no longer important, or may even become meaningless from their point of view.

In his 1991 book, *Angels and Aliens: UFOs and the Mythic Imagination*, Keith Thompson described a dilemma of which few took heed at the time:

> Many UFO witnesses emerge from their sighting experience or close encounter with a surrealistic appreciation that the world is filled with enormous vistas and abysses. It is as if they have glimpsed the edge of reality so precisely defined by the surrealists, and now can never go back to the mechanistic Newtonian world absent of depth, beauty, significance, and soul. In contrast, both extremes of the UFO debate—proponents and debunkers—seem committed to forcing witness interpretations into narrow boxes that witnesses themselves tend to see as inadequate. This is surely one of the richer ironies of the UFO epic.[4]

Witnesses may not be prepared to give the investigator what they are looking for, and, in fact, the two parties may often be talking about very different things. The witness' desire to make sense of their experience moves him or her inexorably closer to any seemingly rational explanation.

Throughout the history of the subject, UFO enthusiasts and researchers have been concentrating on gathering information from witnesses based on presumably unbiased observations of their encounters. It is an established fact that recall of even mundane experiences and witnessed events can vary widely. Over time, memory becomes hazier and the mind tends to fill in details that are either incomplete or that flatter our prejudices or those of the listener or audience. The instrument for recording these encounters is not radar or a video camera: it is the human brain and nervous system, which are notoriously imprecise things.

People who study UFOs are, for the most part, not interested in the murky and complicated issues of human perception and memory. Perhaps what should be called into question is not just the origin of sightings and abductions (which may or may not be connected) but the very way we look at things; how our brains and nervous systems process input and remember events, and how traumatic events and memory affect what was seen and how we recall events after the fact. If we can pick apart these issues as they relate to UFO sightings and close encounters, we may not only gain some level of interest from intelligent people from outside the field, we might also make a breakthrough in understanding, which is far more important.

The idea of an extra-human consciousness is such an enigma that perhaps the key (or one of them) starts with us, sort of like the dog who looks at your finger rather than what you are pointing at. We may be looking at the effect rather than the cause, and the cause may be wrapped up in our visual and nervous systems. A thorough and up-to-date understanding of these issues might give the researcher a way to get at the cause of sightings and encounters rather than the perceptual packaging that surrounds them. In this regard, close encounters (in J. Allen Hynek's definition of a sighting within 500 feet or less) have the potential to be much more profound than sightings of distant objects, and where far more things seem to be happening between the witness and the witnessed. In fact, the outlier cases may be more accurate precisely because they do not fit a pattern that we expect.

Basic questions like "What causes UFO sightings?" and perhaps on an even deeper level, "What do the weirder cases tell us about the phenomenon?" should take center stage. The late abduction researcher Karla Turner said that, "the truth to me more likely is going to lie in the anomalous details."⁵ The stranger cases may contain clues about the nature of the phenomenon and how we perceive it. This probably appears counterintuitive, since most researchers tend to throw out or ignore these reports, but the whole phenomenon can be looked at as counterintuitive, and, when things don't fit a pattern, it should serve as a beacon for attention.

Some very strange and generally little known cases illustrate the variety of human experience with UFOs, and blur the line between the internalized experience and the external world. They suggest that the mind is far more creative than we expect when confronted by cognitively dissonant input. Here are just four among many similar examples that could be presented:

1. Driving to his job as a radio DJ in Long Prairie Minnesota on the night of October 23, 1965, Jerry Townsend rounded a curve in the road and was startled to come upon what looked like a 40-foot tall rocket in the middle of the road, standing on three fins. Three small figures approximately the size and shape of beer cans on two legs waddled towards him, stopped, and put out a third "leg" which they balanced on while apparently "looking" at him. They soon made their way back to the craft and disappeared inside the "rocket." With a humming sound, it took off into the sky and disappeared.⁶

2. In January of 1978, a boy named Cristovao disappeared from an apartment building in Curitiba, Brazil, where he lived with his mother. She searched in vain for him all night while a strange beeping sound and other paraphysical disturbances occurred in the apartment. In the morning, an employee of a local power plant found the boy sleeping on the grounds. Cristovao told his mother that he had been taken away in a "rocket" and encountered a man and woman with no mouths. His mother said that he was emitting a strong odor and had marks on his skin that were not there previously. He said he had gone to a "yellow moon" and that the beings said that they would return for him. Strange paranormal events continued to plague them for a period after the incident.⁷

3. The rural witness in an incident from Emilcin, Poland in 1978 had no exposure to any media or cultural antecedents for his

experience which featured an apparent rectangular or boxlike craft with corkscrewing spirals on it, diminutive humanoids with flippers for feet, a platform with a pulley system to raise him and his visitors into the craft, and a door on the object that looked like a rolled-up carpet.[8]

4. In 1974, a few days after a fiery "meteorite" was seen plummeting to earth a few miles from Bald Mountain, Washington, a hunter, used his binoculars to look at something in the distance that caught his eye. He observed "an incredible glowing creature... It was vaguely horse-like, he said, with four 'legs' that looked like the tentacles of an octopus and a football-shaped head with an antenna-like prong sticking up. The body was covered with scales.[9]

These cases evince almost none of the normal elements of a supposed abduction or what we have become used to as the standard "alien," but they are only very rarely mentioned in surveys and research, mainly because they both don't make any sense and because they don't fit comfortably into a standard narrative.

Many UFO researchers would be tempted to say that these accounts are either faulty recollections (that would fit a humanoid narrative if given enough questioning) or screen memories imposed by aliens, but perhaps extra-human consciousness has no need or method to impose any mind control on us. We have our own built-in screen memories that function quite well in earthly situations such as childhood trauma. How much do we bring to the dance during a paranormal encounter? In other words, how much of the UFO experience is the result of our subconscious minds trying to make sense of unexpected, startling, and/or frightening input, and leaving us with an insane placeholder when it can't decide on anything else?

A legitimate question arises about photos and films or videos of UFOs. These seem to depict, for the most part, what was seen by witnesses. This may be true, but there seem to be very few if any close-up photos of UFOs or their occupants. The close encounter appears to be a very different animal from sightings of distant objects. Besides, images of supposed unidentifieds have not convinced skeptics and others who determine what the greater public believes, and they can be faked very convincingly now. If we can make some sort of headway in understanding how humans encode visual stimuli and remember it, we may begin to crack the mystery, and attitudes and outlooks may change or evolve. There is also the seemingly well-supported idea that the closer a witness is to the phenomenon, the more variety seems to emerge. Perhaps our creativity could even change what a camera sees.

Electronic engineer John Fenderson was a guest on the *Radio Misterioso* podcast in 2015. He described an "experiment," which he conducted sometime in the 1970s, where he and a few friends released hot air balloons made with laundry bags over their hometown after dark. He said that accounts later varied from those who saw exactly what was there to others who thought that there was some sort of alien invasion underway. There are many studies that indicate that the human visual system changes what is seen before we are consciously aware of it. Fenderson said "Most of what you're seeing, you are actually imagining, and consists of what you are filling in based on patterns you expect. When something happens that you don't expect, very often you won't see it at all."[10]

The human mind is well known for editing out what is too painful or useless to us. What is not as well-known is how it does this. In his 1997 book, *Mind Trek*, Remote viewer Joe McMoneagle discussed a model of perception based on his understanding of the human visual system and how our brains process input from our senses:

> We reside and operate in a constantly fluctuating past of our own creation ... By the time our processing is of any use to us, we are already dealing with past events. Our reality is one we in fact invent or make up as we go.
>
> Processing sequence as a Function of Time:
>
> TIME 0: We recognize incoming information about our current reality.
> PLUS .00000: We begin to make sense of the input from our five senses.
> PLUS .00001: We fish out additional information from our hardwired brain memory modules.
> PLUS .0001: We reason a little about the information and decide we lack certain essentials to make any decisions.
> PLUS .001: We insert additional overlay, inaccurate assumptions a prejudice in order to make it more palatable.
> PLUS .01: We reach a conclusion regarding our surrounding physical reality.

PLUS .1: Assured of the accuracy of our reality understanding, we make corrections to our hard-wired memory, file the conclusions for quick reference in the next check to make sure nothing changes too drastically, and begin the process all over again.

Overlap these processing sequences and perform them at fifty times per second and you can see that not only is the accuracy somewhat questionable, but no matter how fast it operates, it will always be just a tad behind reality as it can be observed. We will always be subject to our own observations as well as our own belief concepts.[11]

Think of what is happening to a UFO witness. These complicated, subconscious processes are going on while the mind is furiously trying to stuff everything into the proper mental filing boxes for cognition and recall later. It is a wonder that we get *any* memories of extraordinary experiences. Referring to this conundrum, parapsychologist Dean Radin said, "We're not equipped very well for accommodating and absorbing things which are too different... If you don't have a place to stick a memory, it just doesn't stick at all."[12]

When a witness sees something startling and unexpected they may block it out or transpose or conflate the experience with something else in the same way as a trauma or abuse victim often does. Perhaps there are far more UFOs seen than are ever reported for just this reason. It is so jarring to a sense of everyday reality that the victim creates a story for themselves and others that the he or she can handle without too many problems, and without having to live with the disturbing memory as it happened. Researchers counter that abduction victims often have terrifying memories of ostensibly real experiences, but perhaps the actual reality is either so incomprehensible or so terrifying simply because there is nothing to compare it to, and the victim latches on to whatever makes sense, even if it seems outlandish by most people's standards.

UFOs and anything walking out of them are never expected and always strange. In the act of first experiencing the event, and then, more importantly, in remembering it and telling the story about it to ourselves and others, we are adding many layers of cultural baggage and other input that help us to make sense of the experience. In so doing, we are taking ourselves step-by-step away from our original impressions.

The phenomenon of faulty memory and perception is so common that lawyers and judges are starting to place less emphasis on witness testimony, and this is for events that we all agree happen every day—like assaults and murders.

In a January 2010 article in *Scientific American* on witness reliability, authors Hal Arkowitz and Scott O. Lilienfeld wrote:

> The uncritical acceptance of eyewitness accounts may stem from a popular misconception of how memory works. Many people believe that human memory works like a video recorder: the mind records events and then, on cue, plays back an exact replica of them. On the contrary, psychologists have found that memories are reconstructed rather than played back each time we recall them. The act of remembering, says eminent memory researcher and psychologist Elizabeth F. Loftus of UC, Irvine, is "more akin to putting puzzle pieces together than retrieving a video recording." Even questioning by a lawyer can alter the witness's testimony because fragments of the memory may unknowingly be combined with information provided by the questioner, leading to inaccurate recall.[13]

Most UFO and abduction researchers probably have an idea of what they are looking for before they speak to witnesses. This invariably guides the interview. Recently, some MUFON representatives have claimed their field investigators are now specifically instructed and trained to not ask leading questions. This is a great step, but the investigator may not even need to lead the witness that much, because already they know that the investigator is there to ask them about their UFO encounter, and the image given to us by popular culture is already assuming that the questioner is asking about aliens from other planets. This may be even more implicit when witnesses speak about abductions.

Karim Nader, a neuroscientist at McGill University in Montreal, has proposed that the very act of remembering causes errors to creep into our recall. Journalist Greg Miller wrote in a 2010 article from *Smithsonian* magazine:

> ... it may be impossible for humans or any other animal to bring a memory to mind without altering it in some way. Nader thinks it's likely that some types of memory, such as a flashbulb memory, are more susceptible to change than others. Memories surrounding a major event like September 11 might be especially susceptible, he says,

because we tend to replay them over and over in our minds and in conversation with others—with each repetition having the potential to alter them.

Nader and his colleagues have termed this "memory reconsolidation:"

... recalling the experience to other people may allow distortions to creep in. "When you retell it, the memory becomes plastic, and whatever is present around you in the environment can interfere with the original content of the memory," [postdoctoral researcher Oliver] Hardt says.

Nader suggests that this might be a coping mechanism that the brain uses to make memory useful, rather than accurate. Again from the *Smithsonian* article:

[mental] editing might be another way to learn from experience. If fond memories of an early love weren't tempered by the knowledge of a disastrous breakup, or if recollections of difficult times weren't offset by knowledge that things worked out in the end, we might not reap the benefits of these hard-earned life lessons. Perhaps it's better if we can rewrite our memories every time we recall them. Nader suggests that reconsolidation may be the brain's mechanism for recasting old memories in the light of everything that has happened since. In other words, it might be what keeps us from living in the past.[14]

But what about the initial impressions we receive from our visual system? Could those be wrong as well?

Illustration adapted from Donald Hoffman, *Visual Intelligence: How We Create What We See.* 1998, WW Norton. p. 3.

The diagram above is an illustration of a perception experiment called "The Magic Square." Look at the pattern on the left. You should see a well-defined square appear in the middle of the slanted lines. It may even appear brighter than the background. As we move to the second figure, it appears that the square is not as defined as the first one. When we arrive at the pattern on the right, the perceived square has almost or completely disappeared.

What this suggests is that our mode of perceiving visual input is very adept at filling in what is not there, and may be a way for our brains to quickly analyze the environment by extrapolating what isn't there with something that should be (or that we expect) much of the time. In essence, the less information we are presented with (or can comprehend) the more our minds fill in the blanks with what is expected, or at least what we can comprehend.

This, taken with the research on the susceptibility of memory recall to external (and internal) influences, suggests that the implications for UFO close encounter witnesses and abductees are significant. There is a distinct possibility that whatever is happening to people, from complete illusion to actual contact with non-human entities, may be so far removed from the original experience that we are starting with compromised recall even before the witness talks about it, and extrapolating even further as they describe their encounter to a UFO researcher. Whatever is seen is so well-hidden behind a wall of expectations, perceptual errors and reconstituted memories that any supposed intelligence behind it doesn't need to fool us, control our minds or cover up our memories with other ones.

Is it possible that we really make up what we are seeing, or at least edit it heavily based on our evolutionary heritage?

Donald D. Hoffman is Professor of Cognitive Science at UC Irvine and is the author of a book entitled *Visual Intelligence: How We Create What We See.* He has proposed an evolutionary model of perception that says humans have developed a sense of reality that is rooted in our survival rather than the reality of what is there. In other words, our ways of seeing were not evolved to see things as they are, but to see things in a way that ensured fitness for the species. In fact, Hoffman has developed actual equations of evolutionary survivability that take into account environment, threats, resources, physical state of the organism, and a few other factors. He tested them to make sure that they were consistent with real world data and then started to run computer simulations of differing scenarios. About these experiments, he said: "Across thousands of simulated trials, fitness or survival trumped reality in every case. All organisms that saw only what was best for their survival beat out the rest that saw reality as it was or partially as it was." [15]

What this suggests is that we have evolved our perceptions to deal with factors that give us the best chance to deal with threats or needs, and ignore the rest of the input from our senses. Hoffman also says that we are looking at things one step or more removed from reality (see McMoneagle quote above) and compares our experience of the world to a computer: "Evolution has given us an interface that hides reality and guides adaptive behavior." [16] He compares it to a computer desktop with the observation that "physical objects are simply icons on that desktop." The icons of files are only representations of the data stored in the computer. They are not the physical hard drive, the memory, and all the integrated circuits, etc. that comprise the computer itself. That information is not useful to us. The data and how we access it is what is important. Hoffman is suggesting that physical objects as we perceive them are not the real physical objects in reality, but what we perceive as useful to us. They are approximations of that reality.

He concludes that, "Reality is like a 3D desktop that is designed to hide the real world and guide adaptive behavior." And that "the desktop is not there to show us the reality of the computer, it's there to hide the reality." [17]

A snarky person could suggest that if Hoffman thinks physical objects are not what we perceive, then he should test his theory by jumping in front of a moving train. He responds that the visual representation of the train he sees is a great approximation of what the train actually is. It will still hurt him if he gets hit, in the same way that if you throw away the icon on your desktop that represents a file, you have lost all the work that went into it, even though it is only an electronic or graphic representation of the data and not the data itself.

So, how does this inform our concerns here? What do people see when they are witnessing an unknown object or consciousness or strange paranormal scene?

It would seem that the most important thing our minds would be concerned with when we see a UFO close up is any sort of threat to our survival. Quickly, issues start to arise, such as "How close is it?" or "Is it going to hurt or kill me?" At that point, the witness' brain is furiously trying to figure out if the unknown object or being or whatever it is could be a threat. Since there are no precedents in their lives for what is happening, the mind will latch on to the most familiar or recognizable scenario, or make one up. Then, in the remembering or retelling, the witness' mind may subtly change events as described previously. Many encounters seem to follow dream logic, which is at least within the psyche's experience. In this way, the experience of the paranormal can also be seen as an information-rich event that the mind organizes into its own version of reality and recalls and retells to itself in order to make sense of the experience, no matter what was going on in the local environment at the time.

Almost a decade ago, the late writer, researcher and transhumanist Mac Tonnies said, "I have this hunch that this [UFO] phenomenon comes from some sort of domain of pure information, and the fact that it can interact with us at all suggests that we also inhabit a domain of pure information."[18] This was a most prescient statement. Until recently, scientists have regarded mass and energy as the primary building blocks of nature. Now, some are beginning to regard information as the basic currency of reality. This may be following a trend in science that stretches back over 3000 years.

In ancient Greece, surveying equipment and musical instruments were regarded as the pinnacle of technology, and the Greeks thought of the universe as a series of geometrical relationships and musical harmony. This idea held sway until just after the Renaissance when clockwork mechanisms had reached a high level of development. At that time, people like Isaac Newton thought of the cosmos as a deterministic clock that ran on a precise schedule like a machine. In the 19th century, the steam engine was the rage and scientists at the time thought of the universe as an almost infinite heat machine, gradually running out of fuel and collapsing. A combination of these ideas ruled popular science until just about 90 years ago, when ideas of quantum physics entered the picture. Now, those theories and quantum computing are becoming the new models of how reality is conceptualized, perhaps as a vast information processing system, with us at the center of it.[19]

The concept of quantum computing relies on having the data not only stored in a state of on or off, 0 or 1, as in the computers and phones and tablets everyone uses, but in both states at once. In this way, it can store much more data and perform potentially trillions of computations per second. In theory, it can represent all values of a computation simultaneously and solve certain problems extremely quickly, since it is essentially working on all possibilities at once. These devices are in their infancy and the very first functioning examples have appeared only in the last few months. The theory behind their operation derives from the quantum physics models of entanglement (where the measurement of one particle can affect another irrespective of location) and super-position of states (which says that probabilities of multiple quantum states can be combined) and which are used as the basis to store and analyze data. Probabilities are collapsed when the problem is solved.

In a crude analogy, perhaps the UFO witness may be involved in a strange scenario where the possibility of an improbable event becomes real when they witness or get near it, and that it could evolve in an infinite number of directions until the witness collapses the probability by observation.

This is not to say that we are living in some sort of vast computer simulation, a concept that tabloid science has been drooling over recently. The idea may be closer to Hoffman's concept of perceived objects being like, but not what they are. However, the proponents of information theory are not asserting that the model is a metaphor, but that reality may comprise countless bits of information at a basic level.

Information theory studies the quantification of information. In 1990, the famous American physicist John Archibald Wheeler (who worked on the Manhattan Project and the hydrogen bomb) said that he was beginning to suspect that what we experience as reality is directly and intimately connected to our observation of it, which he termed the "Participatory Anthropic Principle." In simplified form, this is the theory that all physical things arise from a background of infinite possibilities and are quantified only when they are observed—the so-called "it from bit" idea.

In 1990, Wheeler explained in his book *A Journey Into Gravity and Spacetime*:

> ... every *it*—every particle, every field of force, even the space-time continuum itself—derives its function, its meaning, its very existence entirely—even if in some contexts indirectly—from the apparatus-elicited answers to yes-or-no questions, binary choices, bits. It from bit symbolizes the idea that every item of the physical world has at bottom—a very deep bottom, in most instances—an immaterial source and explanation; that which we call reality arises in the last analysis from the posing of yes-no questions and the registering of equipment-evoked responses; in short, that all things physical are information-theoretic in origin and that this is a *participatory universe*.[20]

So, what is done to the "bit" that transforms into "it" when someone sees a UFO (or perhaps even other paranormal phenomena)? Perhaps at that point, the witness is so close to a unique realm or field of infinite possibility, that a quick and almost random series of decisions are made as to the form that the probability will take, that it has no time to be checked against what "should" be there. If we are thinking in terms of an external, non-human intelligence or consciousness, they may be far more conversant with this concept than we are. There is even the possibility (alluded to earlier) that the result is some sort of true co-creation with an external consciousness. The concepts examined so far indicate that anomalous experience is not well-supported by a physics-based view of reality, but is almost a certainty in an informational one.

It appears to some of us that aliens are coming to our planet in structured craft and occasionally taking some of us out of our beds at night to perform strange experiments and sometimes say and do other nonsensical things. In the infinite realm of possibilities, and in our version of reality and the cosmos, this is highly improbable, but not completely impossible. There is also the possibility that we have created this by our expectations and evolutionary heritage of perception, and it is akin to, but not what is actually happening. The reality of it may either be so foreign to our way of thinking or even conceptualizing that this is the closest we can get at this point.

Can we get ourselves out of the equation to see the phenomenon for what it really is, if there is such a thing? If there is a non-human consciousness interacting with us, occasionally, there is probably no way to see them except in relation to us. Any theorizing about their motivations or methods is doomed because it may be self-reflexive at such a basic level as to be meaningless.

There is the old idea that God created the universe in order to see what not being God was like. There was no yardstick for a supreme being's existence until not existing as a supreme being was a possibility. Something similar may be operating here. From the "aliens" (or whatever they are's) point of view, we may not exist except when there is some sort of interaction, and they either accidentally or deliberately create scenarios where we can interact.

I will repeat that I am not trying to "explain away" UFO experiences here. I have never encountered any unidentified flying object at close range, or had what is classically called an "abduction" experience. If I do, someday, there is the possibility that I will be so overwhelmed by my experience that I will immediately switch over to the standard view that aliens from other planets have told me the Truth and that all of this is just silly intellectual games. If that ever happens, I hope that I can maintain my philosophical distance, and still be able to speculate freely on what I saw.

The issues discussed here are essentially beliefs and theories about the phenomenon based on years of observations and data. The area I want to inhabit if I do have a close encounter is a third category that is neither belief nor the certainty of knowing, but that keeps me in between opinions about what happened, because I can never be sure if my conclusions can reflect any concrete external reality. As we have seen, there may be no way that we can have uncompromised access to this external reality, and it may not actually exist until we come to the end of a long line of incalculable questions about what it is.

There is also the issue that science can't answer everything yet, especially questions of how UFOs and paranormal phenomena affect witnesses on an emotional level and how these may change their lives. This aspect is usually forgotten in a rush for some sort of respectability by hamstringing UFO study into a supposedly scientific framework. Many close encounter witnesses have their outlook, beliefs, and even their entire lives changed by one short encounter with the unknown. It involves issues that can't be quantified in a chart or narrowed down in a questionnaire. Perhaps the very act of trying to quantify these life-changing issues robs them of their meaning. It is an area ripe for research by someone who can perhaps forego the making of charts and graphs and instead focus on the documentation of each story as a piece in some sort of larger puzzle that engages our emotional makeup.

Whitley Strieber once mentioned that he heard an extraordinary statement from a government insider who said that what they were trying to suppress in the 1950s and later was *belief* in the visitors, because the more we believed in them, the more chance they had to get at us in some way. He wrote that it was either his deduction, or that he was told by his visitors, that interaction was being performed in the most democratic way possible, literally from the bottom up, by contacting people on an individual basis and letting their personalities and perceptions be affected as a way to introduce us to the idea of contact.

We don't need to take these statements completely literally, and, in fact, as we have seen, many issues of perception, memory, and even the basis of reality may not be literal (at least by popular definition) at all. They do, however reinforce the idea that we shoulder the main responsibility for our thoughts, theories, and feelings about non-human consciousness, whatever form it takes. Perhaps by looking within and at the human mind, our senses, and how we remember things, we can better calibrate our main instrument for measuring UFO encounters. This can only lead to a better understanding of the relationship we have with this mystery and, perhaps, any intelligence that may be associated with it.

DISCOVERING OUR HUMANITY
IN **THE ALIEN** OTHER

Robert Brandstetter

"A human being is a part of the whole called by us 'universe,' a part
limited in time and space. He experiences himself, his thoughts and
feeling as something separated from the rest—a kind of optical delusion
of his consciousness. This delusion is a kind of prison for us, restricting
us to our personal desires and to affection for a few persons nearest to
us. Our task must be to free ourselves from this prison by widening
our circle of compassion to embrace all living creatures and the whole
of nature in its beauty."

—ALBERT EINSTEIN

I am standing alone at night on a wooden bridge that cuts over a
marsh near the Credit River in Mississauga, Ontario, staring into
the sky, looking for signs. The slow drone of cars on the overpass
settles into the background buzz of an insect symphony. Toads sing sad
love songs and a cacophony of crickets create an aural chaos. Clouds
cling to the outer edge of darkness and dance under a scimitar moon
while I look at Mars signaling to me in the distance. Mars appears to
be rising slowly away from its ecliptic as if time is speeding up. Its light
gets brighter in the night sky.

I scan the south-eastern sky where I can see true Mars in its much dimmer red sheath. The light far to the right of it has increased in brightness and is definitely moving towards me. Mystified as the light glows brighter and brighter, I watch a soft orange fireball in the sky. Everything is suddenly quiet, as if someone has thrown a switch on the world. There are no cars or insects, just an anxious silence. The light glows larger now, soundless, the size of a copper penny held at arm's length. Its illumination increases. My heart rate rises and, as I watch, the orange ball rises directly above me and splits into two great glowing spheres of buttery mango. There is an electrical charge on my skin. I should not be seeing what I'm seeing. The silence is instantly cracked open by the sudden sound of hundreds of thousands of bees in the air. The buzzing is tremendous inside my head and comes in steady waves all around me. The two balls of light move further apart to reveal a tiny lemony spark in between them, strobing steady in time to the buzzing reverberations. My body vibrates with this unreal cacophony and the entire marshland in front of me is now illuminated and alive.

There are things dancing in the woods, strange aquatic shapes, like weird pulsing neon jellyfish that swim in and out of trees. They are all around me and I can no longer feel myself standing on the bridge. I am covered in amber light and am subtly stretching. I feel elastic. My fingers are not my fingers; they look thin and long while I float freely in the swirls of light. Above me is a miasma of multi-colored starfish, red ochre seahorses and glowing sea slugs that contort and buckle like a green and blue train. The night is a riot of color. A celestial siren call is singing in the centre of my skull. It is the strobing electrical ball that controls the heavy rhythm in my brain. It is ripples on my skin. My body throbs in time to it. It is saying it wants to speak with me. Over and over again, its buzz blares that it wants to speak to me. And, just as before, a switch is thrown and then there is nothing—total darkness. I am standing alone on the wooden bridge again and there is no sound. No strange sights. Just nothingness. I look to my left into the hollow dark tunnel of the forest path beyond the bridge. I look to my right and a thin alien figure in the shadows is coming towards me...

Dear Witness: Nobody Wants to Hear Your UFO Story!

We are storytellers by nature. There is something that burns deeply in the human experience that compels us to share our stories with those who are near to us. We share our dreams and visions, tales of life and death and survival. We recall our earliest experiences from the outer darkness of childhood when we saw things that we could not explain. All that moves us we want to share.

For tens of thousands of years in cave paintings all around the world we see hand prints: hands outlined by color in Argentina's Cuevas de las Manos 31,000 years ago, mystical spirals painted inside of hands in the Three Rivers location in America and the stencils of mutilated hands in the French Pyrenees in the Grotte de Gargas. On every continent in the world there is a cave stained with human hands, a universal graffiti that in its most base interpretation is a simple symbol of self, as if to say, *"Here is my hand on the wall. I was here once upon a time."*

The UFO experience is one that reaches out to us from the past to provide us with strange tales of horseless carts emerging from metal spheres touching down in farmers' fields, or inexplicable airships anchoring themselves on roofs as they hang in the sky over towns, whose operators wore fur skins or elegant dresses and suits as if preparing for high tea. UFO stories arrive out of every culture in the shape of dragons, phoenixes, pearls, holy spirits, saints, giant tanks, honeycombed spider-webbed ships, glowing orbs, triangles with red lights, and football-field-sized platforms that block out whole chunks of the sky. All these indescribable events are translated by human tongues into stories that must be told. But these are events so far outside the boundaries of common social experience that it makes their telling both a compulsion and a fear to admit seeing such preposterous things.

Such is the traumatic nature of the UFO experiencer. The anomalous experience is a story desperately looking for a way to be told. The trauma survivor is plummeted into a well of abnormality and faced with the task of trying to integrate that which the wider waking world often mocks and sometimes hyper-validates for the sake of perpetuating various myths of ufology, specifically to prop-up the ETH, a theory long in need of a drastic overhaul, if not outright abandonment.

Investigatory approaches towards the UFO witness have been haphazard and, in some cases, quite harmful, leaving the witness as something both to exploit and consume. Yet it is the witness experience that is the primary catalyst for ufology. Their stories have since exploded into an orgy of squabbles over belief systems, and the wringing of hands over the imminence of government Disclosure. What started as a story about seeing something strange in the sky has since been manufactured into a mythology by the whole cabal of gladiators in the arena of ufology. A return to the core component of the narrative is necessary and it must be done with more imagination, ethics and standardization that respect what it means to undergo a traumatic experience. A more compassionate approach to the witness, as well as an appreciation of how the act of seeing works during high-strange experiences, may allow us to gather much more valuable information about how the UFO phenomenon intersects with human perception.

The physiological limits of human perception provide only a glimpse of reality; consequently, it is worth our while to parse out the full experience of the UFO witness—not just how to ameliorate the social rejection, but because the entire container of how the UFO experience is translated must be refashioned. How the UFO witness has been prepared for their individual experience must take priority in any investigation, especially as we learn more about neurobiology and how these scientific examinations define our perceptual experiences. It is imperative to look at the human body as both a memory archive and a perceptual tool translating highly unique external stimuli into words, thoughts and emotions.

Memory, culture and our sensory apparatus combine to create the narratives of consciousness that frame the UFO. In this way, it is both self-creationist muse and active agent of deconstruction. The witness must work to integrate this anomalous experience in the narrative of their own life. Those who come forth to speak must be prepared to have their status and very identity in society challenged. The investigator must seek a deeper understanding of how to approach these subjects as a means to augment our understanding and experience of reality, as well as engage in profound acts of self-discovery. The essence of witness experience is one of change and transformation. People are altered profoundly by the accidental close encounter case turning them into accidents of their former selves. Those who spend time with survivors of trauma know that the internalization of such major life events is profoundly destabilizing. When a police officer becomes witness they are most severely reviled and rejected by the community. How can the embodiment of rationality have possibly seen something so irrational? During the Portage County Ohio Police UFO chase on April 17, 1966, two sheriff's deputies had a close sighting and chased the object into the neighbouring state of Pennsylvania at speeds of up to 100mph. The experience was as profound as the aftermath for all police involved, but especially destabilizing for officer Dale Spaur. His description is certainly alien in nature:

It started moving towards us, and this time he's still looking straight ahead. As it came over the trees and I looked at Barney and he's still watching the car. I mean the car in front of us. The thing kept getting brighter and the area started getting light. And I look at Barney and he's still not saying anything and I told him to look over his shoulder. So, he did and he didn't. He didn't say nothing and he just stood there with his mouth open for a minute and as bright as it was and he looked down and I started looking down and I looked at my hands at both of them Barney, Barney are you....... and then it stopped, parked right over top of us. And the only sound in the whole area was just a hum and it just changed a little bit but it wasn't anything screaming or real loud and, but you, sound like a transformer being loaded when you overload a transformer.[1]

Dale Spaur stands at the centre of an incredible story. This Deputy Sheriff became the accidental witness whose life foundered into a series of tragedies. He was soon after charged with spousal abuse, left his job, moved to a motel room, lost weight and finally lost his family. He also claimed to see the UFO for months afterwards. He was completely destabilized from the event.

No one who is invested in the normal order wants to hear this kind of story. Who is a better UFO witness than the moral guardian who risks social status to tell what they saw? This voice should be the most convincing of them all and yet police are often publicly vilified and have their lives ruined for daring to claim they saw a UFO. The story they dare to tell stands against a number of social constructs and is part of a continuum of narratives across a history of people experiencing a reality society would prefer to call a vision.

The UFO phenomenon takes place at the known borders of society, at the edge of human experience, and still unfolds in ways akin to the experience of the seer or shaman, except, instead of honoring this vision or attempting to integrate it into our social structures, we have laughter, derision, and exclusion. Their stories generated processes that moved society forward by innovating traditional practices. Truly the UFO is a vital and viral image, an agent of change in society that is a disruptive influence and appears as an invitation. The close encounter experience is a sensory overload for both the individual and society. These are things the human creature is not meant to see, and yet they are seen.

While described as a shy phenomenon occurring only in marginal spaces, UFOs often appear with an incredible theatricality. Rare and spectacular, they are a persistent injection into the narrative of consumer pop culture, and still hosted with glee by carnival barkers who will gladly show you the mummified remains of a young child which they claim to be a real-life Roswell alien. The alien meme has permanently entered the human psyche and, in the modern era, is on display for the cost of admission. We do such experiences wrong by haggling about them, bruising internet egos and completely abandoning the true role of the witness. What ufology needs is to have a reorientation and reinvention of the witness paradigm. As any decent investigator of any mystery knows, you need to talk to the witness before their narrative gets consumed and re-scripted by existing structures. Is this even possible in the modern era when everyone "knows" that flying saucers come from outer space? Creating new ways of working with witnesses, defining the nature of what it means to see something as rare as the UFO and comprehending its aftermath is a critical direction for the future.

Symbolic Reality: Witnessing Ultima Thule

> "What the psychedelics seem to me to argue for is that reality is not reality. There may be no reality, but certainly this is not it. This is some kind of highly provisional, culturally sanctioned hallucination that we are all participating in."

—TERRENCE MCKENNA

The world is a riot of color. Everything emits light and, depending on its vibration, we perceive it as a different color. Lava burns red with its photon emissions whereas stars emit not just red and orange but green and blue, and they combine to create white. Human beings are also made of electrically charged particles. We are made of star stuff, and so we are also creatures of light.

One third of the human brain is devoted to vision. It is important to understand, then, what the act of seeing entails. How does this sensory apparatus that is human perception take external photons of light and convert them into a workable virtual reality projected in our minds that allows us to function inside our physical environment?

Each individual has their own distinct virtual reality experience. Only through the medium of language, or other senses, can we communicate the similarity and differences of our experiences with each other. No two realities are the same. If we take time to reflect on those glowing bodies around us we do not have to look very far to see the alien among us. We, who are symbolic representations of stars and light, experience the human other from a distance. The UFO is held even further away. If we can understand better what it means to see, we may be able to participate more productively with the witness who has seen something extraordinary.

In his essay, "Conscious Realism and the Mind-Body Problem," Donald Hoffman explains a unique approach to seeing. Hoffman believes that the sensory perception system that humans have evolved exists to an extent in order for us to survive as a species. If humans had access to all frequencies of sound and light, would we be able to see anything clearly or even learn how to communicate amongst the cacophony of such sensory overload? Our evolving brain has provided us with essential survival skills so that as a species we can thrive:

> According to conscious realism, when I see a table, I interact with a system, or systems, of conscious agents, and represent that interaction in my conscious experience as a table icon. Admittedly, the table gives me little insight into those conscious agents and their dynamics. The table is a dumbed-down icon, adapted to my needs as a member of a species in a particular niche, but not necessarily adapted to give me insight into the true nature of the objective world that triggers my construction of the table icon. When, however, I see you, I again interact with a conscious agent, or a system of conscious agents. And here my icons give deeper insight into the objective world: they convey that I am, in fact, interacting with a conscious agent, namely you.[2]

This does not mean to say that Conscious Realism is Panpsychism, where all objects are conscious, but instead that they are symbols of a reality outside our own perceptual apparatus. What we see are representations of icons in how we as humans interact with reality through what Hoffman describes as a network of conscious agents all around us. When we see something, we have a conscious experience of those agents. But we only see what we need to see in order to survive and thrive.

This is why the UFO is such a unique event in the act of seeing. It appears to come from a land that is outside of normal human experience altogether, as with the maps of old where in the margins we read:

215

Here there be monsters! The high-strange experience of the UFO close encounter event is one in which the witness is able to catch a glimpse of Ultima Thule, that place on the map beyond known borders. Here there be conscious agents, or aspects of these agents, rarely accessible by human perception.

Hoffman describes his definition of a "conscious agent" through the following implications:

> A conscious agent is not necessarily a person. All persons are conscious agents, or heterarchies of conscious agents, but not all conscious agents are persons. Second, the experiences of a given conscious agent might be utterly alien to us; they may constitute a modality of experience no human has imagined, much less experienced. Third, the dynamics of conscious agents does not, in general, take place in ordinary four-dimensional space-time. It takes place in state spaces of conscious observers, and for these state spaces the notion of dimension might not even be well-defined.[3]

What this means is that beyond those experiences of easily visible conscious agents, swimming all around us is a reality beyond the margins of experience—networks of conscious agents who may or may not be conscious that interface with conscious observers in a very limited manner. This theory makes room for the UFO as a conscious agent, operating in a manner that humans cannot properly perceive at all, making the many surreal and strange witness reports of close encounter sightings better understood. Perhaps reality breaks down at the edges of our senses, having both a profound impact on the observer as well as giving them a glimpse of a conscious agent that is literally alien to us.

Researcher and podcaster Greg Bishop often cites the late abduction researcher Karla Turner's advice that the strangest encounter cases may be the most important. In the ever-probing realms of ufology such high-strange events have been compared to dreams, visions, ecstatic or religious experiences, and visits from aliens. Close encounter cases often appear to be hallucinatory and nonsensical. It is a psychedelic experience, more than anything else, filled with odd distortions of familiar realities. If we are to better know the UFO then we must learn first how to disentangle ourselves from the hallucinatory nature of seeing and accept that much of what is reported in closer encounter events is so very strange because it is beyond the borders of what can be witnessed. Greg Bishop has also advocated the concept of the witness event as being co-creative—where the interface of the external stimulus with a conscious observer work together to create a reality inside the mind of the observer. This is basically a very streamlined version of what Hoffman explains as Conscious Realism.

On May 10, 1978, Jan Wolski, a Polish farmer from Emilcin had a remarkable experience while riding his horse and cart out of some thickets. He suddenly spied two beings walking along the path. They had green faces and black uniforms like scuba divers, with tiny slits for mouths and fins between their fingers. He thought at first that they were Chinese with green painted faces when they jumped into his cart. They spoke in a strange rapid language that was unintelligible to Wolski and never once engaged in anything such as telepathic communication:

JW: They were driving ahead for some time and then ordered me to stop—they didn't speak in words but expressed it with hands to stop. So, I understood it and began urging the horse to stop but he [one of the beings] caught the reins and pulled back urging the horse to stop. And when it stopped they got off the cart—in the same way as they previously got on and they gave me a sign with hands to go with them.

I tied my horse, then got off and went after them toward that machine.

There was a tiny elevator of some kind for two people to hold—maybe it couldn't carry two large people but surely could delicate ones… And then he went forth and set his foot onto this craft, I followed him and it soon lifted up rapidly—in front of that craft door. And the whole craft could be about 4m. above the ground, maybe 4.5m. [The corners of the roof and the "small lift" connected with "cord"—cables or wires with a diameter similar to that of an electric cable of modern irons.][4]

It was a purely white craft—from outside. It could be 4.5 maybe to 5m. in height and it was as long as a bus, so it looked in that way [Jan Wolski on other occasion mentioned that there were 4 "barrels" on the craft corners with "drills." Those black drill-like objects seemed to be made of black material and were rotating around its axis with great speed although without creating any disturbances in the air. They generated the hum Wolski mentioned].[5]

This is a fascinating case featuring a visual description of both the small men and their craft. It also featured the requisite medical check-up in which the little green men in scuba suits had Wolski strip down. The seemingly interstellar craft has all the hallmarks of both the surreal and technological magic present in high-strange events. The cable system for the platform and Wolski's own nonchalance throughout the entire event, including his polite refusal of an icicle-shaped cake-like material that the beings were eating and offered to him, all speak to a shared creative event. His perceptions of the experience appear to be drawn from both his own personal life experiences in combination with what must have been an extremely bizarre external stimulus.

There are sociological and cultural symbols that help to organize and structure our society and define a normative representation of reality. There are perhaps also species-specific symbols lurking in the reptilian brain that create emotional responses in the limbic system that we use to navigate the essence of our reality. The value of Jungian concepts such as The Shadow, The Other and The Trickster may be valuable in how they represent common expressions of human experiences as stories. There is also the archetypal experience of "The Visit by The Stranger," where rare external stimuli, which like any stimuli we can never truly perceive in a veridical manner, may cause certain human beings to have what others may define as an irrational experience, like a Polish farmer from Emilcin who meets two strange small green fellows in the middle of the field who hop on his wagon and take him by metal rope system up to their spaceship. This illogical event challenges our cultural ideas about transportation in the sky and positions us as specimen. It is a stimulus being injected into our collective society on a global level—is it a species-specific symbol? It would seem so.

The symbolic structures of society may either see this as dangerous or may conversely welcome the creative narratives of those who can imagine a reality beyond known maps and borders. They are the wayfarers to Ultima Thule, sojourners of the high-strange whose perceptions challenge stagnant structures and reveal other possibilities related to technology and culture. For now, the close encounter UFO witness is rarely cared for, and often exploited or demeaned. Meanwhile, the original narrative is rarely interpreted, but translated into confirmation of the ETH. This leaves little room for imaginative processes to respond to something potentially much more fascinating taking place inside and outside of the witness, who are collaborators with an external stimulus and are often removed from the equation of the event itself. Their story is reduced to singular testimony or event. Who they were before, during, and after the events are equally necessary engagements by any investigator or treating physician. Like all evolving species, we must embrace the innovative narratives in our culture so that the doorways of knowing continue to open. We must welcome the UFO witness and give them a more appropriate response by caring for their narratives in the way we would care for any human being having extraordinarily difficult and traumatic experiences. They have had a glimpse of the unknown country, and they come to us buzzing with a vision of innovative transit and, sometimes, alien beings. In many ways, the close encounter UFO witness event is an invitation to be explored.

The late Bruce Duensing, a highly imaginative commentator on ufology, paranormality and the witness experience, identified the UFO as an overt invitation to explore the limits of how we understand the reality of human transit. There is a distinct history of invention that is being mapped out by what is seen:

> One aspect of everything involved with this phenomenon that struck me this morning relates to the general concepts whose axis is a vehicle to overcome time and space in our three dimensions, and how in a sense our defining of the possibility of how this can be accomplished has evolved from earthbound vehicles to air borne mechanisms to space faring vehicles and now physics that transcends the former materials of earth, then atmosphere and then space, to our changing the materials themselves in a quantum sense. Have the forms of anomalies seen in the sky shown a trending of this by the predominance of one form versus another...? Are these simply semiotic metaphors as a form of feedback... suggesting a form of "transit" always one step ahead of technology? They could reflect a transition from hard craft plying various mediums to changing the medium itself by way of physics.... a changing of 'vehicles'? If so could this be a form of feedback that suggests an invitation? Sometimes I am struck by how this resembles a carrot on a stick... that prods a changing of context in our conceptual models in terms of our means of transit.[6]

The UFO challenges the witness with regards to their own known paradigms of transit in the skies, presenting impossible materials, mediums, shapes and forms. They also leave their mark on the witness as seen in the case of Dr. X, investigated by both Aime Michel and, later, Jacques Vallée. The absurd high-strange events that continued to follow Dr. X and his family, from teleportation and levitation to poltergeist activity, demonstrate the capacity the UFO experience has for the deconstruction of commonly held beliefs about reality. For two years following this experience, Dr. X and his infant son, the only two witnesses to the event, experienced recurring triangular red marks on their stomachs centred around the navel. Michel writes about the wife's experience of events in their home following the incident:

Mme "X" consequently felt at first an unendurable sensation of unreality, as she has often told me. She expected me, and the other people whom she consulted, to find an explanation which would bring everything back once more onto a basis of logic and reason. When she began to perceive that this was impossible and that she and her family would be obliged—at least for the time being—to resign themselves to the realm of the irrational, despair was added to her impression of unreality.[7]

Michel's continued investigation of the many high-strange reports by Dr. X defined unique consequences for the witness who was subjected to a prolonged experience of the destabilization of their previously held beliefs about the physical truths of the world.

Symbolically, the UFO may signal advances in technology. Perhaps we are being prodded, by a conscious agent, to consider how we re-invent aerial vehicular forms of transportation. Each witness to such high drama is imprinted by such visions. When the narrative includes "aliens" it also positions the human being as a specimen, subjected to banal medical experimentation, or at its most torturous and medieval, they become the object of sexual violation and extreme medical experimentation. When reports of such nature are being made, as in any case of violent transgression, the witness must have access to state-provided, professional medical and psychological support systems, rather than an individual collecting new material for their next podcast.

The symbol in the sky is more than mandala. It is an icon that represents a distinct human experience that commands attention when a witness is impacted dramatically by such altered experiential spaces. In an essay titled, "Are UFO's a Cosmic Art Project?," Greg Bishop asks, "When a witness sees something flitting through the sky (or perhaps closer) s/he is often forced to at least temporarily suspend what they think about "reality." Some cases (like great art works) achieve a permanent shift in the witness' worldview. It's strange that most researchers tend to ignore this aspect of the UFO experience." Later in the same essay he closes with the following pertinent observation: "So the non-human intelligences knocking at our collective consciousness may have no other message than 'look,' or 'think,' or perhaps even 'you don't know everything.' Ultimately, what the UFO subject does is throw a mirror in front of us, to look at what we are, and how we perceive our reality, which is of course one of the things that great art is supposed to do."[8] Great artworks should destabilize and alter the viewer through their innovation and intensity. In the wake of the UFO experience our cool reality is shattered. We are forever changed when allowed to see the world in a manner not known before.

If we subtract our own innate bias, context, and psychology from the history of UFO reports, what we have left is the pure art of the universe: energy=information. And that might be all we can grasp at this time. The phenomenon seems to be shifting as it responds to our own technological inquiries. The other possibility is that the mind of the witness creates their own iconic skin to dress whatever the stimulus is behind the UFO in the technological clothing of the times. It is best described as a co-created event.

We might do well to engage in more long-term studies of witnesses who have been altered to get a better measure of the unknown external stimulus. For while we cannot know the UFO, we can know how we've been changed by seeing it. In this way, we have a direct connection to the phenomenon measured by our internal shifts; which, in turn, make us a part of the unknown. In knowing that much about ourselves, we can know something of the phenomenon as well. We are a part of this metaphor, this cosmic art project, for, like the UFO, we are also transitional and transformative beings who live and breathe symbolic reality.

We have evolved to use photons to sense the world and to see things. We will always be seeing things. The colors of the world signal to us, as people signal to us to mate with them, love them, be with them to work and create together. Let us let the alien Other who signals to us from sky and ground merely be one more sign that reaffirms our essential humanity, our essential love of the Other. If we start from such a premise, then treatment of the witness with great compassion will extend beyond their narrative and examine more the one who sees.

Knowing Iris: Finding Humanity in the Alien Other

"Once you realize the phenomenon may be deliberately misleading, then you can use certain safeguards. I'm not saying that safeguards are always going to work. There is an element of danger you really can't avoid. There's no way to do that kind of study just by reading books."

—Jacques Vallée

The alien Other is us. We are alien to each other in all our exchanges with other human beings on this earth. We may speak the same language and see similar things, but our experiences of reality are incredibly different. We want to connect to each other through the tools and symbols we have fashioned. But in our solitary experiences we are still utterly alone and apart from the other. We try to mitigate these distances through common attempts to fashion a shared symbolic reality, to express what we've seen and lived through. Still, there are chasms of meaning that we cannot truly overcome. These chasms are most evident in what Chris Rutkowski describes as Alien Abduction Syndrome. He describes the people who are having the experience of contact with aliens as having difficulty with dealing with reality: "For some reason certain people appear to think they have been contacted by aliens. This could be because of various contributing factors: dissatisfaction with life; stress; domestic problems; peer pressure; rape trauma; chemical imbalances or child abuse. Perhaps any one of these or in combination of them."[9] Trauma appears to be an essential component of the alien contact/abduction experience. For the individual experiencer, there is the highly symbolic event of the stranger who visits us from far away and you are abducted into their realm. Suddenly, it seems as if reality is broken and what you are seeing and feeling cannot be, but it is there nonetheless. This experience has happened twice in my life.

In 1977, at the age of nine I saw two classic illuminated and seemingly metallic ships descend upon me and a friend at night while on an ice rink in Northern Ontario. They made no sound and hung still in the sky. One started moving towards us until it was only about two telephone pole heights above us. Multi-colored lights were on its perimeter and it remained utterly silent. I heard my own voice in my head say, *"You know what's going to happen. You're going to get abducted."* This flying saucer hung in the air for around a minute and then slowly drifted along the edge of the backyards of the houses bordering the ice rink field. I remember hearing the voices of the adults inside calling out about the lights in the sky and one shouted for binoculars, which was strange in retrospect because what I was looking at certainly didn't require magnification. I suspect we were all seeing very different things in the sky at that moment. The 'ship' continued to drift in a straight line until it paused over a roof and tall tree in the backyard of a friend's house. I had the distinct impression it was 'scanning' the people in the house. It slowly went up to join its counterpart and the two of them lazily moved across the neighbourhood to the north and hung above the main intersection of Sault Ste. Marie at Highway 17 North and then they rapidly burst up into the sky at an incredible rate. We watched those two lights join the stars and then fade into nothingness. The next summer, along with a friend, we saw that the top third of the tree described previously now appeared to be dead and burnt. We also noticed that the shingles on the roof where the object had paused now looked as if they had been burned and overturned in a radial arc. I am a UFO witness.

The second of my experiences is captured in the story at the beginning of this essay; it is a visionary description of the events leading up to my first contact with Iris Phalene, a self-described alien living a lonely life here on planet earth. One night in 2005 I had a very strange experience of an object in the sky while walking in the woods at night. While meditating on the light, I allowed my mind to drift into hallucinatory territory, as was often my practice when completing walking mediations in the evening. I allowed the orange light to transform into an altered object and watched with delight as it in turn altered my perceptions of the natural world around me, transforming the woods into a surreal aquatic phantasmagoria, which was followed by meeting a strange woman who came out of the dark woods. She was short and unnaturally thin, and her conversation was immediate. She described herself as an alien that had just arrived on earth.

For as long as I can remember, my significant experiences with human beings have been around their sharing of traumatic experiences with me. I grew up in a space of domestic trauma, have experienced permanent life-altering traumas at various points, and have since found myself to be the receiver of the narratives of many others who are trauma survivors. Beyond being listener and sometimes friend, their life narratives have often become entangled in my own. While some I still maintain contact with, many others, at my own advising, have sought out professional psychological and psychiatric supports to help them navigate the difficulties they were having with their own experiences of reality.

My contact with Iris Phalene lasted for only three months and altered me permanently. Our brief communications were destabilizing at the time, but through her I discovered something about the nature of humanity and what it means to make contact with the alien Other. During our time together I interviewed her over a series of brief and strange meetings, often in the woods:

Robert Brandstetter: Why do you identify with aliens?

Iris Phalene: Because they are far away and they visit earth and that's what I do. I'm from far away and I visit earth.

RB: How long are you here for?

IP: I don't know. I'm stuck here. I fell here by accident because I fell from the moon. I adore her. She is my lover, and my mother and myself.

RB: Did you leave anyone behind there on the moon?

IP: No. It was solitude.

RB: Have you had contact with similar aliens here on earth like yourself?

IP: There's some people who aren't exactly people; they are special. They have minds that work.

RB: Compared to the rest of the people here? Their minds don't work? Are they filled with bad stuff?

IP: They don't necessarily have bad stuff. It's filled with longing and desire. They live this life just to die and that's their mission. They keep staying the same. They don't know what they are working towards and they are working towards death.

RB: Are you working towards death?

IP: No, I wish for death. And then I would have no presence and I would not exist anymore. I would prefer to have quiet and nothingness.

RB: Do you experience desire and longing as well?

IP: Yeah I do. We all do. Some people experience it but don't know what to do with it. It's not bad, but if you have no desire and longing then what else do you have? You are always looking for something but you don't know what it is. Sometimes people call you, or it's death that calls you and you go there because you want to see what that song is.

RB: How else do you recognize the other aliens among us?

IP: Well, you are drawn to their energies. You are drawn to them because they are like poetry and they inspire you when you are around them. Sometimes you are drawn to aliens because being around them would inspire good poetry. You want to take their energy and translate it into words. Because you only exist through those people because they only exist through poetry. And if you don't exist and you are not creating art then what else are you doing?

RB: Is the act of creating important to you?

IP: It's not important per se, but it's all one can ever do and it's a wonderful thing. Well, that and destroy. Destruction happens on its own but you can always dance with that flame. You can watch your world turn to shit because you have nothing else to lose.

RB: Is this a cyclical event for you, creation and destruction?

IP: Every few hours I'm a different person.

RB: Are there any other parts of alien contact that you can describe to me?

IP: Every single contact with an alien is good. Sometimes it's very brief and it lasts only the length of a cigarette. Sometimes it only lasts for one fun wild night. Other times it lasts for an indefinite amount of time. And that only happens with people who you really suspect are aliens. Because strange things happen with them in that great long amount of time and you don't expect it.

RB: Can you describe those strange things?

IP: Strange in that nothing happens in that moment and you don't have to be dead for a time. You are alive and smiling and nothing's happing. And you can share that with someone for a while. It is strange because I am a very solitary person.

RB: You brought up a point earlier in your discussions about your relationship to others and your experiences of them.

IP: I feel so disconnected to others no matter how close they are.

RB: You identified it doesn't really matter what their experience of you is or how they feel about you.

IP: That does matter because I perceive they don't want me there and then I leave. Even with people I'm close to, no matter who they are because I feel more alien from them. We're all aliens but I'm alien from them too.

RB: You still feel this way no matter how much they convince you otherwise that maintaining a dynamic with you is important?

IP: Because you're not actually seeing them. They're not there at all so it doesn't matter if they leave. Because I won't feel the pain they will feel and so I can do whatever and it doesn't matter. I try to feel for them and try to get a glimpse of them but I can't. I want to feel but if I can't feel that, I don't need it.

RB: There's a deep melancholy there.

IP: There is. Because it's always sad when you do that with people. But it's okay. As soon as one thing goes, another comes.

RB: So feelings are a very perplexing thing.

IP: They are perplexing! Feelings are a bitch. And the way we all experience them differently but we share the same words for them. Everyone feels sad yet each sadness is different.

RB: Well we all have our own reality. And in that way, we are all aliens from each other.

IP: But I like to talk with you. It's an alien dynamic this one. You are an alien. We are two aliens. Whenever you have a dynamic with another alien you find your humanity. Which is the goodness in you. You discover a new part of you and you view that part of you as a distinct individual and you sort of become it and you try to hold onto it. It's nice but it's a very individual experience because of the other being. It's a very permanent thing to hold onto that. Because it's discovery, a creation of self.[10]

~

Following this interview in late 2005 Iris has since departed from my life and I have no manner of contacting her again. The experience of my time with her can best be described as a period of my life where it felt like I was swimming with the mermaids. I knew Iris to be suffering from a series of various personal traumas that manifested in great physiological, mental and emotional complication. I do not believe that she was an alien living here on earth but I do know she was very alienated from most of the human beings she made contact with. Knowing her was a great challenge on a deep personal level.

In longing to make contact with the alien Other we can destabilize ourselves in ways that are not always healthy in how we endure our lonely existential hours. If you decide to set out for Ultima Thule, you best take caution. The dialog with Iris taught me that those who are having severely altered perceptions of reality appear to be experiencing Hoffman's "conscious agents" in ways not normally perceived. Iris' discussions on time, memory, perception and human interaction were utterly alien to me but her goodness and kindness as an alien here on earth reminded me, with each successive contact, that human compassion is what must be at the root of all our interactions with those whose narratives descend from trauma.

The longing to see the ship and share time with its pilot, Aura Rhanes, is a simple fantasy of sexual union, participating in grainy explosions along the Milky Way.[11] There is a stress and distress to such spaces that can evolve into addictions and self-destruction. To dare to know the song the siren sings is to sink oneself into a void of self-design. The pursuit of the UFO mystery offers much of the same. There is a danger in surrendering the ego and identity, and so the call of the UFO may simply be one that is mirroring something much simpler to us. *Do not try to penetrate the mystery, for that is not the way, but learn about yourself and what you are at the edges of the capacities of your biology.* In a world where we are symbol we may best use our biology to create positive networks for our collective mindspace in order to share more fully with one another, and in kinder ways. Each human conscious agent has perceptions so different from one another that we all qualify as alien to each other. To learn to be with each other may be the first thing the UFO mystery has to offer humanity, a chance to reflect on the best of what we can be as a social species.

ABOUT THE **CONTRIBUTORS**

CHRIS **RUTKOWSKI** is a Canadian science writer and educator with degrees in astronomy and education. Since the mid-1970s, he's also been studying reports of UFOs and writing about his investigations and research. He has eight published books on UFOs and related issues, including *Unnatural History* (1993), *Abductions and Aliens* (1999), *A World of UFOs* (2008), *I Saw It Too!* (2009) and *The Big Book of UFOs* (2010). He has appeared on numerous radio programs, podcasts and documentary TV series, including *Unsolved Mysteries, UFO Hunters, Sightings, Eye2thesky, The Paracast*, Discovery's *Close Encounters* and A&E's *The Unexplained*. He is past president of both the Winnipeg Science Fiction Society and the Winnipeg Centre of the Royal Astronomical Society of Canada.

MIKE **CLELLAND** is an avid outdoorsman, illustrator and UFO researcher. He is the author of *The Messengers: Owls, Synchronicity, and the UFO Abductee* (2015, Richard Dolan Press), inspired by his own first-hand experiences. Outside of the UFO arena, Mike is considered an expert in the skills of ultralight backpacking, and has authored or illustrated a series of instructional books focused on advanced outdoor techniques. He spent nearly 25 years living in the Rockies, and now lives in the Adirondacks. For access to Mike's extensive research on the mysteries of UFOs, synchronicity, and related weirdness, including extended audio interviews with visionaries and experts, visit his blog, hiddenexperience.blogspot.com

JACK **BREWER** is the author of the nonfiction book, *The Greys Have Been Framed: Exploitation in the UFO Community*, which explores the ways deception, sensationalism and questionable ethics distort public perception of the UFO phenomenon. He writes the blog, the UFO trail, where he posts credible info on incredible topics. Brewer's research interests include social dynamics surrounding reported UFO sightings, alleged alien abduction, and the overlapping of the UFO and intelligence communities. Connect with him on twitter @theufotrail or by email at jackbrewerblog@yahoo.com

JOSHUA **CUTCHIN** is a North Carolina native with a longstanding interest in Forteana. He holds a Masters in Music Literature and a Masters in Journalism from the University of Georgia, and currently resides in Roswell, Georgia. He is the author of two books: 2015's *A Trojan Feast: The Food and Drink Offerings of Aliens, Faeries, and Sasquatch* (translated into Spanish as *Banquete Troyano*) and 2016's *The Brimstone Deceit: An In-Depth Examination of Supernatural Scents, Otherworldly Odors, & Monstrous Miasmas*. Both are published by Anomalist Books. Cutchin is also a published composer and maintains an active performing schedule as a jazz and rock tuba player, having appeared on eight albums and live concert DVDs. Joshua has appeared on a variety of paranormal programs discussing his work, including Coast to Coast AM, Mysterious Universe, Binnall of America, and The Gralien Report. He can be heard on the weekly podcast Where Did the Road Go? and maintains an online presence at JoshuaCutchin.com

MICAH **HANKS** is a writer, podcaster, and researcher whose interests cover a variety of subjects. His areas of focus include history, science, philosophy, current events, cultural studies, technology, unexplained phenomena, and ways the future of humankind may be influenced by science and innovation in the coming decades. He is author of several books, including *The Ghost Rockets*, a survey of drone-like technologies of unexplained origin, and his 2012 New Page Books release, *The UFO Singularity*, which focuses on purported "exotic" aerial phenomena, and how anecdotal reports of such observations mirror some technological innovations occurring in the present day, along with those expected for tomorrow. Micah lives in the Appalachian Mountains near Asheville, North Carolina, and, in addition to writing, podcasting, and research, he enjoys traveling, and maintains a passion for science fiction, fine art, music from around the world, and the pursuit of all things unique and interesting.

LORIN **CUTTS** became fascinated with UFOs and the paranormal after his first experience with anomalous aerial phenomena in 1993. He began researching other people's UFO-related events in 1995, and, after co-founding a UFO and paranormal Internet talk radio network in the USA, he became interested in the sociological, cultural and mythological implications that the UFO subject would seem to present. Lorin has written for magazines in both the U.S. and the UK; he also presents the *High Strangeness* podcast on iTunes. Lorin lives in the Pacific Northwest and is currently working on his first book.

CURT **COLLINS** is the author and researcher behind Blue Blurry Lines (blueblurrylines.com), a website focused on mysteries, hoaxes and legends about UFOs. After retiring from a career in retail management, Curt began writing about UFOs, with a special interest in re-investigating the paradoxical 1980 Texas Cash-Landrum UFO case. More recently, Curt was on the investigative team known as the Roswell Slides Research Group. Curt lives in the southern United States, near Jackson, Mississippi.

SMILES **LEWIS** has had a lifelong interest in all things anomalous. He led the local MUFON chapter and UFO Experiencer Support & Study Group for several years. He organized the ill-fated National UFO Conference in September 2001. He's been described as an "Informationalist & Gonzo Alt-Media Proprietor" for his decades of counter-culture media publishing in print, web, and radio (both terrestrial and Internet) on the subjects of the paranormal and parapolitical. In 2003 he founded the 501(c)3 nonprofit Scientific Anomaly Institute, Anomaly Archives, which now boasts a lending library and archive with thousands of rare books, periodicals, and research files. He served as an inside observer with the Roswell Slides Research Group (RSRG). He is active with several local nonprofits and has served on the board of directors for the Institute for Neuroscience and Consciousness Studies (INACS) and Human Potential Center (HPC). For the past 20 years, he has worked for the Texas Talking Book Program, providing audio books for the blind and print-disabled. He's served as Studio Manager for that program since 2003. He lives in Austin, Texas.

MJ **BANIAS** is a writer and blogger who critically explores the modern UFO phenomenon and other Fortean subjects from a philosophical perspective. With a background in Critical Theory, History, and Cultural Studies, he enjoys exploring all things weird and anomalous. He is a field investigator with MUFON, has been featured on multiple podcasts, and writes for *Mysterious Universe* and *Rogue-Planet*. His blog, Terra Obscura, is where philosophy, critical theory and high strangeness meet. Visit www.terraobscura.net for the collection of his work.

RED PILL **JUNKIE** Agnostic gnostic, walking conundrum & metaphysical oxymoron (with emphasis in the 'moron'), the mysterious RPJ leads a double life: By day he serves as Grand Master in the International Sacred Order of Lucha Libre, but at night he pursues his life-long study of everything considered mysterious and/or 'paranormal'—a term he personally detests. When he's not exploring the web looking for his daily fix of Forteana, he can be found blogging, doodling, fooling around and offering his services as news administrator at The Daily Grail. He also participates regularly in other websites and podcasts like Mysterious Universe, The Grimerica Show and Where Did the Road Go? He awaits impatiently for the return of the mothership in Mexico City.

SUSAN **DEMETER-ST. CLAIR** is a professional research assistant, author, editor, and PSI experimenter. Her research interests include individual and institutional responses to anomalies and exceptional human experiences, and how they interact and enact change within groups and large institutions, such as the military. Her life took on the framework of UFO experience after an encounter in 1990, and she considers anomaly studies to be her true life's work. She has established both ParaResearchers of Ontario, and Paranormal Studies and Inquiry Canada as online educational resources for those wishing to explore the subject of anomalous events. Susan has conducted field research on unusual light phenomena and lectured on this subject at the Ontario Institute for Studies & Education, University of Toronto. She is currently collaborating with Eric Ouellet, Ph.D. of the Canadian Forces College on new approaches to UFO studies through the lenses of scientific Parapsychology. At the time of this publication Susan is conducting a series of independent experiments based in part on the work of the late mathematician, Dr. A.R.G Owen and psychotherapist Dr. Joel Whitton that will be the focus of a planned future book on

UFOs, social PSI, and Magick. More info can be found through her website: www.susanstclair.com

RYAN **SPRAGUE** is the author of *Somewhere in the Skies: A Human Approach to an Alien Phenomenon* (Richard Dolan Press, 2016). He has written for numerous publications, including *Omni Reboot, Open Minds Magazine, Phenomena Magazine U.K.*, and *UFO Truth Magazine*. Speaking on the UFO topic, he has been featured on ABC News, Fox News, and The Science Channel, and is a regular on The Travel Channel's *Mysteries at the Museum*. He is also the co-host for both the *Into the Fray* & *UFOmodPOD* podcasts. When he's not writing about UFOs, he is a professional playwright and screenwriter, living in New York City. He is the co-founder of THIRD KIND Productions, a multi-media company dedicated to promoting the work of independent artists. More information on Ryan's work can be found at www.somewhereintheskies.com and at www.thirdkindproductions.com

GREG **BISHOP** In 1991, Greg Bishop co-founded a magazine called The Excluded Middle, a journal of UFOs, conspiracy research, psychedelia and new science. *Wake Up Down There!*, a collection of articles from the magazine, was published in 2000.

Greg's second book was *Project Beta: The Story of Paul Bennewitz, National Security, and the Creation of a Modern UFO Myth*, which documented a government campaign of disinformation perpetrated against an unsuspecting U.S. citizen. Weird California, a portrait of strange history and places in the Golden State, was released in 2006. From 2007 to 2011, Greg blogged for the UFO and paranormal site Ufomystic. His current book, *It Defies Language*, is composed, for the most part, of entries from that blog and new articles written specifically for the collection. For two years, Greg hosted The Hungry Ghost, a radio show of interviews and music airing on pirate FM station KBLT in Los Angeles. His current show, Radio Misterioso, can be heard live at radiomisterioso.com, and podcasts are available for download. Interviews with fringe-topic researchers and weird music are the usual fare. He is licensed to fly drones for commercial clients, and is also a certified paraglider and ultralight pilot as well as holding a private pilot license.

ROBERT **BRANDSTETTER** has occupied many roles as a writer, anti-racist, teacher, equity activist and a trauma survivor. He is a mindfulness and self-regulation instructor and an ethnographer of trauma.

He spends his time conducting long term interviews of trauma survivors and spends the remaining free time, when not parenting and focussing on family, contemplating the nature of reality, memory, the biological functions of perception, and how these intersect, using the UFO trauma experience as a lens. He is focused primarily on how individuals destabilize as a result of their own witness experience, resulting in personal acts of both creation and destruction. His major influences in the field include McDonald, Vallée, Bishop, Rutkowski and Duensing. His primary professional writing is concerned with the fields of equity, social justice and self-regulation, designing curriculum and training for staff and students in a high school setting. This essay is his first published work inside the UFO field. He defines himself as both witness and experiencer.

ENDNOTES

FOREWORD

1 Jacques Vallée, *Messengers of Deception: UFO Contacts and Cults* (Daily Grail Publishing, 2008), Appendix.

2 Whitley Strieber and Jeffrey J. Kripal, *The Super Natural: A New Vision of the Unexplained* (TarcherPerigee, 2016), 3, 5-6.

CHRIS RUTKOWSKI

1 "Extra-Terrestrials and other Stranger Things: Four-in-Five Canadians believe," *Angus Reid Institute*, Aug. 24, 2016, http://angusreid.org / extra-terrestrials-stranger-things/

2 Chris Rutkowski, *Abduction and Aliens* (Toronto: Dundurn Press, 1999), 78.

3 Stephan Lewandowsky and Klaus Oberauer, "Motivated rejection of science," *Current Directions in Psychological Science*, Aug. 2016. Vol. 25, no. 4, 217-222.

4 Leon Festinger, Henry W. Riecken, Stanley Schachter, *When Prophecy Fails* (Minneapolis: University of Minnesota Press, 1956).

5 Susan Perry, "When facts fail: UFO cults, 'birthers' and cognitive dissonance," *MinnPost*, 2011, https://www.minnpost.com/second-opinion/2011/04/when-facts-fail-ufo-cults-birthers-and-cognitive-dissonance/

6 See: http://www.disclosureproject.org/

7 Nick Pope, "Disclosure has happened!" *UFO Digest*, 2015, http://ufodigest. com/article/disclosure-happened-0501/

8 See: http://omnec-onec.com

9 Howard Menger, *From Outer Space to You* (New York: Pyramid Books, 1959), 88, http://www.universe-people.com/english/svetelna_knihovna/ htm/en/en_kniha_from_outer_space_to_you.htm

10 Ibid, 117.

11 Luke Turner, 2011. See: http://metamodernism.org

12 Alain Morin, "Levels of Consciousness and Self-Awareness: A Comparison and Integration of Various Views," *Consciousness and Cognition*. Vol. 5, no. 2, 2006, 358–371, http://www.sciencedirect.com/science/article/pii/S1053810005001224

13 cf. Jayaram V, "The Concept of Advaita Vedanta," *Hinduwebsite*, http:// www.hinduwebsite.com/hinduism/concepts/advaitaconcept.asp

14 Gary Zukov, *The Dancing Wu Li Masters: An Overview of the New Physics* (New York: William Morrow and Company, 1979).

15 cf. The Universal Hierarchy, *A Pictorial Tour of Unarius* (El Cajon, California: Unarius Educational Foundation, 1982).

16 Clifford Stone, *The Arcturians*, http://www.bibliotecapleyades.net/vida_ alien/alien_races01.htm

17 Sir James Jeans, *The Mysterious Universe* (London: Cambridge University Press, 1930).

18 Lisa Zyga, *PhysOrg*, 2009, http://phys.org/news/2009-06-quantum- mysticism-forgotten.html

19 Trevor Wozny, blog post, *The Angry Ufologist*, Jun. 22, 2016, http://www. theangryufologist.us/black-knight-ufo-satellite-explained/

20 cf. Robert Balch and David Taylor, "Making Sense of the Heaven's Gate Suicides," in: David G. Bromley and J. Gordon Melton *Cults, Religion, and Violence* (London: Cambridge University Press, 2002).

21 cf. "Strange vigil in North Woods ends in tragic death," *Galveston Daily News*, Dec. 16, 1982, 18; "Death watch," *Arizona Republic*, Dec. 25, 1982, 22.

22 cf. Chris Rutkowski, *Unnatural History* (Winnipeg: Chameleon Press, 1993), 47-48.

23 Paul Harris, "Review: Cold War hysteria sparked UFO obsession, study finds," *The Guardian*, May 5, 2002, https://www.theguardian.com/science/2002/ may/05/spaceexploration.research

24 Donald Warren, "Status Inconsistency Theory and Flying Saucer Sightings," *Science, New Series*. Vol. 170, no. 3958 (Nov. 6, 1970), 599-603, http://www. jstor.org/stable/1731501

[25] cf. Kimberly Ball, "UFO-Abduction Narratives and the Technology of Tradition." *Cultural Analysis*. Vol. 9. 2010, 99-128, http://socrates.berkeley.edu/~caforum/volume9/pdf/ball.pdf

[26] Menger, *From Outer Space to You*, 117-118.

[27] Michael Persinger, *The Most Frequent Criticisms and Questions Concerning the Tectonic Strain Hypothesis*, 1999, https://www.god-helmet.com/tectonic.htm

[28] Ibid.

MIKE CLELLAND

[1] Audio interview with Dr. Leo Sprinkle, Hidden Experience podcast, Jan. 5, 2011, http://hiddenexperience.blogspot.com/2011/01/audio-conversation-with-dr-leo-sprinkle.html

[2] Audio conversation with the crew from Open Minds, Hidden Experience podcast, Jun. 4, 2014, http://hiddenexperience.blogspot.com/2014/06/audio-conversation-with-crew-from-open.html

[3] Mike Clelland, "The Possible Unsettling Implications of UFO Sightings," Jul. 30, 2014, http://www.openminds.tv/possible-unsettling-implications-ufo-sightings/29256

[4] Audio interview, *Where Did the Road Go*, Jeffery Kripal, May 28, 2016, time count 42:30, http://www.wheredidtheroadgo.com/show-archive/2016/item/290-jeffrey-kripal-on-the-super-natural-part-1-may-21-2016

[5] Whitley Strieber and Anne Strieber, *The Communion Letters* (Harper Collins, 1997).

[6] The line "Disclosure with a capital D" is a catchphrase used by activist Stephen Bassett, who has long been at the forefront of the UFO disclosure movement.

JACK BREWER

[1] See: *Anachronism*, http://historydeceived.blogspot.co.uk/2016/03/blog-post.html#more

[2] James Carrion, "Human Deception at Play During the UFO Wave of 1947," *Anachronism*, Aug. 20, 2016, http://historydeceived.blogspot.co.uk/2016/08/human-deception-at-playduring-ufo-wave.html

[3] RAND Corporation, *The Exploitation of Superstitions for Purposes of Psychological Warfare*, 1950, http://www.rand.org/pubs/research_memoranda/RM365.html

4 Lydia M. Fish, "General Edward G. Lansdale and the Folksongs of Americans in the Vietnam War," *Journal of the American Folklore Society. Vol. 102, Oct.-Dec., 1989. No. 406,* http://faculty.buffalostate.edu/fishlm/folksongs/lansdale.pdf

5 See: *Majestic Documents*: Project Grudge August 1949: Part 1, http://www.majesticdocuments.com/pdf/project-grudge_part1.pdf

6 Robbie Graham, *Silver Screen Saucers: Sorting Fact from Fantasy in Hollywood's UFO Movies* (White Crow Books, 2015), 28-29, 98-102.

7 Marc D. Bernstein, "Ed Lansdale's Black Warfare in 1950's Vietnam," *HistoryNet,* Feb. 16, 2010, http://www.historynet.com/ed-lansdales-black-warfare-in-1950s-vietnam.htm

8 Gerald K. Haines, "CIA's Role in the Study of UFOs," 1947-90, *Central Intelligence Agency,* https://www.cia.gov/library/center-for-the-study-of-intelligence/csi-publications/csi-studies/studies/97unclass/ufo.html

9 U.S. Department of State Office of the Historian, *Foreign Relations of the United States, 1952-1954, Guatemala, Document 89,* https://history.state.gov/historicaldocuments/frus1952-54Guat/d89

10 Lynn Picknett, *The Mammoth Book of UFOs* (Brown Book Group, 2012).

11 Julia Shaw, "What Experts Wish You Knew about False Memories," *Scientific American,* Aug. 8, 2016, http://blogs.scientificamerican.com/mind-guest-blog/what-experts-wish-you-knew-about-false-memories/

12 Joe Keohane, "How Facts Backfire," *boston.com,* Jul. 11, 2010, http://ruby.fgcu.edu/courses/tdugas/ids3332/acrobat/factsbackfire.pdf

13 Lawrence Robinson, Melinda Smith, and Jeanne Segal, "Coping with Emotional and Psychological Trauma," *HelpGuide.org,* Jan. 2017, http://www.helpguide.org/articles/ptsd-trauma/emotional-and-psychological-trauma.htm

JOSHUA CUTCHIN

1 James M. Lattis, *Between Copernicus and Galileo* (Chicago: The University of Chicago Press, 1994).

2 B.S. Eastwood, "Heraclides and Heliocentrism – Texts, Diagrams, and Interpretations," *Journal for the History of Astronomy, 23(4),* 1992, 233-260.

3 Lattis, *Between Copernicus and Galileo.*

4 Albert Einstein, *Ideas and Opinions* (London: Crown Publishers, 1954).

5 Stephen Hawking, *A Brief History of Time* (New York: Bantam Books, 1996). Original work published 1988.

6   Thomas E. Bullard, *UFO Abductions: The Measure of a Mystery. Vol. 1* (Bloomington: The Fund for UFO Research, 1987).

7   Richard Dolan, *UFOs for the 21st Century Mind* (Rochester: Richard Dolan Press, 2014).

8   Budd Hopkins, *Missing Time* (New York: Richard Marek Publishers, 1981).

9   "We know that an abductee can receive an impression from his own thoughts, translate it into his words, and think that the words are coming from aliens. Naive researchers often accept alien dialog at face value, not realizing that all or portions of it could be generated from the abductee's mind." David Jacobs, *The Threat* (New York: Simon & Schuster, 1998).

10 David Jacobs, *Secret Life: Firsthand, Documented Accounts of Ufo Abductions* (New York: Simon & Schuster—Fireside, 1992).

11 Alex, Tsakiris, *Skeptiko 159: Stanton Friedman on Extended Human Consciousness and Mind Control* [Audio podcast], Jan. 31, 2012, http://skeptiko.com/stanton-friedman-on-extended-human-consciousness-and-mind-control/

12 Jacques Vallée, *UFOs: The Psychic Solution* (Frogmore: Granada Publishing—Panther Books, 1977). Original work published in 1975 as *The Invisible College.*

13 John Herlosky, *A Sorcerer's Apprentice: A Skeptic's Journey into the CIA's Project Stargate* (Walterville, OR: Trine Day LLC, 2015).

14 Central Intelligence Agency, *Experiments—Uri Geller at SRI, August 4-11, 1973,* https://www.cia.gov/library/readingroom/docs/CIA-RDP96-00791R000100480003-3.pdf

15 Herlosky, *A Sorcerer's Apprentice.*

16 Ingo Swann, *Penetration* (Rapid City, SD: Ingo Swann Books, 1998).

17 Mario Bunge, *Treatise on Basic Philosophy: Volume 6—Epistemology & Methodology II: Understanding the World, Dordrecht,* (Holland: Springer Science+Business Media, B.V., 1983).

18 National Research Council, *American Psychological Association Monitor,* Jan. 1988, 7.

19 Rupert Sheldrake, *Dogs That Know When Their Owners Are Coming Home and Other Unexplained Powers of Animals: Fully Updated and Revised* (New York: Three Rivers Press, 2011). Original work published 1999.

20 Pirn van Lommel, Ruud van Wees, Vincent Meyers, Ingrid Elfferich, "Near-death experience in survivors of cardiac arrest: a prospective study in the Netherlands," *The Lancet,* Dec. 15, 2001, 358.

21 Ian Stevenson, *Reincarnation and Biology: A Contribution to the Etiology of Birthmarks and Birth Defects, Vol. 1 & 2* (Westport, CT: Praeger Publishing, 1997).

22 Daryl J. Bem, "Feeling the future: Experimental evidence for anomalous retroactive influences on cognition and affect," *Journal of Personality and Social Psychology 100*, 2011, 407-425.

23 Alex Tsakiris, *Why Science is Wrong... About Almost Everything* (San Antonio, TX: Anomalist Books, 2014).

24 *Science Daily*, "Experiment confirms quantum theory weirdness," May 27, 2015, https://www.sciencedaily.com/releases/2015/05/150527103110.htm

25 Greg Carlwood, *The Higherside Chats: Gordon White | Understanding Gnosticism, Parapolitics, and Chaos Magic* [Audio podcast], Jan. 23, 2015, http://thehighersidechats.com/gordon-white-understanding-gnosticism-parapolitics-chaos-magic/

26 Gordon White, *Star.Ships* (Bucknell: Scarlet Imprint, 2016).

27 Jacques Vallée, *Passport to Magonia* (Chicago, IL: *Henry* Regnery Co., 1969).

28 Gordon White, *Pieces of Eight: Chaos Magic Essays and Enchantments* (Seattle: Amazon Digital Services LLC, 2016).

29 N. Laos, *Methexiology: Philosophical Theology and Theological Philosophy for the Deification of Humanity*, (Eugene, OR: Pickwick Publications, 2016).

30 Gordon White, "*Earth is Outside Our Delivery Zone*," *Runesoup*, Aug. 2016, https://www.runesoup.com/2016/08/earth-is-outside-our-delivery-zone/

31 White, *Star.Ships*.

MICAH HANKS

1 Allan Hendry, *The UFO Handbook: A Guide to Investigating, Evaluating and Reporting UFO Sightings* (New York: Doubleday, 1979).

2 Ibid.

3 Ibid.

4 Ibid.

5 Ibid.

6 Ibid.

7 J. Allen Hynek, *The UFO Experience: A Scientific Inquiry* (New York: Ballantine Books, 1972).

8 Richard F. Haines, *CE-5: Close Encounters of the Fifth Kind* (Naperville, Illinois: Sourcebooks, 1999).

9 Hynek, *The UFO Experience*.

LORIN CUTTS

1 Popular Mechanics/CUFOS study, 1947-2005. Yakima County came in 4th place of all the lesser populated counties in the USA.

2 *Oregon Journal*, Jul. 4, 1947, 2.

3 "Report on the Wave of 1947," *Ted Bloecher*, NICAP, 1967.

4 Stan Gordon on *High Strangeness*, Apr. 15, 2012, http://highstrangenessshow.com/high-strangeness-episode-3-bigfoot-the-ufo-connection-with-stan-gordon-apr-15th-2012/

5 Author's own research.

6 Ibid.

7 Laura Magdalene Eisenhower, "The Grail of Venus: Completing Magdalene's Legacy and the Story of Goddess Sophia," *Cosmic Gaia*, http://cosmicgaia2012.com/journey.html

8 Laura Magdalene Eisenhower, "Global Mission and Life Expenses," *gofundme*, https://www.gofundme.com/23n8qnk4

9 Solreta Antaria, "Sirian Star Language Message for August 2016 Ep51," May 8, 2016, http://www.solretapsychicreadings.com/sirian-star-language-messages/sirian-star-language-message-for-august-2016-ep51?

10 James Gilliland biography, *ECETI*, http://www.eceti.org/Eceti.James.html

11 For an honest attempt at reporting an early visit to ECETI, see: http://highstrangenessshow.com/lorin-cutts-journey-to-the-field-of-dreams/

12 Lots of good information about previous work done in Yakima here: http://web.archive.org/web/20161104105653/http://vogelstudy.org/archives.htm

13 Austin Hill, "What Do I Do Next?' Actor Dwight Equitz Navigates UFO's, A Hit TV Series, And Owning A Small Business," Jan. 29, 2015, *Austin Hill's Big World of Small Business*, http://austinsbigworld.com/next-actor-dwight-equitz-navigates-ufos-hit-tv-series-owning-small-business/

14 Douglas Main, "Most People Believe Intelligent Aliens Exist, Poll Says," *Newsweek*, Sept. 29, 2015, http://www.newsweek.com/most-people-believe-intelligent-aliens-exist-377965

15 James Carrion, "Human Deception at Play during the UFO Wave of 1947," *Anachronism*, Aug. 20, 2016, http://historydeceived.blogspot.co.uk/2016/08/human-deception-at-playduring-ufo-wave.html

16 The very first thing the CIA recommends you do if you want to investigate flying saucers is to start a group. See: https://www.cia.gov/news-information/featured-story-archive/2016-featured-story-archive/how-to-investigate-a-flying-saucer.html

17 "It [MUFON] also gave Bigelow Aerospace access to the MUFON Case Management System [CMS]." See: http://www.mufon.com/mufon-history2. html. Much has been written and said about this, but suffice to say that Bigelow Advanced Aerospace Studies (BAAS) paid MUFON for full CMS access and BAAS appeared to investigate the best cases and leads themselves.

18 MUFON Field Investigators Manual 4th Edition, Chapter 22.

19 Margie Kay, MUFON Assistant State Director, Missouri, interview on *MUFON UFO Radio*, Jul. 26, 2016. At one point, Kay notes: "In some cases I will actually know more than the witness did because I will see more and they have actually been blocked from seeing it."

20 Jack Brewer, "MUFON Chief Investigator Requests Ban on Roswell Slides Promoters," *The UFO Trail*, Jun. 18, 2015, http://ufotrail.blogspot. com/2015/06/mufon-chief-investigator-requests-ban.html

21 See: http://www.tricksterbook.com/ArticlesOnline/LindaCase.htm

22 Whitley Strieber describing memories of CIA mind control experiments as a child. *Dreamland*, Jan. 9, 2010, https://archive.org/details/WhitleyStrieber-MemoriesOfMindControlAndChildhoodAbuse. See also: Frederick C. Crews, *Follies of The Wise: Dissenting Essays* (Berkeley: Counter Point Press, 2006), 206-207.

23 Ralph Keyes, "The Post-Truth Era: Dishonesty and Deception in Contemporary Life," *Ralph Keyes*, http://www.ralphkeyes.com/the-post-truth-era/

24 'Disclosure' as defined by Steven Bassett and the UFO Disclosure movement. The announcement of extraterrestrial life is not the same as the US government coming clean on the so-called truth embargo or the UFO cover up. It will also happen regardless of political lobbying.

CURT COLLINS

1 Michelle Basch, "UFO experts say 'we are not alone'," *WTOP*, Nov. 13, 2014, http://wtop.com/news/2014/11/ufo-experts-say-we-are-not-alone/

2 Jaime Maussan, BeWitness Press Conference, *Conferencia de Prensa Jaime Maussan beWITNESS / Sé Testigo Auditorio Nacional*, Feb. 4, 2015, https:// www.youtube.com/watch?v=6TB_Tn4KpJ8

3 Narrenschiffer, Der Ufo-Absturz bei Roswell, 08.02.2015 at 21:30, *Allmystery*, Feb. 8, 2015 https://www.allmystery.de/themen/uf25902-212

4 Kevin Randle, "Roswell Slides Today's Update," *A Different Perspective*, Feb. 10, 2015, http://kevinrandle.blogspot.com/2015/02/roswell-slides-update-february-10-today.html

5   David Hunt, "A Child's Mummy," *AnthroNotes.* Vol. 33, Spring 2012, https://repository.si.edu/bitstream/handle/10088/22464/anthronotes_33_1_2.pdf

6   WGN News, "Vivian Maier Meets the X-Files: Has Chicago Man Uncovered Secret Alien Pics?" Feb. 18, 2015, https://www.youtube.com/watch?v=QyoCiLv31d8

7   Paul Kimball, "The 'Roswell Slides' Witness," *The Other Side of Truth*, Feb. 27, 2015,

    http://redstarfilms.blogspot.com/2015/02/the-roswell-slides-witness.html

8   Rich Reynolds, "The [New] Roswell Slides Group," *UFO Conjecture(s)*, Mar. 2, 2015, https://ufocon.blogspot.com/2015/03/the-roswell-slides-group.html

9   José Antonio Caravaca, "Es Esta la Momia, El Famoso 'Extraterrestre' de las Diapositivas de Roswell?" *Esos Misteriosos Objetos Celestes y sus Tripulantes*, Mar. 25, 2015, http://caravaca.blogspot.com/2015/03/es-esta-momia-el-famoso-extraterrestre.html

10 Gilles Fernandez, "The Roswell Slides Saga: Some Claims vs. Facts," *Sceptiques vs. les Soucoupes Volantes*, Mar. 25, 2015,

    http://skepticversustheflyingsaucers.blogspot.com/2015/03/the-roswell-slides-saga-claims-versus.html

11 "12am Roswell Slides," *The Conspiracy Show with Richard Syrett*, Apr. 12, 2015, http://www.richardsyrett.com/10-past-show-archive/372-sunday-april-12-2015

12 Tim Printy, *SUNlite.* Vol. 7, No. 3, May/June 2015, http://www.astronomyufo.com/UFO/SUNlite7_3.pdf

13 BeWitness Parts 1 and 2, *The Face of Roswell*, May 19, 2015, http://www.thefaceofroswell.com/biography

14 Curt Collins, "The Placard of the Roswell Slides: The Final Curtain," *Blue Blurry Lines*, May 8, 2015, http://www.blueblurrylines.com/2015/05/the-placard-of-roswell-slides-final.html

15 Slidebox Media, "Real Placard," *Kodachrome: Documentary about the Roswell Slides 1947*, May 9, 2015. Original screenshot archived at: http://www.anomalyarchives.org/public-hall/wp-content/uploads/slideboxmedia-calls-rsrg-trolls.jpg http://web.archive.org/web/20150511150511/http://slideboxmedia.com/placard/

16 Rich Reynolds, "The Roswell Team's placard scans and the new Anti-Slider's placard scan," *UFO Conjecture(s)*, May 8, 2015. Archived at: http://www.blueblurrylines.com/p/anthony-bragalia-has-provided-these.html

17 Press Release, *The 'Roswell Slides' Research Group*, May 8, 2015, http://www.roswellslides.com/

18 Isaac Koi, "Roswell Slides Solve the mystery in 1.5 minutes," *Above Top Secret*, http://www.abovetopsecret.com/forum/thread1066804/pg1

19 Nab Lator, "Analysis of the 'Roswell Slides' (FAQ)," *Nabbed*, May 18, 2015, http://nabbed.unblog.fr/2015/05/18/analysis-of-the-roswell-slides-faq/

20 Anthony Bragalia, "The 'Roswell Alien Slides' and My apology to a Dead Child of the Mesa Verde," *A Different Perspective*, May 10, 2015, http://kevinrandle. blogspot.com/2015/05/tony-bragalia-and-end-of-roswell-slides.html

21 Tom Carey and Don Schmitt, "Statement," *Blue Blurry Lines*, May 12, 2015, http://www.blueblurrylines.com/2015/05/roswell-slides-tom-careys-statement-on.html

22 Curt Collins, "Shepherd Johnson finds documents that finish the Roswell Slides," *Blue Blurry Lines*, Jun. 13, 2015, http://www.blueblurrylines. com/2015/06/shepherd-johnson-finds-documents-that.html

23 Jorge Peredo, post on *Facebook*, Jun. 9, 2015, https://www.facebook.com/ jorge.peredo/posts/10200675048716200

24 Curt Collins, "Shepherd Johnson finds documents that finish the Roswell Slides," *Blue Blurry Lines*, Jun. 13, 2015 http://www.blueblurrylines. com/2015/06/shepherd-johnson-finds-documents-that.html

25 "Jaime Maussan Video Evidence That UFOs are real" (at 57m, 23s), YouTube channel, *Mutual UFO Network (MUFON)*, Aug. 27, 2015, published, Jan. 6, 2016, https://www.youtube.com/watch?v=82TiX84LokA

26 "Interview with Tom Carey & Don Schmitt," *Podcast UFO*, Jul. 20, 2016, https://www.youtube.com/watch?v=LQ4TlBcjsjU

SMILES LEWIS

1 Stephen Miles Lewis, "UFOs and Consciousness: The Fantastic Facts About UFOs, Altered States of Consciousness, and Mind-at-Large," 2011/2013. See: http://www.anomalyarchives.org/public-hall/events/past/UFOs-and-consciousness/ http://www.anomalyarchives.org/public-hall/events/past/UFOs-and-consciousness-part-two/

2 Serena Roney Dougal, "UFOs, States of Mind and The Pineal Connection: Parts I & II," *UFO Times*, 16 & 17, 1991/1992, http://www.psi-researchcentre. co.uk/publications.htm

3 Norman S. Don and Gilda Moura, "Topographic Brain Mapping of UFO Experiencers," *Journal of Scientific Exploration*. Vol. 11, No. 4, 1997, 435-453. http://citeseerx.ist.psu.edu/viewdoc/download;jsessionid=157027E0B AA383985DDC857FD8C521E6?doi=10.1.1.680.8482&rep=rep1&type=pdf

4 Alan Vaughan and Peter Guttilla, "Testable Theory of UFOs, ESP, Aliens, and Bigfoot," *MUFON UFO Journal*, Nov. 1998, 8-10, http://atestabletheoryofUFOsespalien. blogspot.com

5   Robert C. Beck and Eldon A. Byrd, "Bibliography on the Psychoactivity of Electromagnetic Fields," *Archaeus* magazine, 1986, 4, http://www.vxm.com/bib.doc.html

6   Robert C. Beck, "Extreme low frequency (ELF) magnetic fields and EEG entrainment: A psychotronic warfare possibility?" *Association for Humanistic Psychology Newsletter*, May, 1978, Biomedical Research Associates, Los Angeles, CA. See: http://www.elfis.net/elfol8/e8elfeeg1.htm, and: http://www.elfis.net/elfol8/e8elfeeg2.htm

7   Whitley Strieber, *Communion* (New York: Beech Tree Books, 1987), 103-104.

8   Jeffrey Mishlove, Jeffrey (host), "Aliens and Archetypes," *Thinking Allowed* video series. See: http://www.intuition.org/txt/mckenna.htm; http://www.thinkingallowed.com/2tmckenna.html; and https://www.youtube.com/watch?v=4LnOoUCh_8c

9   Jacques Vallée, "Five Arguments Against the Extraterrestrial Origin of Unidentified Flying Objects," *Journal of Scientific Exploration*. Vol. 4, No. 1, 1990, 105-117, http://www.jacquesVallée.net/bookdocs/arguments.pdf

10 Paul Devereux, "Beyond UFOlogy: Meeting With The Alien," *New UFOlogist* magazine, *MUFON UFO Journal*, Oct. 1995. See: http://www.UFOupdateslist.com/digest/DIGEST10.TXT, and: http://www.slideshare.net/mUFOnnexus/mUFOn-UFO-journal-1995-10-october

11 Kenneth Ring and Christopher J. Rosing, "The Omega Project: An Empirical Study of the NDE-Prone Personality," *Journal of Near-Death Studies*, 8 (4), 1990 (Summer), http://newdualism.org/nde-papers/Ring/Ring-Journal%20of%20Near-Death%20Studies_1990-8-211-239.pdf

12 John S. Derr and Michael A. Persinger, "Fluid Injection Causes Luminous Phenomena," 11th Annual Meeting, Society for Scientific Exploration, Princeton, NJ, Jun. 11, 1992, http://www.science-frontiers.com/sf082/sf082g14.htm

13 Albert Budden, *Allergies and Aliens: The Electromagnetic Indictment*, http://www.bibliotecapleyades.net/ciencia/ciencia_astralplano2.htm http://www.abduct.com/books/b31.php

14 Jeff Wells, "Spirit of the Beehive," *Rigorous Intuition*, Dec. 4, 2005, http://rigorousintuition.blogspot.com/2005/12/spirit-of-beehive_04.html

15 Karla Turner, *Taken: Inside the Alien-Human Agenda*, 1994, http://www.viewzone.com/ebooks/KarlaTurnerTaken.pdf. See also: Karla Turner, "Alien Abduction Researcher Karla Turner in Austin, Texas." [Video of Austin MUFON lecture], Sept. 26, 1992, https://www.youtube.com/view_play_list?p=15672147BFE4E557

16 Rupert Sheldrake, "Sir John Maddox - Book for Burning," http://www.sheldrake.org/reactions/sir-john-maddox-book-for-burning

[17] Jacques Vallée, *UFO Chronicles of the Soviet Union: A Cosmic Samizdat* (Ballantine Books, 1992), 89-90.

[18] Jenny Randles, *Mind Monsters: Invaders from Inner Space?* (Harper Collins, 1990), https://issuu.com/dirkthedaring11/docs/jenny_randles_-_mind_monsters_-_invaders_from_inne

[19] Jenny Randles, *Beyond Explanation? The Paranormal Experiences of Famous People* (Robert Hale, 1985).

[20] Jenny Randles, "J.R. Comments ..." *Northern UFO* News. No. 115, 1985, 2-3, http://www.afu.se/Downloads/Magazines/United%20Kingdom/Northern%20UFO%20News%20(Jenny%20Randles)/Northern%20UFO%20News%20-%20No%20115.pdf

[21] Danielle Sedbrook, "Must the Molecules of Life Always be Left-Handed or Right-Handed? They are on Earth, but life on other planets could play by different rules," *Smithsonian*, Jul. 28, 2016, http://www.smithsonianmag.com/space/must-all-molecules-life-be-left-handed-or-right-handed-180959956/

[22] Jenny Randles, "Re: Abductee Files/Our Children," *UFO UpDates*, Aug 1. 2000. See: http://web.archive.org/web/20111106085049/http://UFOupdateslist.com/2000/aug/m01-023.shtml

[23] Dennis Stillings (ed.), *Cyberbiological Studies of the Imaginal Component in the UFO Contact Experience* (Archaeus Project, 1989).

[24] Smiles Lewis, "ELFIS Researcher Dialog: The UFO is a Psychic Bomb," *E.L.F. Infested Spaces*. Issue 9, 1999, Spring/Summer, http://www.elfis.net/rd/rd9/smle.htm

[25] Thomas Bearden, *Excalibur Briefing: Explaining Paranormal Phenomena. The interaction of mind and matter* (Strawberry Hill Press, 1980), http://www.cheniere.org/books/excalibur/

[26] Steven Mizrach, "UFO Abductions and Race Fear," Feb. 24, 2001, https://web.archive.org/web/20010224063942/http://www.fiu.edu/~mizrachs/abductions-and-race-fear.html

[27] Jacques Vallée, *Messengers of Deception: UFO Contacts and Cults* (Daily Grail Publishing, 2008).

[28] Gregory Bishop (ed.), "Issue 8, Interview: Parapsychologist Dean Radin," *Wake Up Down There! The Excluded Middle Collection*, 2000, 293-294.

[29] Michael A. Persinger and — Gyslaine F. Lafrenière, *Space-Time Transients and Unusual Events*, 1977 http://books.google.com/books?id=x41QAAAAMAAJ

See also: B.P. Mulligan, L.S. Cloes, Q.H. Mach, and M.A. Persinger, "Geopsychology: Geophysical matrix and human behavior," (Chapter 4) in: Florinsky, Igor V. (ed.), *Man and the Geosphere*, Jan. 2010 & 2011, 115-141. https://www.novapublishers.com/catalog/product_info.php?products_id=11475

https://www.researchgate.net/publication/286611854_Geopsychology_
Geophysical_matrix_and_human_behavior

30 Chris Rutkowski, "Michael Persinger's theories make sense? Not," Comments
at *Daily Grail*, May 2011, http://www.dailygrail.com/Mind-Mysteries/2011/5/
Michael-Persinger-No-More-Secrets-Telepathy#comment-53261

31 H.P. Albarelli, Jr., *A Terrible Mistake: The Murder of Frank Olson and the
CIA's Secret Cold War Experiments* (Trine Day, 2009).

32 Jerome Clark, "Interview: Vallée Discusses UFO Control System," *FATE*
magazine, 1978,

http://web.archive.org/web/20090304002113/http://www.nidsci.org/articles/
clark.php http://www.ufoevidence.org/documents/doc608.htm

33 Martin Cannon, "The Controllers: A new hypothesis of Alien Abduction,"
MUFON UFO Journal (1989), http://www.constitution.org/abus/mkt/
cannon_controllers.pdf

34 Philip Coppens, "A lone chemist's quest to expose the UFO cover-up," *Philip
Coppens.* http://www.philipcoppens.com/davidson.html

35 H.P. Albarelli, Jr., *A Secret Order: Investigating the High Strangeness and
Synchronicity in the JFK Assassination* (Trine Day, 2009).

36 Kenn Thomas, "UFO Crash at Maury Island and the Murder of JFK with
Kenn Thomas," [Video], https://www.youtube.com/watch?v=qDHA5hfkiUU

37 Peter Levenda, "Peter Levenda: The Origins of the Secret Space Program
(2011)," [Video], https://www.youtube.com/watch?v=SBelUmWuLOE

38 Alston Chase, "Harvard and the Making of the Unabomber," *The Atlantic*,
Jun. 2000, http://www.theatlantic.com/magazine/archive/2000/06/
harvard-and-the-making-of-the-unabomber/378239/

39 Kathy Curran, "Whitey Bulger's Notebook Chronicles LSD Prison Testing,"
WBZ-TV / CBS Boston, Jul. 7, 2011, http://boston.cbslocal.com/2011/07/07/i-
team-whitey-bulger-volunteered-for-lsd-testing-while-in-prison-in-1950s/

40 Julie Vanderperre, "Declassified: Mind Control at McGill," *The McGill
Tribune*, http://www.mcgilltribune.com/mind-control-mcgill-mk-ultra/

41 Nick Redfern, "Is This the Flatwoods Monster?" *There's Something in the
Woods*, Sept. 23, 2010, http://monsterusa.blogspot.com/2010/09/is-this-
flatwoods-monster.html

See also: Nick Redfern, "Conspiracies and Visions," *Mysterious Universe*,
Dec. 9, 2011, http://mysteriousuniverse.org/2011/12/conspiracies-and-visions/

42 J. M. Hungerford, "The Exploitation of Superstitions for Purposes of
Psychological Warfare," *RAND Corporation*, 1950, http://www.rand.org/
pubs/research_memoranda/RM365.html

43 Rich Reynolds, "Is the 1957 Antonio Villas Boas 'abduction; still grist for discussion?" *UFO Conjecture(s)*, Jan. 24, 2016, http://ufocon.blogspot.com/2016/01/is-1957-antonio-villas-boas-abduction.html

Nick Redfern, "Alien Abduction or Mind-Manipulation?" *Jim Harold*, Jan. 28, 2016, http://jimharold.com/alien-abduction-or-mind-manipulation-nick-redfern/

Nick Redfern, "UFOs: Microwaved to Death?" *Mysterious Universe*, Mar. 25, 2015, http://mysteriousuniverse.org/2015/03/ufos-microwaved-to-death/

Philip Coppens, "Doctoring Villas Boas and aliens on ice," *Philip Coppens*, http://www.philipcoppens.com/ufo_fontes.html

Rich Reynolds, "The Carlos Alberto Diaz abduction, not unlike the Antonio Villas Boas episode," *UFO Conjecture(s)*, Sept. 12, 2011, http://ufocon.blogspot.com/2011/09/carlos-alberto-diaz-abduction-not.html

Mark Pilkington, "Orfeo Angelucci's acid test?" *Mirage Men*, Oct. 4, 2010, https://miragemen.wordpress.com/2010/10/04/orfeo-angeluccis-acid-test/

44 "MK-ULTRAViolence: Or, how McGill pioneered psychological torture," *The McGill Tribune*, Sept. 6, 2012, http://www.mcgilldaily.com/2012/09/mk-ultraviolence/

45 Jason Colavito, "Alien abduction at... The Outer Limits: meet the alien that abducted Barney Hill," *Jason Colavito*, 2012/2014, http://www.jasoncolavito.com/alien-abduction-at-the-outer-limits.html

46 Nick Redfern, "UFOs and Out-of-Body Experiences," *Mysterious Universe*, May 10, 2013, http://mysteriousuniverse.org/2013/05/ufos-and-out-of-body-experiences/

47 Hank P. Albarelli, Jr., and Zoe Martell, "Did the U.S. Army help spread Morgellons and other diseases?" *Voltaire Network*, 2010, http://www.voltairenet.org/article165450.html

48 Jacques Vallée, *Revelations: Alien Contact and Human Deception* (Ballantine Books: 1991), 154-165.

49 Jacques Vallée, *Forbidden Science—Volume Three: Journals 1980-1989*, Feb. 10, 2016, 75.

50 "The Aviary: A UFO Secrecy Group," *Biblioteca Pleyades*, http://www.bibliotecapleyades.net/esp_sociopol_aviary.htm

Ryan Dube, "Christopher 'Kit' Green," *REALITY uncovered*, Aug. 9, 2008, http://www.realityuncovered.net/ufology/articles/kitgreen.php

51 Sacha Christie, "Rendlesham Revealed UPDATED 2015. What Really Happened," *Sacha Christie—Infomaniac Housewife*, Feb 2. 2012, http://sacha-christie-infomaniachousewife.blogspot.com/2012/02/rendlesham-revealed.html

Greg Bishop (Producer), "Peter Robbins: Rendlesham Controversy," *Radio Misterioso*, [Audio Interview], http://radiomisterioso.com/2012/05/09/peter-robbins-rendlesham-controversy/

52 Gerald K. Haines, "CIA's Role in the Study of UFOs, 1947-90: A Die-Hard Issue," *Central Intelligence Agency. Studies in Intelligence–1997*, Semiannual Edition. No. 1., 1997, https://www.cia.gov/library/center-for-the-study-of-intelligence/csi-publications/csi-studies/studies/97unclass/ufo.html

53 Bruce Maccabee, "CIA's UFO Explanation Is Preposterous," 2000, http://brumac.8k.com/cia_explaination.html

54 Philip Coppens, "Driving Mr. Bennewitz Insane," *Philip Coppens*, http://philipcoppens.com/bennewitz.html

Micah Hanks, "Was J. Allen Hynek Secretly Involved in U.S. Air Force Misinformation?" *Mysterious Universe*, Jun. 6. 2016, http://mysteriousuniverse.org/2016/06/was-j-allen-hynek-secretly-involved-in-u-s-air-force-misinformation/

55 Chris Keall, "The Best Kept Secret of World War Two—Project Seal, the tsunami bomb," Jan. 17, 2013, extracted from: Ray Waru, *Secrets & Treasures: Our stories told through the objects at Archives New Zealand*, (Random House, 2012), https://www.nbr.co.nz/article/best-kept-secret-world-war-two-%E2%80%94-project-seal-tsunami-bomb-ck-134614

56 James Carrion, *The Rosetta Deception*, aka *Anachronism*, 2014,

https://www.keepandshare.com/doc13/11670/anachronism-pdf-2-2-meg

http://followthemagicthread.blogspot.com

http://historydeceived.blogspot.com

http://rosettadeception.blogspot.com

57 "Carnegie Endowment for International Peace, Division of Intercourse and Education, Publication No. 15," *The Imperial Japanese Mission 1915* (The Endowment, 1918), http://bit.ly/2hhtnyo

58 Philip Taylor, "The Mystic and the Spy: Two Early British UFO Writers," *Magonia* Issue 61, Nov. 1997, http://magonia.haaan.com/1997/the-mystic-and-the-spy-two-early-british-ufo-writers/

59 "Address to the 42d Session of the United Nations General Assembly, NYC, September 21, 1987," *Ronald Reagan Presidential Library & Museum*, https://reaganlibrary.archives.gov/archives/speeches/1987/092187b.htm

60 "Remarks to the Students and Faculty at Fallston High School in Fallston, Maryland, December 4, 1985," *Ronald Reagan Presidential Library & Museum*, https://www.reaganlibrary.archives.gov/archives/speeches/1985/120485a.htm

61 "Remarks and a Question-and-Answer Session With Members of the National Strategy Forum in Chicago, Illinois, May 4, 1988," *Ronald Reagan*

Presidential Library & Museum, https://www.reaganlibrary.archives.gov/archives/speeches/1988/050488a.htm

62 Josh Sanburn, "Paul Krugman: An Alien Invasion Could Fix the Economy," *TIME* magazine, Aug. 16, 2011,

http://business.time.com/2011/08/16/paul-krugman-an-alien-invasion-could-fix-the-economy/

63 Paul Krugman's alien invasion strategy, *Real Time with Bill Maher*, [Video], https://www.youtube.com/watch?v=CgAUW_zcN9k

"Real Time with Bill Maher, Ep 250, May 25, 2012: Quotes," *HBO*, http://www.hbo.com/real-time-with-bill-maher/episodes/0/250-episode/synopsis/quotes.html

64 Gene Poteat, "Stealth, Countermeasures, and ELINT, 1960-1975," *Studies in Intelligence*, "Some Beginnings of Information Warfare," 1998, 51-59, https://www.cia.gov/library/readingroom/docs/DOC_0006122549.pdf

65 Scott Corrales, "Holograms and High Strangeness," *FATE* Magazine, Mar. 2003, http://www.fatemag.com/holograms-and-high-strangeness/

See also: Nick Redfern, "Faking the Second Coming," *Mysterious Universe*, Aug. 21, 2012, http://mysteriousuniverse.org/2012/08/faking-the-second-coming/

66 Scott Simmie, "The scene at NORAD on Sept. 11: Playing Russian war games... and then someone shouted to look at the monitor," Profile: Operation Northern Vigilance, *Toronto Star*, Dec. 9, 2001. See: http://www.historycommons.org/entity.jsp?entity=operation_northern_vigilance

See also: http://web.archive.org/web/20100705173410/http://www.historycommons.org/entity.jsp?entity=operation_northern_vigilance

Also: http://911research.wtc7.net/cache/planes/defense/torontostar_russiangame.html

Also: http://pqasb.pqarchiver.com/thestar/doc/438380580.html

John J. Hamre, Deputy Secretary of Defense, "U.S. Department of Defense, Office of the Assistant Secretary of Defense (Public Affairs) - News Transcript," *US Department of Defense*, Jan.15, 1999, http://web.archive.org/web/20061002103645/http://www.defenselink.mil/Transcripts/Transcript.aspx?TranscriptID=863

67 "Dr. Carol Rosin - National Press Club - May 9th 2001," [Video],

https://www.youtube.com/watch?v=naUlF5O2ciU

68 "Reporting on an alien landing," *Everybody Writes and the National Literacy Trust*. See:

http://web.archive.org/web/20081203151325/http://www.everybodywrites.org.uk/everybody-writes-day/reporting_on_an_alien_landing/

See also: http://www.everybodywrites.org.uk/downloads/primary/alien/Broomwood%20Case%20Study.pdf

69 Craig A. Copetas, "Extraterrestrial edge helps the balance sheet," *Bloomberg News / Houston Chronicle*, Jan. 22, 2004,

http://www.chron.com/business/article/Extraterrestrial-edge-helps-the-balance-sheet-1597771.php

70 Nick Pope, "Latest News - Global Competitiveness Forum," *Nick Pope*, http://www.nickpope.net/latest-news.htm

71 "Robertson Panel," *Wikipedia*, https://en.wikipedia.org/wiki/Robertson_Panel

72 Grant Cameron, "Disney, UFOs, and Disclosure," *The Presidents UFO Web Site*, http://www.presidentialufo.com/old_site/ufo_films.htm

73 Vallée, *Revelations*, 22.

74 Robbie Graham, *Silver Screen Saucers: Sorting Fact from Fantasy in Hollywood's UFO Movies* (White Crow Books, 2015), 17-18, 31-34.

75 Thomas DeLonge, "Fwd: Interesting news," *WikiLeaks - The Podesta Emails*, Feb. 2016, https://wikileaks.org/podesta-emails/emailid/33552. See also: Robbie Graham, "The DeLonge Delusion: Part One," *Mysterious Universe*, Nov. 3, 2016, http://mysteriousuniverse.org/2016/11/the-delonge-delusion-part-one/

76 Smiles Lewis, "Majestic Art of Mind Kontrol Majestic Art of Electronic Disinformation," *ELFIS Journal of Possible Paradigms*, Spring 2001, http://www.elfis.net/mkc/mkcx/majesticarts.htm

77 Craig Medred, "'The Fourth Kind' pays for telling a big fib," *Alaska Dispatch News*, Nov. 11, 2009, https://www.adn.com/features/article/fourth-kind-pays-telling-big-fib/2009/11/12/

78 "PRESS RELEASE: H.R. MacMillan Space Centre reveals starring role in UFO hoax," *H.R. MacMillan Space Centre*, Sept. 10, 2013, http://www.spacecentre.ca/images/spacecentre-drone-creates-buzz-091013.pdf

79 Paul Herman, "New UFO sighting in Sandton a fake," *News24*, Dec. 1. 2015, http://www.news24.com/SouthAfrica/News/new-ufo-sighting-in-sandton-a-fake-20151201

80 Raymond D. Duvall and Alexander Wendt, "Sovereignty and the UFO," *Political Theory*. Vol. 36, No. 4., 2008, 607-633,

http://minotb52ufo.com/pdf/Wendt-Duvall-Sovereignty-and-the-UFO.pdf

See also: Raymond D. Duvall and Alexander Wendt, "Militant Agnosticism and the UFO Taboo: A call for reason and responsible action" in: Leslie Kean (ed.), *UFOs: A call for reason and responsible* action, 2010, 269-281, https://experts.umn.edu/en/publications/militant-agnosticism-and-the-ufo-taboo-a-call-for-reason-and-resp, and: Russ Wellen, "To the U.S. Government, UFOs Are a Threat to Its Sovereign Rule. Few

Americans actually fear UFOs, but the U.S. government treats them like an existential threat," *Foreign Policy In Focus*, Oct. 24, 2011, http://fpif.org/to_the_us_government_ufos_are_a_threat_to_its_sovereign_rule/

MJ BANIAS

1 "The True Cost of the Bank Bailout," *PBS.org*, Sept. 3. 2010, www.pbs.org/wnet/need-to-know/economy/the-true-cost-of-the-bank-bailout/3309/

2 Mike Collins, "The Big Bank Bailout," *Forbes.com*, Jul. 14, 2015, www.forbes.com/sites/mikecollins/2015/07/14/the-big-bank-bailout/#6e05e25b3723

3 Slavoj Žižek, "Looking Awry; An Introduction to Jacques Lacan through Popular Culture" (October Books, 1991).

4 Alejandro Rojas, "Chris Rutkowski, 2015 Canadian UFO Report," *Open Minds UFO Radio*, 2016.

5 Katie Levine, "Neil deGrasse Tyson Returns Again," *Nerdist Podcast*, Mar. 7, 2014, www.nerdist.com/nerdist-podcast-neil-degrasse-tyson-returns-again/

6 "Heads They Win, Tails We Lose; How Corporations Corrupt Science at the Public's Expense," *The Scientific Integrity Program of the Union of Concerned Scientists*, Feb. 2012, 13, www.ucsusa.org/sites/default/files/legacy/assets/documents/scientific_integrity/how-corporations-corrupt-science.pdf

7 Ibid, 18.

8 Jennifer Washburn, "Science's Worst Enemy: Corporate Funding," *Discover Magazine*, Oct. 11, 2007, www.discovermagazine.com/2007/oct/sciences-worst-enemy-private-funding

9 John Sides, "Fifty Percent of Americans believe in some conspiracy theory. Here's why," *Washington Post*, Feb. 19, 2015, www.washingtonpost.com/blogs/monkey-cage/wp/2015/02/19/fifty-percent-of-americans-believe-in-some-conspiracy-theory-heres-why/

10 "Noam Chomsky on the (in)compatibility of democracy and capitalism," *Can We Do It Ourselves?* 2015, www.youtube.com/watch?v=Xz9HWMX4oT8

RED PILL JUNKIE

1 Episode 3: "Harmony of the Worlds," *Cosmos: A Personal Voyage* (1980).

2 The Terence McKenna Wiki: Shamanic Approaches to the UFO. Angels, Aliens and Archetypes Conference, San Francisco, California, Nov. 21, 1987,

terencemckenna.wikispaces.com/Shamanic+Approaches+to+the+UFO

See also: https://youtu.be/22F6pZU_PC8

3 J.M.R. Higgs, "From Operation Mindf**k to the White Room: The Strange Discordian Journey of the KLF," *Darklore*. Vol. 7, 2012, Daily Grail Publishing, www.dailygrail.com/Guest-Articles/2013/5/The-Strange-Journey-the-KLF

4 For example, the Shaver Mystery, as popularized by Ray Palmer, editor of *Amazing Stories*. See: Raymond Hall, The Andreasson Affair (New York: Prentice Hall, 1979).

5 Grimerica Talks to Crop Circle Maker Matthew Williams, The Grimerica Podcast, Nov. 28, 2014, www.grimerica.ca/williams

6 Episode 12: "Encyclopaedia Galactica," *Cosmos: A Personal Voyage* (1980).

   See also: *Contact*. Dir. Robert Zemeckis, Warner Brothers (1997).

7 Colm A. Kelleher Ph.D. and George Knapp, *Hunt for the Skinwalker: Science Confronts the Unexplained at a Remote Ranch in Utah* (Paraview Pocket Books, 2005).

8 John A. Keel, *The Mothman Prophecies* (Panther Books, 1975).

9 Loren Coleman, "Red Dawn Again," Jul. 26, 2012, http://copycateffect. blogspot.co.uk/2012/07/red-dawn-again.html

10 *Batman: The Dark Knight*, Dir. Christopher Nolan, Warner Brothers (2008).

11 Larry Warren and Peter Robbins, *Left at East Gate: A First-Hand Account of the Rendlesham Forest UFO Incident, Its Cover-Up and Investigation* (Da Capo Press, 1997).

12 Nick Redfern, *Contactees: A History of Alien-Human Interaction* (New Page Books, 2010).

13 Richard M. Dolan, *UFOs & the National Security State Volume 2: The Cover-Up Exposed*, 1973-1991, (Keyhole Publishing Company, 2009).

14 Jacques Vallée, *Passport to Magonia: From Folklore to Flying Saucers* (Daily Grail Publishing, 2014).

15 Red Pill Junkie, "Portents & Politics: UFO Apparitions Connected to Social Disturbances?", Aug. 10, 2011,

   http://dailygrail.com/blogs/red-pill-junkie/2011/8/ Portents-Politics-UFO-Apparitions-Connected-Social-Disturbances

16 Ronald D. Story (ed.), *The Mammoth Encyclopedia of Extraterrestrial Encounters* (Constable and Robinson, 2001).

17 Mack Maloney, *UFOs in Wartime: What They Didn't Want You to Know* (Berkley: Original Edition, 2011).

18 *Where Did the Road Go?* Radio Show. Live on WVBR Every Saturday at 11 PM Eastern, wheredidtheroadgo.com

[19] Seriah Azkath, broadcaster of the New Aeon, Radio Misterioso Podcast, Mar. 29, 2016, radiomisterioso.com/2016/03/29/seriah-azkath-broadcaster-of-the-new-aeon/

[20] See: hiddenexperience.blogspot.com

[21] Dave Lifton, "That Time John Lennon Spotted a UFO in New York," *Ultimate Classic Rock*, Aug. 23, 2015, www.ultimateclassicrock.com/john-lennon-ufo/

[22] Timothy Green Beckley, "David Bowie, UFOs, Witchcraft, Cocaine and Paranoia," *UFO Digest*, 2010, http://ufodigest.com/article/david-bowie-ufos-witchcraft-cocaine-and-paranoia

[23] Gary Johnson, "Lam I Am," *Aleister Crowley 2012*, Oct. 20, 2012, https://ac2012.com/2012/10/20/lam-i-am/

[24] Yabba Dabble Doo: How Aleister Crowley Introduced the Iconic Gray Alien, By Richelle Hawks (2007), http://www.ufodigest.com/news/1107/dabbledoo.html

[25] Alan Moore and David Lloyd, *V for Vendetta*, DC Comics, 1988.

[26] Richard M. Dolan and Bryce Zabel, *A.D., After Disclosure: When the Government Finally Reveals the Truth about Alien Contact* (New Page Books, 2012).

[27] "Timothy & Terence," Podcast 369, *Psychedelic Salon*, Sept. 17, 2013, https://psychedelicsalon.com/podcast-369-timothy-terence/

SUSAN DEMETER-ST. CLAIR

[1] Personal correspondence with UFO witness, Aug. 24, 2010. All UFO witness interviews cited within this essay were conducted in confidentiality. Names of interviewees are withheld by agreement.

[2] Massimo Teodorani, *The Hyperspace of Consciousness* (Sweden: Elmenta, 2015), 206, 208-209.

[3] J. Allen Hynek, Speaking at the United Nations, Nov. 27, 1978, http://www.ufoevidence.org/documents/doc757.htm

[4] Jacques F. Vallée and Eric W. Davis, "Incommensurability, Orthodoxy and the Physics of High Strangeness: a 6-layer model for anomalous phenomena." In *Proceedings*, 2003, 223-239.

[5] Personal correspondence with UFO witness, and telephone interviews, 2014.

[6] J. Allen Hynek, personal correspondence with Iris Owen dated Aug. 24, 1977, Henry McKay UFO Archives, http://psican.org/index.php/ufological-information/947-hynek-letter-to-iris-owen

7 Jacques F. Vallée and Eric W. Davis. "Incommensurability, Orthodoxy and the Physics of High Strangeness: a 6-layer model for anomalous phenomena," In: *Proceedings*, 2003, 223-239.

8 Ibid.

9 Ibid.

10 Ibid.

11 Teodorani, *The Hyperspace of Consciousness*, 208-209.

12 D. Scott Rogo, *The haunted universe* (Anomalist Books, 2006).

13 Eric Ouellet, *Illuminations: The UFO Experience as a Parapsychological Event* (San Antonio and Charlottesville: Anomalist Books, 2015), 25-26, 28-29.

14 Ibid.

15 Susan Demeter-St. Clair, "Parapsychology and UFOs: Are UFOs a psychic event?" *Susanstclair*, Jan. 2016, http://www.susanstclair.com/index.php/podcast/14-parapsychology-and-ufos-are-ufos-a-psychic-event

16 Ouellet, *Illuminations*, 25-26, 28-29.

17 David Halperin and Eric Ouellet, "(Para)psychology and the UFO," *Davidhalperin*, Sept.23, 2016, http://www.davidhalperin.net/eric-ouellet-parapsychology-and-the-ufo-2/

Further Reading

Hilary Evans, *Visions, apparitions, alien visitors* (Aquarian Press, 1984).

Carl Jung, *Flying Saucers: A Modern Myth* (Princeton University Press, 1970).

Jacques Vallée, *The Invisible College* (New York E. P. Dutton, 1975).

Jacques Vallée, "The Psycho-Physical Nature of UFO Reality: A Speculative Framework," AIAA Thesis-Antithesis Conference Proceedings, Los Angeles, 1975, 19-21.

RYAN SPRAGUE

1 Jasper Copping, "UFO enthusiasts admit the truth may not be out there after all," *The Daily Telegraph*, Nov. 4, 2012, http://www.telegraph.co.uk/news/newstopics/howaboutthat/ufo/9653499/UFO-enthusiasts-admit-the-truth-may-not-be-out-there-after-all.html

2 Max Miller, *Saucers Magazine*. Vol. 7, Issue 1, 1959.

3 Jenny Randles, "Ufology: Is There Life After Death?" *UFO Evidence*, http://www.ufoevidence.org/documents/doc584.htm

4 Jim Keith, "UFOs at the Edge of Reality," *Paranoia Magazine*, Issue 17, 1997, http://www.paranoiamagazine.com/2016/05/ufos-edge-reality-lecture-jim-keith/

5 Ibid.

6 Jacques Vallée, *Messengers of Deception: UFO Contacts and Cults* (Daily Grail Publishing, 2008), 20.

7 Eric Wargo, "Consciousness Inside-Out," *The Nightshirt*, Nov. 2014, http://thenightshirt.com/?p=1952

8 Jacques Vallée, *Passport to Magonia: From Folklore to Flying Saucers* (Daily Grail Publishing, 2014).

9 Carl Jung, *Flying Saucers: A Modern Myth of Things Seen in the Skies* (Princeton University Press, 1979), vii.

10 David Clarke, *How UFOs Conquered the World: The History of a Modern Myth* (Aurum Press, 2015).

GREG BISHOP

1 Ralph Coon (Producer), *Whispers from Space* (1995). DVD (out of print).

2 Bruce Duensing, "Behaviorism Beyond Physicality," *A Transit of Contingencies*, May 16, 2015, http://tarnsitsandstations.blogspot.com/2015/05/behaviorism-beyond-physicality.htm

3 "Pyrrhonism," *Wikipedia*, https://en.wikipedia.org/wiki/Pyrrhonism

4 Keith Thompson, *Angels and Aliens: UFOs and the Mythic Imagination* (Addison Wesley Publishing, 1991), 191.

5 Greg Bishop and Wes Nations, "Karla Turner: Don't Exclude the Anomalous" in *Wake Up Down There!* (Adventures Unlimited Press, 1995), 94.

6 Jerome Clark, *The UFO Encyclopedia: The Phenomenon from The Beginning Volume 1* (Omnigraphics, 1998), 228.

7 Albert Rosales. See: http://ufoinfo.com/humanoid/

8 "Abductee Jan Wolski Interviewed-30th Anniversary of Emilcin Abduction," *ufocasebook.com*, http://www.ufocasebook.com/2008/wolski.html

9 Jim Brandon, *The Rebirth of Pan* (Firebird Press, 1983), 9.

10 Greg Bishop (Producer), "John Fenderson and Adam Gorightly—Perception, Magick, and the "Missing Fundamental," Audio podcast, *Radio Misterioso*,

Aug. 15, 2015, http://radiomisterioso.com/2015/09/05/john-fenderson-and-adam-gorightly-perception-magick-and-the-missing-fundamental/

11 Joseph McMoneagle, *Mind Trek: Exploring Consciousness, Time, and Space Through Remote Viewing* (Hampton Roads Publishing, 1993/1997), 187-188.

12 Greg Bishop, "Interview with Parapsychologist Dean Radin" in *Wake Up Down There!* (Adventures Unlimited Press, 1995), 313.

13 Hal Arkowitz and Scott O. Lilienfeld, "Why Science Tells Us Not to Rely on Eyewitness Accounts" *Scientific American*, Jan. 1, 2010.

14 Greg Miller, "How Our Brains Make Memories," *Smithsonian* magazine, May, 2010.

15 Donald Hoffman, *Do we see reality as it is?* [Video file], March, 2015, http://www.ted.com/talks/donald_hoffman_do_we_see_reality_as_it_is

16 Ibid.

17 Ibid.

18 Greg Bishop (Producer), "Mac Tonnies: Cryptoterrestrials" [Audio podcast], *Radio Misterioso*, Jul. 9, 2009, http://radiomisterioso.com/2009/07/27/mac-tonnies/

19 Paul Davies and Niels Henrik Gregerson, *Information and the Nature of Reality: From Physics to Metaphysics* (Cambridge University Press, 2010), 1-2.

20 John Archibald Wheeler, *A Journey Into Gravity and Spacetime*, Scientific American Library (New York: W.H. Freeman, 1990), 5.

ROBERT BRANDSTETTER

1 Wendy Conners, *Faded Discs: UFOs and Law Enforcement 1957-1981 Guide.* Officer Dale Spaur & Officer Barney Neff statement at the Ravenna, Portage County, Ohio police station. Interview by Major Hector Quintanilla, Jr., May 11, 1966.

2 Donald D. Hoffman, "Conscious Realism and the Mind-Body Problem," *Imprint Academic Mind & Matter Vol. 6(1)*, Department of Cognitive Science, University of California at Irvine, USA, 2008, 87-121.

3 Ibid.

4 Alberto Francisco Do Carmo, "UFOVIA internacional." *UFOVIA internacional*. The Nautilus Foundation, Warsaw, Poland, 2004. Web. 20 Nov. 2016.

5   Tomek Wierszalowicz, "Abductee Jan Wolski Interviewed-30th Anniversary of Emilcin Abduction," *UFO Casebook—UFOs, UFO Sightings, UFO Case files, Photographs, Aliens*, 2008.

6   Bruce Duensing, "Understanding Reality." Letter to TDOS Discussion Group, May 24, 2015.

7   Aime Michel, "The strange case of Dr. 'X' – part 2," *Flying Saucer Review* 17.6, 1971.

8   Greg Bishop, *It Defies Language!: Essays on UFOs and Other Weirdness* (Los Angeles: Excluded Middle Press, 2016), 183.

9   Chris A. Rutkowski, *Abductions & Aliens: What's Really Going On* (Toronto: Dundurn Press, 1999), 234.

10 "Iris Phalene Interview 3." Personal interview, Oct. 13, 2005.

11 In the early-1950s, one of the most notable of the UFO contactees, Truman Bethurum, claimed to have made contact with a voluptuous female Captain, Aura Rhanes, who piloted a ship from the planet Clarion hidden on the other side of the moon. He wrote her poetry and claimed she was the primary reason why his wife left him.

INDEX

Paperbacks also available from
White Crow Books

Elsa Barker—*Letters from
a Living Dead Man*
ISBN 978-1-907355-83-7

Elsa Barker—*War Letters from
the Living Dead Man*
ISBN 978-1-907355-85-1

Elsa Barker—*Last Letters from
the Living Dead Man*
ISBN 978-1-907355-87-5

Richard Maurice Bucke—
Cosmic Consciousness
ISBN 978-1-907355-10-3

Arthur Conan Doyle—
The Edge of the Unknown
ISBN 978-1-907355-14-1

Arthur Conan Doyle—
The New Revelation
ISBN 978-1-907355-12-7

Arthur Conan Doyle—
The Vital Message
ISBN 978-1-907355-13-4

Arthur Conan Doyle with
Simon Parke—*Conversations
with Arthur Conan Doyle*
ISBN 978-1-907355-80-6

Meister Eckhart with Simon Parke—
Conversations with Meister Eckhart
ISBN 978-1-907355-18-9

D. D. Home—*Incidents in my Life Part 1*
ISBN 978-1-907355-15-8

Mme. Dunglas Home; edited,
with an Introduction, by Sir
Arthur Conan Doyle—*D. D.
Home: His Life and Mission*
ISBN 978-1-907355-16-5

Edward C. Randall—
Frontiers of the Afterlife
ISBN 978-1-907355-30-1

Rebecca Ruter Springer—
Intra Muros: My Dream of Heaven
ISBN 978-1-907355-11-0

Leo Tolstoy, edited by Simon
Parke—*Forbidden Words*
ISBN 978-1-907355-00-4

Leo Tolstoy—*A Confession*
ISBN 978-1-907355-24-0

Leo Tolstoy—*The Gospel in Brief*
ISBN 978-1-907355-22-6

Leo Tolstoy—*The Kingdom
of God is Within You*
ISBN 978-1-907355-27-1

Leo Tolstoy—*My Religion:
What I Believe*
ISBN 978-1-907355-23-3

Leo Tolstoy—*On Life*
ISBN 978-1-907355-91-2

Leo Tolstoy—*Twenty-three Tales*
ISBN 978-1-907355-29-5

Leo Tolstoy—*What is Religion
and other writings*
ISBN 978-1-907355-28-8

Leo Tolstoy—*Work While
Ye Have the Light*
ISBN 978-1-907355-26-4

Leo Tolstoy—*The Death of Ivan Ilyich*
ISBN 978-1-907661-10-5

Leo Tolstoy—*Resurrection*
ISBN 978-1-907661-09-9

Leo Tolstoy with Simon Parke—
Conversations with Tolstoy
ISBN 978-1-907355-25-7

Howard Williams with an Introduction
by Leo Tolstoy—*The Ethics of Diet:
An Anthology of Vegetarian Thought*
ISBN 978-1-907355-21-9

Vincent Van Gogh with Simon Parke—
Conversations with Van Gogh
ISBN 978-1-907355-95-0

Wolfgang Amadeus Mozart with Simon
Parke—*Conversations with Mozart*
ISBN 978-1-907661-38-9

Jesus of Nazareth with Simon Parke—
Conversations with Jesus of Nazareth
ISBN 978-1-907661-41-9

Thomas à Kempis with Simon
Parke—*The Imitation of Christ*
ISBN 978-1-907661-58-7

Julian of Norwich with Simon
Parke—*Revelations of Divine Love*
ISBN 978-1-907661-88-4

Allan Kardec—*The Spirits Book*
ISBN 978-1-907355-98-1

Allan Kardec—*The Book on Mediums*
ISBN 978-1-907661-75-4

Emanuel Swedenborg—*Heaven and Hell*
ISBN 978-1-907661-55-6

P.D. Ouspensky—*Tertium Organum:
The Third Canon of Thought*
ISBN 978-1-907661-47-1

Dwight Goddard—*A Buddhist Bible*
ISBN 978-1-907661-44-0

Michael Tymn—*The Afterlife Revealed*
ISBN 978-1-970661-90-7

Michael Tymn—*Transcending the
Titanic: Beyond Death's Door*
ISBN 978-1-908733-02-3

Guy L. Playfair—*If This Be Magic*
ISBN 978-1-907661-84-6

Guy L. Playfair—*The Flying Cow*
ISBN 978-1-907661-94-5

Guy L. Playfair —*This House is Haunted*
ISBN 978-1-907661-78-5

Carl Wickland, M.D.—
Thirty Years Among the Dead
ISBN 978-1-907661-72-3

John E. Mack—*Passport to the Cosmos*
ISBN 978-1-907661-81-5

Peter & Elizabeth Fenwick—
The Truth in the Light
ISBN 978-1-908733-08-5

Erlendur Haraldsson—
Modern Miracles
ISBN 978-1-908733-25-2

Erlendur Haraldsson—
At the Hour of Death
ISBN 978-1-908733-27-6

Erlendur Haraldsson—
The Departed Among the Living
ISBN 978-1-908733-29-0

Brian Inglis—*Science and Parascience*
ISBN 978-1-908733-18-4

Brian Inglis—*Natural and Supernatural:
A History of the Paranormal*
ISBN 978-1-908733-20-7

Ernest Holmes—*The Science of Mind*
ISBN 978-1-908733-10-8

Victor & Wendy Zammit —*A Lawyer
Presents the Evidence For the Afterlife*
ISBN 978-1-908733-22-1

Casper S. Yost—*Patience
Worth: A Psychic Mystery*
ISBN 978-1-908733-06-1

William Usborne Moore—
Glimpses of the Next State
ISBN 978-1-907661-01-3

William Usborne Moore—
The Voices
ISBN 978-1-908733-04-7

John W. White—
The Highest State of Consciousness
ISBN 978-1-908733-31-3

Stafford Betty—
The Imprisoned Splendor
ISBN 978-1-907661-98-3

Paul Pearsall, Ph.D. —
Super Joy
ISBN 978-1-908733-16-0

**All titles available as eBooks, and selected titles available in Hardback and
Audiobook formats from www.whitecrowbooks.com**

Printed in July 2019
by Rotomail Italia S.p.A., Vignate (MI) - Italy